BUSINESS TALK

SENDING, PRESENTING, AND RECEIVING MESSAGES IN A PROFESSIONAL SETTING

J. Kanan Sawyer

D1402630

Hayden-McNeil Sustainability

Hayden-McNeil's standard paper stock uses a minimum of 30% post-consumer waste. We offer higher % options by request, including a 100% recycled stock. Additionally, Hayden-McNeil Custom Digital provides authors with the opportunity to convert print products to a digital format. Hayden-McNeil is part of a larger sustainability initiative through Macmillan Higher Ed. Visit http://www.macmillanhighered.com/Catalog/other/sustainability to learn more.

Printed in the United States of America

10 9 8 7 6 5 4 3 2 1

ISBN 978-0-7380-5631-9

Hayden-McNeil Publishing
14903 Pilot Drive
Plymouth, MI 48170
www.hmpublishing.com

Sawyer 5631-9 W13

Table of Contents

ACKNOWLEDGEMENTS

This text is a collection of personal experience, research, and the significant contributions of many; heartfelt thanks go to: Karen L. Sawyer, Lisa Millhous, Eryn Travis, Tyler Daniels, Elizabeth Saldan, Jessica Alicea, Mike Willis, Virginia Smith, the 9 book reviewers whose comments led to a far more worthy text, the WCU adjunct staff and their contributions in all editions, Whitney Kerns, Karly Moeletteri, and Mabel.

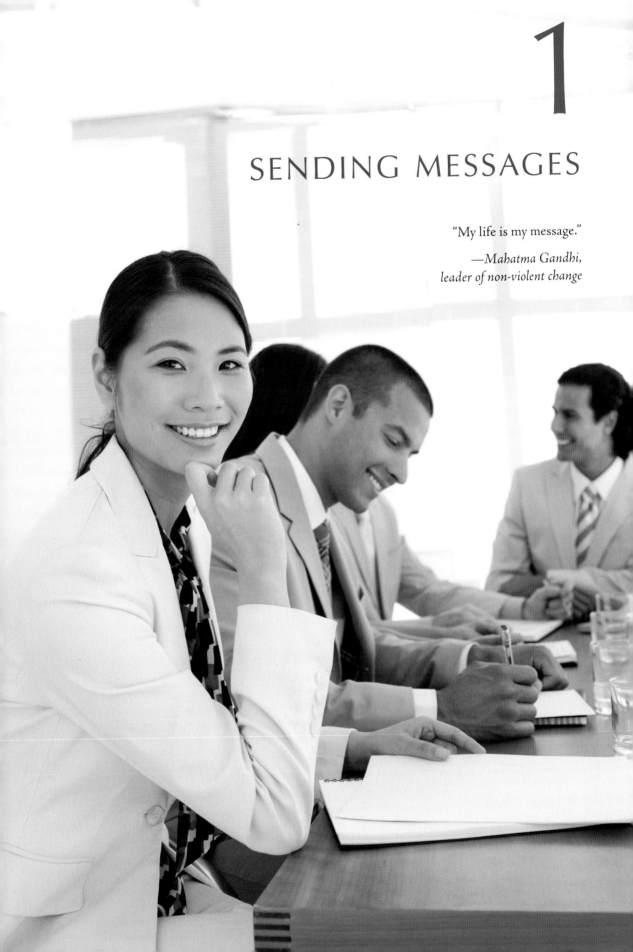

1

SENDING MESSAGES

"My life is my message."

—*Mahatma Gandhi,*
leader of non-violent change

WHAT BUSINESSES WANT

In survey after survey of major employers, communication skills are stated as one of the top qualities that companies desire in applicants (Morreale, 2001; Morreale & Pearson, 2008; NACE, 2011). But what does that actually mean? If you know how to talk, does that mean that you have strong communication skills? Unfortunately, it does not.

Communication is what connects one person to another. In a professional setting, communication is how tasks are assigned and clarified as well as how projects are managed. Using clear communication is how the work actually gets done. Whether a person is in accounting, management, medicine, government service, or any other industry, that person has a stronger chance of career advancement if he or she has mastered effective communication. You want "that person" to be you! The first step toward developing these skills is learning how communication works and occurs in a professional setting.

With so much expectation on the giving and sending of messages in professional settings, it would be ideal for companies to train you in this important skill. True, but remember that employers expect you to *come in* with strong communication skills (NACE, 2011). Even when employers offer seminars in developing sales presentations or giving business presentations to clients, your post-graduate communication training will likely be extremely limited. Companies are in the business of making money—not offering speech training. If you come through the door having those communication skills in your repertoire of experience then you are well ahead of your colleagues and likely to be far more successful.

This text will help you to understand the most effective means of sending and receiving messages when engaging in "business talk." Our focus will be on the verbal and nonverbal messages sent to others with a brief look at some written business messages. While certain written skills such as crafting an effective business letter or proposal or mastering the art of professional email messages is important, this text will take you beyond the writing to the crucial element of explaining and expanding upon your ideas in a verbal context. This text will give you the tools for crafting and delivering effective business *talk*.

In the chapters ahead, you will learn about the sending of business messages, critical choices made in the context of sending business messages, how to collect needed evidence, organization for business speeches, how to construct visual elements for business talks, and then how to deliver them to achieve your desired impact. We will also provide you with the tools to become a master in the interviewing process, including putting together résumés and standout cover letters. Finally, you will learn how to apply all of these skills to become a true business leader! We begin our conversation with the most foundational aspect of the business talk— what it means to communicate.

Defining the Communication Exchange

In its most simple form (put together way back when, in ancient Greek times, by Aristotle!), the art of communication is seen to involve two parties in the exchange of messages: senders and receivers.

If this were all that there were to communication then you would hardly need training in it. You would open your mouth, messages would come out, and receivers would understand. Sadly, it is not that simple. (If you have ever sent out a message that did not have the result that you intended then you already know this.) Communication is the *complicated process* of attempting to achieve shared meaning between message senders and receivers. Why is this complicated? Because getting someone on the same page with you, especially in a business setting, is a complex endeavor.

First, consider the concept of shared meaning. **Shared meaning** is the process of coming to a common understanding of key elements and topics (Perelman, 1969) and it is difficult to reach. How often do we pause and considerately ask others what they actually mean by the words or phrases that they are using? Typically, we assume that we know without doing any clarifying. Although this practice is more problematic in confrontational exchanges, it impacts friendly conversations as well. "*You haven't learned how to manage the budget,*" your co-worker states when looking at your spreadsheets. You retort, "*I don't know how to manage budgets?! You're so vague and incomprehensible—who would ever want to have you manage their budget?*" In the subsequent minutes these two otherwise happy co-workers have launched in a button-pushing, dirty-look exchanging relationship that will define their interaction for the foreseeable future. And yet, neither of them ever clarified what process, part, or even what the other defined as budget management. The first may have intended a slur on the other's work product but may also have simply realized when seeing the chosen format that his new co-worker had not gone through the required budget format training. Who knows? They never attempted to share a meaning!

Second, there are so many elements to consider when attempting to reach shared meaning that communication breakdown seems almost inevitable. Don't worry…it's not. Our understanding of how communication variables interact has grown over time to lead us to better means of developing and sending messages in professional settings. We have gone from the basics of Aristotle's model of "sender-message-receiver" to a far more evolved understanding of how communication moves from one to another—and once you understand those connections, you've got a leg up on your co-workers! The first step in your understanding is to evaluate *models*.

OUR EVOLVING UNDERSTANDING OF COMMUNICATION

Before you wonder if this is the swimsuit version of business communication texts or think that you are about to turn the page and find a pop-up book, put simply, **models** are basic visual representations of all the components that make up a construct. Models are a fantastic means of grasping the complex notion of communication. You may find them so easy to understand that you cannot fathom why anyone would think that communication is so complicated. Hold off on that thought.

Models help us understand the key components of communication, but, do not be fooled, they are not the full picture! Mortenson (1972) reminded us that any use of models to understand a concept will help us to clarify or organize complex ideas, ask better questions, and see how elements operate in terms of one another—while at the same time leading to oversimplification and potentially limiting our thinking. So, use these as only the beginning of your exploration of business talk!

There are more than a dozen theoretical models that attempt to explain the components of communication. Knowing all of them is not necessary to have functional business talk. Understanding the few communication models that help improve your own talk in a professional setting will be invaluable. The next few pages will enable you to picture how communication works by demonstrating the concepts that top business leaders use today. Some of these notions are extremely old and you may wonder why our very top executives are still tied to them. It's because they work!

Aristotle (384 BC–322 BC)

It would be a huge failing to begin any talk of communication without first looking at the father of communication—Aristotle. The basic model of communication is diagrammed on the previous page, but, even more, the origins of any sort of *systematic* approach to understanding communication go back to ancient Greek origins. The ancient Greeks had a democratic kind of government and, in all fields of business (such as public administration or law or education), civilians had to be their own public advocates. They had to stand up in front of others and convince audiences or argue for any kind of service that they wanted.

To ensure that Greek citizens could rise to this task, education had a focus on *oral/verbal* expression (rather than nonverbal or written components), which focused Aristotle's own view of communication as a *verbal* activity in which the **speaker/rhetorician** (the sender of the message) tries to convince the **listener** (the receiver or audience), by using the strategic construction of an argument and the presentation of the speech itself. While the terms may be slightly different depending on the discussion, this one-directional model is:

The Sender/Speaker

The key element for this original understanding of communication was the sender (also referred to as the speaker or orator). **Senders** are the originators of any message—where it all starts. At first you may think that this will always be you. Sometimes it will be but you should be aware of when this is and is not the case. If you are the person with which a message originates then, yes, this is right. If you come into existing communication (as is the case in most business meetings where there is a history behind every topic discussion) then you are a receiver of a message and may *later* become a sender once you come up with something to say. So what does it mean to be the "sender"?

Communication always *starts* with a sender—one or more people who want to get an idea across to someone else. Because of this, we have a tendency to focus on the speaker, particularly in U.S. culture where speakers have more status than listeners (Han & Shavitt, 1994). Yet, scholars have known since Aristotle that receiver acceptance of the message is key to any successful communication.

If you have ever sat in a class or a work meeting and thought, "Oh...please do not call on me," then in that case you would prefer not to be a sender. After all, a sender must be first *stimulated* and then *motivated* to send a message. You may have many reasons for not wishing to send a message, such as being new to a company or having little information on a subject. However, avoiding verbal responses does not mean that you are not sending messages. Watzlawick, Beavin, and Jackson (1967) argued that it is impossible *not* to send messages. We may be sitting in silence, but our nonverbal communication screams loud and clear. We may be hoping to restrain our impressions, but they shine through. While Aristotle focused on the quality of the argument sent *verbally*, we have since come to know that we are sending messages all of the time. Therefore, effective business communicators keep an eye on every way and situation in which they are the message sender.

Appealing to Message Receivers

Senders are not the only parts of communication models. Receivers and the message itself complete the basic model. Aristotle argued that speakers send messages that are *for audiences, about audiences, and to audiences.* This does not mean that speakers must pander to the preferences of audiences and tell them only what they want to hear—absolutely not! What it does mean is that you need to understand where your audience is coming from if you want to get them where you want them to go (emotionally or behaviorally). *You have to meet them where they are.* Aristotle argued that we can only do this by appealing to our audience in three ways—through the appeals of ethos, logos, and pathos.

+ **Appeals to Ethos**

   Appealing to our audience's **ethos** directs us to be sure that our information is of the highest quality and credibility in the eyes of our audience. In other words, unless we want to distance ourselves from our audience, we should present the best possible research and arguments to our audience and never deceive them or withhold efforts to find out all that we can (Dunleavy, Chory, & Goodboy, 2010). If you are attempting to provide financial advice to investors and you have taken your lead from Bernie Madoff, the infamous swindler of our day, then you have not attempted to appeal to ethos. Similarly, if you are speaking to a group of college students about the connection between sports and the video gaming world, it would serve you well to provide examples from EA Sports'™ games, but if you are speaking to a group of Wall Street brokers then what you can grasp from the *Financial Times* will provide you with the best ideas.

   Matches between sources and audiences are crucial because credibility comes when our audiences believe that we have ethically done our best to provide them with what they need. Additionally, appealing to your audience's sense of ethos will set you apart in a business setting. If you are the third sales group to give your pitch—but the only ones to have research and evidence to back up your claims—then you will sail above the others in the eyes of any audience. Do not let anyone tell you that this appeal is not necessary just because so many business professionals have left if off their radar. You know better.

+ **Appeals to Logos**

Logos is the appeal to our audience's idea of what makes sense. Ideas should be presented through examples and evidence that support the main argument but these must be organized in a form that is easily grasped by our audience (Parra, Nalda, & Pereles, 2011). If you, for example, give a speech on the development of your company's three products over time but instead of presenting them in the order that they were developed (such as 1,2,3), you instead talk about the first then the third then the second, your audience might be a bit confused. Similarly, if you tell your audience that you will talk about A, B, then C and go on to talk about C, B, and 2, your audience is likely to be so busy trying to figure out where you are in your message that they will not be listening to your evidence.

Whether it is the structure to an entire presentation or just a single idea within a larger speech, audiences should never think, "Huh?" when you are laying out your examples. While we will spend significant time later in this text discussing logos and presentation order, you should keep it in mind right from the beginning so you know how important and foundational this appeal is to your success.

+ **Appeals to Pathos**

Arguments are not all about research and sense-making alone. Our presentations must emotionally resonate or connect with our audiences. **Pathos** is the appeal to what an audience will find emotionally touching (Parra, Nalda, & Pereles, 2011). No—this does not mean that you should attempt to make your audience cry or that you should do it yourself, especially at work!

Too many speakers consider the notion of pathos to be, "I must show emotion in my presentation." They force fictitious anger, enthusiasm, or concern into their talks. Audiences know—they can tell when you are faking it! Remember that you lose ethos when you fake pathos. Remember that pathos is not about *your* emotion but a sense of connectedness experienced by the message receivers.

Aristotle's understanding of communication, where communication is described in terms of the *sender* of the message, continued from Greek times through history and, for all practical purposes, until the modern era. We began to shift how we thought about communication when new forms of sending messages emerged through technology that directly impacts professional contexts.

Harold Dwight Lasswell (1948)

The next major shift in our understanding of communication came from Harold Lasswell. Lasswell was not a businessman; he was an American sociologist and political scientist who started to see that our embrace of technology (even before the iPhone® or DVR) would change the face of communication. Lasswell (1948) gave us a model of communication in a sentence. He asked, "Who says what to whom in what channel with what effect?" and, with that sentence, he shifted our focus from the senders to the channel! Put into a visual model, Lasswell's model would look like:

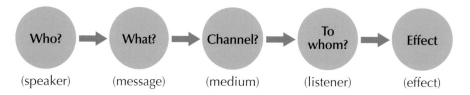

What became so monumental about Lasswell's (1948) theory was that it was influenced by the study of propaganda. Although Lasswell's model was simple and, like Aristotle, saw communication as moving in one direction from the sender to the receiver, it gave significant attention to the definition of **channels**, such as the newly relevant mass media, and included **message effects** in his model.

Message Channels

Email or phone call? Brief or go into details? Lasswell (1948) was the first to point out that messages are more complicated than we had previously considered. They are the sum total of both content (what we say) and channel choice (through what means we say it).

Channel refers to the various kinds of *mechanisms* for conveying a message from one person to another (Lasswell, 1948). Message channels take the form of either **face-to-face** (messages sent using direct contact between senders and receivers—such as two people standing in a room having a conversation) or **mediated** (messages sent using indirect contact between senders and receivers—such as the use of phones, written text, Skype, emails, or other media). How does someone select a channel? Unfortunately, it is not as easy as selecting one with your television remote control! However, it is often done with just as little thought.

Selecting the most appropriate channel for your message is critical to achieving shared meaning. So, in order to keep you on the right path at work, let's consider all of the elements that help you to make a good choice: a) **channel richness**, b) **task ambiguity**, and c) **relationship maintenance**.

Channel richness in channel selection

Have you ever given notes to a friend who missed class? You are happy to provide that friend with your notes but when the test comes, you know the information whereas your friend (with the same notes) does not. Why do you think that this is? Communication models suggest that the *richness* of your channel was the differentiating factor. **Channel richness** is the amount of information that can be transmitted during a communication episode (Daft & Lane, 2008). For instance, the richest channel is **face-to-face** communication (where you get information from all five senses), while the least rich channel might be a telegram (which do still exist) or any other "single sense" targeting method.

When selecting a channel, consider that the more nonverbal cues that are sent, the better. This targeting of many senses creates **redundancy**—or recurrence of the same message in a variety of ways. (Redundancy is good!) Johnson and Lederer (2005) found, in their management information systems research, that the more frequent the communication and *the richer the communication channel* between CEOs (Chief Executive Officers) and CIOs (Chief Information Officers), the more that these corporate leaders are able to agree on future goals and long-term financial decisions. So, rich channels lead to strong corporate leadership and, for your life, strategic professional success!

Task ambiguity in channel selection

Your next task during channel consideration will be what kind of job or task that you want accomplished. Consider the following: you are having trouble with your computer. You find out that you must take the computer apart to fix it, and you have not done anything like this before. Would you like a bulleted list of directions—or would it be better to have a video to watch someone who goes through the process? Most folks before doing this task themselves would want to see, hear, and experience this task because of its complicated nature. Video is a rich channel that would hit all of these senses.

Not all business tasks, however, are as difficult or intricate as computer surgery. If we are asked by our boss to send out a memo to our division about a change in the cafeteria menu, do we need a video from him or her on how to create a memo? This would be both annoying and time consuming. A quick email of the key points to cover would be far more appropriate for this uncomplicated task. Russ, Daft, and Lengel (1990) explain that managers who choose more rich channels for more ambiguous tasks and more lean channels for unambiguous tasks are by far the most effective!

+ **Relationship maintenance in channel selection**

Finally, messages play a role in building relationships. Choose the wrong channel, and the message will be unclear. You will not create shared meaning and you risk alienating your audience. Choose the right channel, and you can develop a strong bond with your audience. If you have recently been hired as the boss at a new company, you can imagine that people will be somewhat skeptical of you. Newness, after all, creates levels of tension (Bisel, Messersmith, & Keyton, 2009). Newness is a time when you will need to be careful about the channels that you select. If you decide to change the décor in the company lunch room, you are probably just fine selecting a company-wide email to announce the change. If you have decided to completely revise employee vacation allotments, then you should have a meeting with your new colleagues that allows you to go through your decision face-to-face and shows value of the relationship.

Channel selection is powerful, and your decision should be based on the goal of your communication. Lasswell (1948) helped us to better understand the impact of our communication channel; however, the models that came next give us insight into other parts of communication that impact the effectiveness of the sender, the receiver, and the channel.

Shannon-Weaver (1949)

About a year after Lasswell's publication, Shannon and Weaver (1949) released their own model of communication based on "signal transfer," which came from their engineering backgrounds. Claude Shannon was an engineer for the Bell Telephone Company™ (which is now AT&T™). He was hoping to engineer an efficient way of transmitting (sending) electronic phone signals from one location to another (receiving) with as little potential interference in the electronic transfer (which he termed **noise**). In other words, he wanted to get all that static off the line that you can hear when you pick up an old landline phone.

In a phone system, words are **encoded** into electrical signals that then need to be **decoded** on the other end. Bad lines or loose connections result in messages not being clear when they reach their final destination. While this model was created for a technical environment, it quickly became adopted by communication scholars who saw that it added key components to the sender-message-receiver idea—notions of **encoding**, **decoding**, and **noise**.

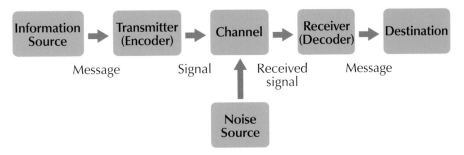

The Shannon-Weaver Mathematical Model, 1949

While we are familiar with senders and channels, Shannon and Weaver (1949) added elements to the communication model that shed light on why some messages make sense to some and are a mystery to others.

+ **Senders will encode a message**

   Encoding means to put an idea into a system of letters, numbers, or symbols. The importance of sender encoding is part of most communication theories and practices including interpersonal communication (Jakobson, 1960), mass communication (McQuail, 1983), and even media context theory (Hall, 1980).

   Think of it this way…do you speak Mandarin? If so, then this would likely be how you would encode a verbal message. If you primarily use sign language then that would be your "code." You will choose how you encode a message based upon: a) your **sender experience**, such as personal knowledge, background, understanding, and familiarity, and b) your **culture**, such as socialized traditions, customs, and ways of life. If two communicators are not from the same culture then they will have more trouble creating shared meaning than those from the same culture (Hall, 1980).

+ **Receivers will decode a message**

   Once messages are taken in by the receiver, they are **decoded** (i.e., translated to a system of letters, numbers, or symbols intended to be understood by the receiver). Decoding involves knowing what message was *intended* and working to share that meaning. This process requires appreciation of both the **denotative** (actual dictionary definitions) and **connotative** (ideas and images associated with the word) meanings. Why? Because the *meaning* of workplace language is often a mystery to those new to the office.

   Let's say that it is your first day on the job. All of your co-workers are using jargon and abbreviations to refer to necessary tasks. How effective can you be in performing your tasks if, as of yet, you do not even understand the directions? It will take time for you to learn how to decode incoming data and reach shared meaning. Time will allow you to have all of the denotative and connotative information needed to get there!

+ **Message clarity can be hindered by noise**

Shannon and Weaver (1949) may have been the first to articulate the idea of noise but they were hardly the first to feel its impact. **Noise** is the verbal and environmental impediments on message clarity. It seems so obvious to say that things outside the message will impact the clarity of a message. Think of your own life. Do you have a cell phone that automatically spells words for you as you are texting? Have you ever sent a word that you did not mean to send? Or even a *message* that you did not mean to send? We have all had our communication thwarted by noise, which can take on a variety of forms:

a. **psychological noise**: distractions from your head (e.g., thinking about hunger, dismay, distress, discomfort, or even hatred)

b. **semantic noise**: the problem associated with differences in the meaning that people assign to words (e.g., the many interpretations of the word "business": an industry, "getting down to business," an affair, an amount of work, etc.)

c. **mechanical noise**: an actual interruption of a message signal (e.g., a wireless printer creates static on your television)

d. **cultural noise**: differences in worldview expectations (e.g., wishing a group of people a *Merry Christmas* when some of them are Muslim)

e. **physical noise**: disturbances that surround and overrun the message (e.g., sitting in an uncomfortable chair, thunder, or a marching band)

Controlling for noise is the best way to have your receiver get the message that you had intended. Given how useful this model has been to language scholars, it is ironic that Claude Shannon (1948) wrote, "(language) aspects of communication are irrelevant to the engineering problem," (p. 1) and then his work guided communication/language models for decades! From a business perspective, we can see the absolute utility of his model. Some channels naturally lend themselves to noise. The next model will help us to understand if our receivers are influenced by that noise.

Schramm (1954)

Have you ever sat in a meeting and someone looks right at you and asks, "Which part didn't you get?" How did they know that you were confused? They probably knew because it was written all over your face. Had that person ignored your facial reaction, he or she would have been *speaking*, but not, according to Wilbur Schramm (1954), *communicating*. Schramm saw that all earlier models of communication failed to talk about the impact of two key ideas: interpretation and feedback!

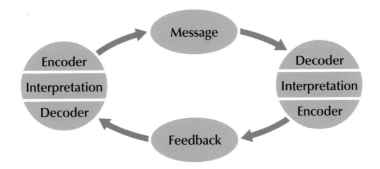

Schramm's Model of Communication, 1954
Schramm actually developed several models;
this is a compilation of those ideas from his 1954–1977 publications.

When we take in a message, we use all of our training and culture and life experience to understand that message—this is called **interpretation**. Any time you say something that makes perfect sense to you and someone of a different age, race, socioeconomic status, or even geographical upbringing (among other differences) does not understand your message, consider that both of you are using those backgrounds to interpret the meaning of the message. Your results can be quite different!

How do you know when interpretations differ? **Feedback** is the information or messages sent from the receiver *back to the sender* to show the extent of receiver understanding. (It is that odd face you make when you have no idea what your boss is asking you to do; it is the email that you receive asking why you are angry when all you did was ask a question; it is every time that you know your significant other is in a bad mood without exchanging a word.) Feedback and interpretation work together. When receivers send feedback, senders know if their messages were accurately interpreted…or not. When this goes back and forth several times (as it should to truly comprehend one another), we call this a feedback loop.

A **feedback loop** refers to the multiple back and forth cycles between sender and receiver until both are satisfied that they are on the same page. Easy, right? Well, it is not actually that simple. Think of these as the **feedback loop rules**:

- feedback itself is a message that must be encoded, sent, and decoded

- without a feedback response, the sender will not know if shared meaning was achieved

- it typically takes *several cycles* of sending and receiving feedback to achieve shared meaning

- when the sender and receiver have overlapping experiences then their interpretations will be more similar, and it is easier to reach a mutual understanding/shared meaning

Schramm in the Real World

Schramm's (1954) model, along with each of the others previously discussed, only depicts a single sender and a single receiver. This is hardly the case in most business settings. As you send a message to Person X, another person is also sending a message to Person X. At the same time that you are both sending a message to Person X, both of you (the senders) are bombarded with messages about any variety of topics. You know that becoming effective with your communication is not about sending messages into a vacuum, but receiving and reacting to as many messages and as much feedback as you get. The whole thing can get a bit sloppy.

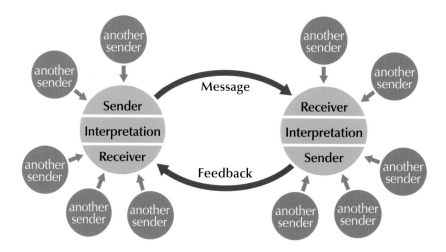

The nice thing about this type of **multiple incoming messages** communication is that by the time we get into a professional setting, we're used to it. Think about your life: your mom calls just as your roommate is in the middle of telling a story and, all the while, you are on your computer trying to finish a report that is due tomorrow when suddenly the song that reminds you of your ex comes on the radio. That is a whole lot of information! But, somehow, we process all of those messages. With time, you will be able to be just as effective in processing numerous simultaneous work messages coming at you. You will be better prepared to do so if you understand everything that makes up each element of the communication model—the source/sender, the message, the channel, and the receiver.

Berlo (1960)

If you are sending a message, you are "the sender." But you are more than that, right? You are perhaps an entry-level employee who has an extensive background with blogs and online social media and is from a Catholic background who was raised in Texas with a middle income family. David K. Berlo (1960) understood that you are more than a label. When Berlo fleshed out his idea of communication, it was not about identifying the elements (folks had already done that). Instead, he gave his attention to what *made up* each of the individual communication elements. He called his model **SMCR** (from the elements of source-message-channel-receiver).

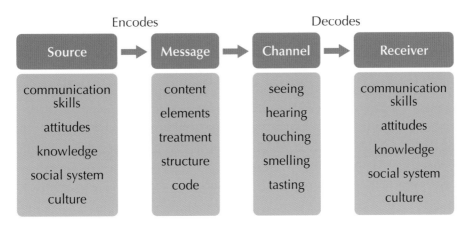

Berlo's SMCR Model

Berlo (1960) starts by elaborating on what it means to be the message sender, or **source**. The source, he says, is more than where the message originates but is a collection of aspects that determine how a source will encode a message. These five influential aspects include: 1) **communication skills** (individual ability to speak, read, write, draw, etc.), 2) **attitudes** (positive or negative association with the idea), 3) **knowledge** (the clarity of the information portrayed), 4) **social system** (values, beliefs, religion, and general understanding of society), and 5) **culture** (socially constructed rules and expectations).

Once the source goes about encoding a message, the **message** itself should be understood as having a particular makeup and is comprised of: 1) **content** (data), 2) **elements** (the various combined means of sending the message such as when a speech is given along with visual or auditory aids), 3) **treatment** (behavior or tone directed toward the content), 4) **structure** (how the message is organized), and 5) the **code** (means by which a message is sent such as language, gestures, music).

The third element Berlo considers is the **channel** of the message or how the audience will take in ideas via **smelling, tasting, feeling, hearing,** or **seeing** (one's senses). If you are confused and considering our above discussion where channel is described as the means by which the message will be transmitted (email, newspaper, radio, speech), don't be. Each of those types of channels is taken in by the audience through a type of input or sense (for instance, we hear a radio ad or see a newspaper...but we also smell a new car!). In a business setting, you may want your audience to select the conference location not only because they *see* the financial benefits or *hear* about the great venues but because they also can *smell* the new paint and fantastic catering. The kind and number of channels you use will largely depend on your intended purpose and audience/receiver.

The final link in communication is, as in all of our models, the **receiver.** The receiver is the person or persons who make up the audience of your message and *who is comprised of all the same elements that make up a sender.* As we remember from Schramm (1954), the receiver then becomes a sender of a message when producing feedback. The SMCR model points our attention to what is *inside* each element of communication. Without this, we may believe that all messages of the same content will be sent and received in the same way—leading us to potentially make huge faux pas at work!

Berlo (1960) understood that who we are determines what message we will send through which channel, and how the person to whom we send our message will be able to receive it. His model built on each model that had come before and, by offering to you what may now seem obvious in a modern-day context, each of these scholars helped us to refine our own message clarity. Professional people communicate successfully without *actively* thinking about every element of their communication process but doing so takes time and practice. As someone who is new to business communication, you will not have had years of experience testing and receiving feedback on your messages. You can, however, have a good idea of and will be more attuned to how these elements of communication work in the specific context of your business setting.

COMMUNICATION IN CONTEXT

Indeed, the perfect exchange of communication, which leads to shared meaning in one company will have people in the next company scratching their heads—or worse, creating significant and disruptive conflict. If you have ever worked with a family member as a boss then you know that how the two of you interact at work is far different than how you talk when you are sitting around the table for

Thanksgiving dinner. Context matters! In the realm of business talk, professionals tend to be concerned with elements such as whether or not the microphone works or if the meeting should be right after lunch. These are valid concerns about environmental impacts on communication, yet limiting ourselves to those tangible concerns without understanding the larger rhetorical context or *situation* will inevitably lead to miscommunication.

The Context of the Rhetorical Situation

Lloyd Bitzer (1968) coined the phrase **rhetorical situation**. Before you become too concerned about the word "rhetoric" (which may seem far too theoretical and vague for such an applied topic as business talk), know that Bitzer simply asked us to be aware that communication occurs in context. This was a simple concept that somehow had been missed in all of those communication models. It is simple, and perhaps obvious, but until we articulate the idea it is far too easy to miss this crucial point. Bitzer just asked, "What sorts of interaction occur between the speaker, audience, subject, and occasion?" (p. 3).

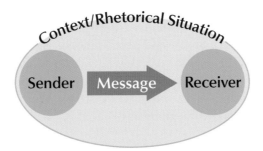

It is hard not to see how this notion of the rhetorical situation is guiding all that we do in our professional lives and business communication. The key task of considering our context means that we should always ask ourselves:

+ if we should speak at all

+ if what we have to say will make a difference

+ if the environment dictates that some messages are more appropriate than others, and

+ do we understand what impact the environment has on those receiving our message?

We can answer these questions by looking at Bitzer's three key elements of the rhetorical situation: **exigence**, **audience**, and **constraints**.

Exigence

Exigence is the most crucial part of Bitzer's (1968) rhetorical situation and refers to the need (or urgency, which is a more direct definition of the word) to engage in communication at all. This is the time when you ask yourself while sitting in your very first department meeting, "Will what I want to say make sense in this discussion and will it make a difference?" Bitzer did not want us to keep quiet—something to which new employees often resign themselves. Instead, he brought to our attention the idea that true communication (the achieving of shared meaning) does not occur between speakers and receivers unless the speaker is reacting to a *need* for a message. He argued that there are times when we really need to speak to respond to an "exigent or urgent situation," and other times when simply launching words into the air is nothing but noise—and not actual communication.

For example, your company might have a sudden dive in sales over the past fiscal year. If no one at the company addressed this issue then the stockholders would be confused, irritated, or even decide to remove their investments. Someone must say something! This is an exigent situation! Alternatively, if you called a department meeting to discuss the viability of a product that was no longer produced and well past its time (such as rotary dial phones or the pet rock...yes, old folks had these in the '80s), then your employees would wonder if you had lost your ability to read the needs of their company or your industry—after all, there is no need for such things and your *"response"* would seem pointless. Keep in mind that not all responses and messages are appropriate. How do you craft an appropriate response? We look at what is fitting for a given moment in time. Much of that decision is determined by who will be in our audience.

Audience

All of the communication models that we have discussed thus far have included an element called the receiver. We have given a fair bit of consideration to this element but, from Bitzer's (1968) perspective, we have not considered how the receivers are impacted by their situational context. Bitzer told us that the **audience**, or, what he called *agents of change*, consists of people who are capable of "mediating change," which means that they can actually change their minds or do something about our message (p. 8). For example, we would not attempt to give our sales pitch for why one must install

new windows in their home to the 5-year-old girl playing in the front yard. No—we would need to knock on the door and talk to her parents, the homeowners, about such a task. Bitzer asks us to consider the audience as part of our communication. If "agents of change" do not exist (e.g., no one can do anything about the information that you give them, won't understand it, or feel that it was useful to them in some way), then true communication cannot occur.

Remember that all models of communication, going back to Aristotle, show us that speakers send messages that are *for audiences and *about* audiences *to audiences. The context will determine the audience! Good business practice means seeing what your audience can and cannot do, which is often dictated by the constraints of the situation.

Constraints

Constraints are likely the most contemplated element of communication for business professionals because many professionals think of these as the actual things that they see around them—such as those concerns about if the microphone works or if the meeting should be right after lunch when everyone seems sleepy. Bitzer (1968) saw **constraints** as those elements of the situation that will either limit or open opportunities to have effective communication. He said that this would be *anything* with which the speaker had to contend, including (but not limited to): **the speaking surroundings** (e.g., the size of the room or the time of the day), **the speaking context** (e.g., a speech about company layoffs during a profitable quarter or an announcement of a merger in tough financial times), and **the speaking occasion** or reason for the speech (e.g., to celebrate the career of a pending retiree or to persuade a group to support company layoffs). If you are not in touch with constraints specific to your speaking/rhetorical situation, especially in *any* business context, then you hurt your potential for success!

Such a limited discussion of situational constraints may have you pondering how to manage these in your particular company. Whereas Bitzer (1968) did not go into the applications of this element in a professional context (because he was focused on developing our understanding of communication in any context), business and managerial methods have developed over time to provide their own unique take on situational constraints. These methods have become known as **business models** and this chapter would be remiss to ignore the fact that *all business talk and business communication is constrained by the business model in which it occurs.*

The Context of Business Models

Placing our communication within any business context means looking at the *expectations* of that particular industry or company. These expectations are derived from the pre-set means of operations that every company has. We might call these organizational models or "pecking orders." A **pecking order** is a hierarchy of status seen among members of a group of people or animals (originally as observed among hens!). This pecking order will determine to whom you will report and who will send information to you. How are these orders determined? They are the result of how the business is organized—or structured.

All of the business communication models that follow describe either **tall** or **flat** structures. This, rather simply, means that every business model intentionally dictates how many *levels* of supervision exist in a company. These levels respond to situational needs as well as management styles. J. C. Worthy (1950) conducted a famous study of the *Sears and Roebuck*™ company (yes, Sears at one time had a partner!). He used his study to determine that not all companies have the same number of *levels* of supervision. He was likely the first to coin the terms of tall and flat structures, which are today regularly used in business communication. According to Worthy, a **flat structure** (also called a **horizontal structure**) has fewer levels of administration and a wide span of supervision. In flat structured businesses, there are not really any levels *between* the employees and managers (i.e., if your boss or the company owner is the only person above you to whom you can report then your organization is flat!).

On the other hand, **tall structures** have multiple levels of organization with a narrow range of supervision. For instance, if you have a supervisor who reports to a department head who reports to a division head who reports to a vice-president who reports to a president who is responsible to a board (and on and on), then you are working in a tall structure. As you may imagine, some structures work better than others given the specific environmental and situational needs. The following business models adopted either tall or flat organizational structures because they were fitting to the time, the industry, and expectations for how to achieve professional success.

Scientific Management

At a time when "business" meant just one man and his apprentice, neither employee needed to articulate a specific corporate structure. The pecking order was clear, and the communication model was no more complex than what Schramm (1954) laid out previously—one person sending messages to one other person who gave feedback. This model stopped working in the United States when, in the 1900s, manufacturing developed and suddenly companies consisted of only a few bosses and tens to hundreds of employees. These new constraints and changed rhetorical situation meant that we needed a more clearly laid out strategy for communication (who should report to whom) and how to manage employees.

In 1911, Philadelphia native Frederick Taylor (1911) published *The Principles of Scientific Management*. He explained how the application of scientific principles such as routinized tasks could benefit company production and he, unintentionally, proposed a new standard in business communication. In Taylor's eyes, companies should have one optimal means of production (e.g., the one best way to make a dress or other product) and then that process should be replicated again and again. Sounds fantastic, right? Isn't this what quality control is all about in a modern age? Not quite. Taylor applied his system to the idea of production but failed to adjust for basic human needs and communication.

Taylor (1911) was known for his **time trials**. He would stand behind an employee with a stopwatch and ask the employee to work as diligently, accurately, and quickly as possible. He would note how long it took under these circumstances to complete a product and then insist that all other work be done just like this— for hours. Can you do that? Can you work at your optimal level for your entire shift? Some folks need to have water, visit the bathroom, stretch, etc. (and this was long before ergonomic workstations!). The result was that employees could not meet employer set standards and were often let go. Employees were not permitted to give feedback on the process because *scientific management only sends information from the top down*. The boss in this flat business model sends a message and no consideration of interpretation or audience feedback is considered. Scientific management was the ideal managerial model and business communication strategy for decades, with only slight modification.

In 1947, Max Weber wanted to take scientific management just a bit further. He agreed that communication should still be top down and that employee feedback was not necessary—or, more accurately, he never even considered that employees would have feedback (note that Schramm's model came around not too long after this). What he added that is still in use today is the notion of *specialization*. Weber's spin, called **Bureaucratic Theory**, argued that tasks should be specialized because not all employees are good at all parts of a job (for example, some could sew the body of a dress very well but others excelled at putting on the trim). Weber believed in continuing the top down, flat process of communication, where bosses simply dictated to employees, but was the first to initiate functional departments. His development helped lead to the next business model, which encouraged bosses to consider that employees did talk to one another and that employees themselves should be considered in business structures and communication.

Organizational Humanism Management

As you might imagine, a widespread scientific management method of management could not last. Workers had goals that differed from that of management (like needing to take a bathroom break!) and managers could not reliably count on this structure for long-term production. Business began to branch out and develop from flat toward tall structures.

Organizational humanism is a set of organizational theories that stress the role of the *employee* in how productivity (and, ultimately, communication) happens in a company. Organizational humanists suggest that the best focus for a manager to have is to challenge employees, develop employee decision-making skills, and give employees workplace responsibility. If jobs allow employees freedom to achieve their own professional goals then those employees will be motivated and satisfied. Conversely, if jobs limit employees' sense of personal achievement and growth, then employees will be less productive and less satisfied even with other incentives. The two prominent organizational humanism philosophies include **Human Relations Theory** and **Human Resources Management**.

- **Human Relations (1949)**

  Elton Mayo (1933) believed that workers would be far more effective if they were not simply told what to do but had some stake in the process—this is the crux of **Human Relations** management. (The only way, of course, to find out what employees want is to ask them…and wait for their feedback.) Elton Mayo's (1949) experiments, known as the **Hawthorne Studies** because they were conducted at the Western Electric Hawthorne Works in Cicero, Illinois, outside Chicago, hoped to find out how different workplace environments (e.g., rest breaks, work hours, lighting, temperature, and humidity) would change productivity. What he actually discovered was that the environment did not matter nearly as much as just giving the employees any kind of attention that showed them that they mattered!

  Mayo's experiments altered workplace environments to encourage employee feedback as a means of increasing worker productivity. He helped managers to realize that employee happiness depended on employees' ability to give feedback and their interaction within social groups at work. It was the first time that any business model recognized that employees talk to one another!

- **Human Resources Management (1960)**

  Douglas McGregor (1960) used his training as a social psychologist to expand upon Mayo's (1949) earlier work by developing a strategy called **Human Resources Management**. In this management model, employees were treated as company resources that required investment (much the same as machinery, buildings, or software). Consider how much time and money it takes to hire and train a new employee. We, employees, *are* investments!

The feedback that McGregor (1960) got from employees let him know that there are two kinds of employees: those that want to be there and those that do not. He proposed using two different types of management styles and feedback approaches for each. **Theory X** is an *authoritarian management* style used to direct employees that dislike work and must be controlled through threats or rewards. Using this style can encourage productivity in workers who will not ever take initiative or seek out additional responsibilities. **Theory Y** is a *participative management* style used to direct employees who will see the job itself as a reward, and the more satisfying the job, the more productivity. Using this style can encourage productivity in workers through improving workplace conditions.

Classic organizational and humanistic business models clearly dictate the type of communication that is expected between managers and employees. Yet, each of these models, once in place, does not change. These models are based on the assumption that there is one communication style regardless of circumstances. Modern business models are more in sync with Bitzer's (1954) **rhetorical situation**—where communication must be based on the ever-changing environmental constraints.

Systems Contingency Models

Systems contingency refers to any organizational model that works to be flexible for ever-changing needs in management and communication. It is the idea that "the best way to organize depends on the nature of the environment to which the organization relates" (Scott, 2003, p. 89). If the environment changes, then the company and the communication must change as well.

This idea flies in the face of what Frederick Taylor (1911) would deem the most effective way to manage and direct communication. Taylor might contend: "If it ain't broke, don't fix it." But, **Systems Contingency** demonstrates that what may work one day, may be "broke" the next. This is the crux of seasonal shopping in the United States.

Who hasn't been shopping during the U.S. holiday season? (Well, probably smart people.) If you ever have been shopping during this hectic time then you know that you will encounter crowds and a frenzy unlike any other time of year. If companies made no changes in their management structures and general business practices during the holiday season then you would likely come across a whole host of ill-prepared and ill-equipped retailers. Instead, we do see changes! We see things like extra employees, new setups for checkout and customer service, and perhaps even temporary standards for managing the retail floor. Perhaps this is a time where temporary employees will want and be given less responsibility (moving from a Theory Y to a Theory X model). Whether it be short or long term, such changes are *contingent* or dependent on changes in the environment.

Moving into a global environment where teams may be spread throughout countries or even continents led to the last business context model.

Transformational Model

The **Transformational Model** (first conceptualized as a leadership model by James MacGregor Burns in 1978) focuses on organized employee supervision and communication around a *vision* rather than around products, seasons, or a bureaucratic model. Timothy Johnpress (2003) looked at the difference between *transactional* businesses and *transformational* businesses. A **transactional** company is clearly defined by its name—transaction. Employees will show up, do work, and get paid. Examples of transactional businesses are trade unions, construction companies, and "old school" manufacturers. This varies greatly from a **transformational organization**. Rand Stagan states that, "A transformational company provides a clear sense of purpose grounded in an unchanging set of core values and guiding principles. These companies maximize human capital by capturing the positive emotional energy of their workforce towards a common vision." (See Johnpress, 2003, p. 2)

Examples of transformational companies include Starbucks, Southwest Airlines Co., and Home Depot Inc., along with employee-focused Google,™ IKEA®, and Richard Branson's Virgin Mobile (Johnpress, 2003). These are the places where we can assume that feedback loops and receiver culture are invaluable parts of communication and long-term planning. While transformational models of business may give more attention to the individual elements articulated in the SMCR model, we cannot assume that they are the best organizational model for our needs. What we can do with any organizational model is look to see how that model influences our rhetorical situation...and respond with appropriate communication!

LOOKING BACK ON THE SENDING OF BUSINESS MESSAGES

Models and Structures

Communication models are an excellent place to start our business and professional communication journey. By understanding how communication flows, we can see how it moves through corporate structures. By understanding the communication needs of employees, we can dictate the business structures that will help us to be productive. When it is your time to put together a workforce for a huge sale at your company, what type of communication will you encourage from your co-workers or hope for from your boss? When someone proposes a new type of business development plan to you, will you consider how effective it will be with the specific audience and within particular constraints? Will you think about the exigence of the plan…is it needed at all?

If you are beginning to see business communication in a whole new light then you are well on your way to having enlightened and more successful business ventures! You are also prepared to consider the vast array of choices that you will make in the business world. In fact, the **narrowing of choices** both defines what your business communication must *do* and is even how many have defined rhetoric and communication itself (Hart, 1994). Your next step to becoming a successful business communicator is to look at your choices to take information in and the ethics of what you do with that information!

2

CHOOSING TO
RECEIVE MESSAGES

"When it comes down to it, it isn't the major choices
we make in life—career, marriage, etc.—
that count the most. It is the everyday, minor decisions
that make life work for us."

—*Dr. Shad Helmstetter, author of* Choices

MAKING BUSINESS CHOICES

Goal setting in the workplace is about making strategic choices. Should you apply for that promotion? Can your company afford to expand into the Western region? Where should you have your company retreat? Is now the time to revise your corporate image, social media, and business plan? Some of your decisions will seem easy and others will leave you feeling a bit overwhelmed. This many choices (too many choices), as we know, can leave us unsure, ineffective, or even in a position to make unethical decisions. Here are a few things to remember:

+ No one else can make your choices for you.

+ When you have a problem, make a choice—you'll feel better.

+ You cannot manage your life if you do not manage yourself. You cannot manage yourself if you do not manage your choices. Manage your choices, and you will manage your life.

+ Those who choose to succeed always do better than those who never choose at all (Helmstetter, 2006).

But we know that language is best used in a business context to help people narrow their choices (Hart, 1994). Part of this process is to put ourselves in the best position to make decisions between choices.

Consider the following choice-based scenario. For the sake of the context of this book (and because, let's face it, you aren't likely to have this scenario actually happen to you), let's put the dilemma into a business setting.

> You manufacture cars. You are happily conducting your business when someone comes to you and says, "This car has a flaw and if you don't fix it, people will die." Sadly, we have seen news lately that car manufacturers have been in this situation. We are now in the position to pose some important questions: Is it ethical to let some people die if it will save your business and the jobs of thousands of people? How many people need to die and have their jobs saved before ignoring the issue is an ethical choice? Are you an ethical person if you decide to fix the cars in some instances and not in others? Ah…it just isn't that simple, is it?

You are left at an ethical crossroads and now must make some incredibly important choices.

This is a chapter about choice. The best foundation for any business talk in any rhetorical situation is to know all of your choices and then to select the best possible one. In other words, business talk is about choosing whether to listen or not, choosing the best questions to ask, and choosing your own ethical path.

THE CHOICE TO HEAR OR LISTEN

Considering what you know about business communication thus far, you likely have a good initial idea of how listening fits into business structures and communication models. For instance, senders send messages through channels to receivers. If the message is never received, then there is no feedback and no communication. But simply taking in the message does not mean that the person was actually listening let alone interpreting and decoding as the sender hoped.

We have all experienced making a statement and, subsequently, knowing that the person to whom we were speaking just didn't get it. Perhaps you have told someone something incredibly tragic and they said, "Hey, that's great!"—clearly having not heard the meaning of your message.

Too often we send messages that are received but not clearly processed. Too often this is an issue of *listening* that, in the business context, can have disastrous, even fatal, results. As the *Encyclopedia of Business and Finance* (2010) explains:

> Most people make numerous listening mistakes every day, but the costs—financial and otherwise—are seldom analyzed. Because of listening mistakes, appointments have to be rescheduled, letters retyped, and shipments rerouted. Any number of catastrophes can arise from a failed communication regardless of the type of industry. Productivity is affected and profits suffer. (p. 1)

On a more dramatic note, Edward Tufte (2005) makes the argument that the choice to use PowerPoint® as a message channel prevented audiences from listening to arguments from NASA engineers that the *Columbia* space shuttle had a potentially (as it turns out, absolutely) fatal design flaw. While the validity of Tufte's PowerPoint argument is highly debatable, the notion that choosing to listen in business settings is crucial cannot be overstressed (DiSalvo, 1980; Sypher, Bostrom, & Seibert, 1989).

Reasons to Choose

It (listening) is a choice. We can choose to tune in and we can choose to tune out. Technology consultant and the author of *Leading Geeks*, Paul Glen (2011), identifies five common ways of **choosing not to listen**:

1. Just Keep Talking

2. When You're Not Talking, Think about What You're Going to Say Next

3. Interrupt Frequently

4. Look Away

5. Never, Ever Ask Clarifying Questions

Would you intentionally choose to do these things? Likely not. However, sometimes we make choices without thinking about them and those choices work against us.

"Choose?", you might be thinking. As an employee, I will just take what I am given and work with it. That may sound right to you at this moment but it is just not how life works. We make intentional and unintentional choices about what gets our attention. This is the difference between hearing and listening.

Choosing Hearing versus Listening

At its most clinical level, **listening** is an intentional act that involves taking in and processing all of a message (Fredriksson, 1999). It is a task that requires discipline, emotional control, focus and commitment (Cheesebro, O'Connor, & Rios, 2010; Ferrari, 2012). Contrast this to **hearing**, which is what most of us do, that can be either a conscious or unconscious behavior involving the physical awareness of sound (Fredriksson). Given this description, there are direct benefits to selecting listening rather than hearing, and those benefits will have an immediate and direct impact on our careers.

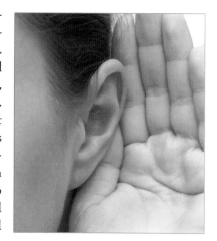

Benefits of Choosing to Listen

As you are building your client base, participating in group projects at work, or even negotiating over who will clean the office refrigerator, you will be building your career through relationships. None of us ever enters the business world set on mediocrity—okay, hopefully most of us don't. For the vast majority of us, excelling in our careers is important. If you are not sure where to begin, remember that effective listening also translates into improved working relationships (Flynn, Vilikoski, & Grau, 2008).

You only need to recall the fallout of your relationship with a disliked co-worker to understand the value of good working relationships. So how can listening help? Flynn, Vilikoski, and Grau (2008) found that creating an organizational culture that values listening will boost employee identification with the company and result in higher employee satisfaction! *New York Times* columnist Glenn Rifkin (1994) found in one of his interviews with top executives that, "June Rokoff, Senior VP for Software Development at Lotus credits her success in turning around the company's position in the software industry to building a team that listens: she made listening the culture of her team" (p. 2).

These relationships are the foundation for long-term successful careers. If that is not enough for you, listening has numerous other benefits such as: increased profit, reduced waste, employee retention, superior leadership and effective teams (Ferrari, 2012 and Gergen, 2011), persuasive influence (Ames, Maissen, & Bockner, 2012), increased upward mobility, (Hartman & McCambridge, 2011), relationship building (Brunner, 2008), positive perceptions of sales staff (Ramsey & Sohl, 1997) and even the development of a professional reputation of maturity, trust and competence (Alleyne, 2011).

You do not need to wait for your boss or senior colleagues to craft this culture for you. You can begin to create this standard and others will follow. In this vein, listening works as a marketing tool for the company to build a long-term clientele and has worked in this way for successful strategists across a variety of industries.

Consider all of the day-to-day workplace tasks that need your listening skills. Taking notes, conducting interviews, receiving instructions, and even handling complaints all demand alert and active listening. Effective listening is crucial to running a business efficiently, and we should know if we are doing it well.

How Well Do I Listen?

With so much riding on listening, ask yourself, "How well do I listen? Am I just hearing the noise and not processing the information? How can I know?" To determine whether you spend more time listening or hearing, take the Listening Quotient (LQ) Test (Wheeless, 1975). Compare your answers to the accompanying scale. (Do not panic if you find that you have been overestimating your listening skills. We all have room for improvement! This is just a *first* step.)

Listening Quotient (LQ) Test

For each of the following statements, select one of the following: (Y) Yes, (S) Sometimes, or (N) No.

_____ I feel comfortable when listening to others on the phone.

_____ It is often difficult for me to concentrate on what others are saying.

_____ I feel tense when listening to new ideas.

_____ I have difficulty concentrating on instructions that others give to me.

_____ I dislike being a listener as a member of an audience.

_____ I seldom seek out opportunities to listen.

_____ I find myself daydreaming when others ramble on.

_____ I often argue mentally or aloud with what someone is saying even before he or she finishes.

_____ I find that others often repeat things to me.

_____ I seem to find out about important events too late.

Now count your answers.

_____ Number of times you answered "Yes"

_____ Number of times you answered "No"

_____ Number of times you answered "Sometimes"

Finally, score your listening adeptness.

If you answered Yes or Sometimes on less than three questions, you perceive yourself as a good listener.

If you answered Yes or Sometimes on three to six questions, you perceive yourself as an average listener.

If you answered Yes or Sometimes on seven or more questions, you must give immediate attention to your listening skills.

Finished? How did you score? If you did well, then you have an excellent foundation on which to develop your current skills. If you struggled, do not worry. This does not mean that you have made bad choices but only that you likely were not aware that your choices were creating listening barriers. Now is the time to reduce or remove those barriers.

Minimizing Listening Barriers

Consider this interesting tidbit about how we listen: average speaking rates range from 100 words per minute (wpm) to 175 wpm. On the other hand, estimated message comprehension rates range from 400 to 800 wpm (Lee & Hatesohl, 1993; Zofi and Metzler, 2007). This means that our minds have the ability to take in information far faster than the person speaking can deliver that information. So what is the significance of this differential? The lag between speaking and message intake is called the **listening gap**, and it is where and when our minds tend to wander.

Recognizing what disrupts effective listening, **listening barriers** that encourage our minds to wander during gaps, is the first step toward improving these skills. Some external and environmental barriers like noise, hunger, or room temperature are easily understood. But other, more psychological, aspects can wreak havoc on our message comprehension without us fully realizing their influence.

Listening Selections

Shramm (1954) told us that we can figure out whether or not our messages are understood by paying attention to listener feedback. But what if someone has the *ability* to understand our message and *chooses* not to? Yes, listening is a choice, but not all of our listening decisions are good ones—like allowing our minds to wander. In psychological terms, we refer to these choices as **selections**.

+ **Selective Exposure**

We tend to seek out information consistent with our existing worldview. If you have ever deliberately avoided a person at work who always talks about their religion (one that is different from yours) or not gone to a social gathering when you learned that everyone attending was from a different sorority or fraternity than the one to which you belonged then you are selectively choosing the situations to which you will expose yourself. You can think of this in terms of Bitzer's (1968) rhetorical situation! We have selected our audience and constraints rather than allowing them to be given to us. If you have made a choice like this, you have certainly missed information that would not be sent in any other scenario (Festinger, 1957).

+ **Selective Attention**

Like the difference between listening and hearing, simply exposing ourselves to alternative viewpoints does *not* necessarily translate into listening. If you have seen the Sarah McLachlan commercial for the American Society for the Prevention of Cruelty to Animals (ASPCA) (the one where abused animals stare pitifully at the camera while McLachlan's song "Angel" plays in the background) and have just tuned it out because it is too rough to watch—then you have *chosen* not to pay attention.

If your co-worker begins to give a presentation on a business strategy with which you whole-heartedly disagree and know that your boss will squash in an instant, do you spend your time keen on every word? Of course not. You begin to go through your workday list (or even your grocery list!) in order to make better use of your time. You do what neurologists and psychologists (see Posner and Peterson, 1980) have long considered a natural reaction— you tune things out. You, in fact, *embrace* the listening gap! This process of selective attention is actually considered to be our brain's way of best utilizing resources but works against us when, buried in the middle of the message that we tuned out, is a key detail to our future success.

+ **Selective Perception**

Perception is the interpretation of messages. Because communication is ambiguous by nature, messages are open to interpretation (remember Schramm, 1954!). Through selective perception, we tend to assign meanings that are consistent with *our* expectations ("But, I did send the project on Friday...11:45 p.m. is still Friday"). When a message does not fit with our expectations or our assigned meanings, we deny the validity of the message, dismiss it as irrelevant, or compartmentalize the message to isolate it from our conflicting views (for original scientific analysis, see Hillyard, et al., 1973).

♦ **Selective Retention**

The worst part about how our brains listen is that we may actually, first, listen and, secondly, *discard* important details. Selective retention allows us to drop from memory both those nagging inconsistencies that do not fit with our worldview or those details that we do not evaluate as vital information (McCroskey, Richmond, & McCroskey, 2006).

Has your boss ever said, "I have told you how to do this twice already!" Do you feel like you are losing your mind? Relax. You are not *losing* your mind… your mind is *letting go* of information for strategic reasons. (Perhaps you have too much on your plate already and can't manage another work task.) This does not make it a good thing to forget the details but it might allow you to understand why you do it and get better at not doing it later.

How are you impacted by your selections? Are you aware of them? (Most of us are not.) Are you aware how these choices impact your daily life, let alone your professional life? Michael Maccoby (2000), author of *Narcissistic Leaders*, writes of these people: "They only listen to the feedback and information that matches what they want to hear. When they say they want teamwork, what they really mean is that they want a group of yes men" (para. 2). This is not the way you want to be viewed in your professional life! The choice now? Improve your listening.

Improving Listening

So, how do we get better? The first—and most straightforward steps—are to, whenever possible, *choose* to acknowledge and eliminate anything that would get in the way of our listening (such as listening selections or physical barriers like hunger or fatigue). The second step is to embrace actual strategies that put us in the best condition to receive messages. (For the record, multitasking is not the answer!)

Be Aware of Choices: 75/25

Shhh. Did you hear that? If you were talking, you were not likely to give attention to the incoming message. Sometimes listening is as easy as…not talking. Conflict resolution and negotiating expert Robert Mayer (2005) has given a label to what most sales trainers recommend—the **75/25 Partnering Secret**. This concept is simple: spend 75% of your time listening and 25% talking. When we do this, we allow speakers to deliver more of their message, reduce our natural tendency to employ listening filters, and improve relationships along the way.

Set the Scene

There is a time and place for everything, right? Effective listening is no different. In order to maximize your listening ability, you need to look around—literally. See what surrounds you in this particular environment. Lloyd Bitzer (1954) told us to be aware of the situational constraints that predetermine what is appropriate to say. Richard Vatz (1968, 2007) would argue that we can control these situations by manipulating the constraints. Perhaps some of the constraints that you need to manipulate include:

- **Allowing Sufficient Time**

  If you are pressed for time, you cannot give your undivided attention to understanding what is being communicated to you (King, 2010). Make an appointment for a time when you can focus on listening fully. If you have been given 5 minutes then know that you cannot listen as well as push a 20-minute sell into that time. Ask for the time that you need—and work with the time that you have.

- **A Lack of Physical Distractions**

  Make sure that you have a setting that supports giving the other party your undivided attention. Bierck (2001) advised avoiding having *serious* conversations in your office. Why? Unfinished projects, your phone, your email, and other distractions can draw your attention away from the conversation, which is *especially* problematic if the interaction is emotionally sensitive (like listening to someone explain that a serious health crisis will prevent him or her from finishing a project). It can be hard not to think about personal distractions but remember that your focus is on creating a listening culture, which starts with you!

  Smart organizations create spaces that promote effective listening opportunities (Hartman & McCambridge, 2011). Find a conference room or a private nook where you can talk without distractions and interruptions. (If you think that this is only for folks getting fired or more stodgy industries…at Skywalker Ranch, George Lucas has seating nooks in numerous locations in order to allow staff to brainstorm without interruption at any time.)

- **A Lack of Mental Distractions**

  You know from our discussion of listening selections that distractions come from our environment but also from *within* us. Give yourself time before any meeting or interaction to remove these internal distractions. Choose to arrive for your meeting early, which will give you some transition time to get out of the thinking mode you needed for whatever you were doing just before the meeting, and to get into an appropriate mindset for this interaction.

Bierck (2001), again, recommends that we all review the purpose of meeting or interaction and then identify ideal outcomes. Yes—get your mind wrapped around why you are there and not wrapped around your own issues. A little assessment time makes for better listening!

Attention to Ethos, Pathos, Logos

Aristotle (in *Nicomachean Ethics*, trans. 1980) told us that sending messages is *about* the audience, *for* the audience, and *to* the audience. So, now, you are the audience. Understanding Aristotle's audience appeals, as they are presented to you in the audience, will help you pay attention. Look specifically for the presence or absence of these appeals and this will give you something with which to engage the speaker at the end.

- **Logos—Can I Follow the Outline?**

  Not everyone has had (or remembers) a public speaking class but we know that having a clear speaking outline, where the message "makes sense" to the audience is crucial. Unfortunately, the speaker to whom you are listening may not make this so clear; therefore, it becomes your job to look for the organizational flow by:

  1. *Making Mental Summaries:* You can write arguments down, but you can also simply track in your head the central arguments, main ideas, and supporting evidence. A good listener takes advantage of natural pauses in the flow of ideas to think back and recap what has been said. These listener-generated summaries significantly reinforce overall understanding (Lee & Hatesohl, 1993).

  2. *Anticipating:* What is coming next? Wait—does the subsequent argument make sense given what was just said? By foreshadowing (guessing!) what arguments *should* be made and anticipating them ahead of time, we play a mental game with ourselves. If we guess right, we win because learning is reinforced (Lee & Hatesohl, 1993); if we guess wrong, figuring out why helps to increase attention.

- **Ethos—What Type of Support Am I Offered?**

  The worst part of persuasive messages outside the academic setting is that speakers want us to buy their arguments just because "they said so." Why is it that journalists, professors, and authors must have external support for their claims, but we do not maintain these requirements for business speakers? We should!

  Lee and Hatesohl (1993) observed that, "By and large, we use only three ways to build points: We explain the point, we get emotional and harangue the point, or we illustrate the point with a factual illustration" (para. 31). Figuring out how someone is supporting (or not supporting) an argument can increase our listening efficiency—and also keep us from believing something that simply has no foundation!

+ **Pathos—Am I *Feeling* It?**

Emotional resonance, as we discussed earlier, does not mean that the speaker made your cry (or laugh out loud or shake with anger). Emotional resonance simply means that we feel connected to the message in some way. As an audience member, *you* need to determine if what the speaker offers reaches you emotionally. ("Has the speaker made efforts to connect the subject matter to me personally in a way that is meaningful and useful?") Choosing to ask yourself this question throughout a speaking interaction puts you in a better place to hold on to the message long term (Aristotle, in *Nicomachean Ethics*, trans. 1980).

Enact Listening Behaviors—Showing Feedback

At this point, you may be thinking that you are well aware of your choices to listen or not—and that you will make good choices. Excellent. That is the right path for professional success...as long as the person speaking *knows* that we are listening. Wilbur Schramm (1954) advanced the idea of **feedback**—letting the message sender know that we comprehended the message.

Imagine (or perhaps you have experienced) a scenario where a speaker goes over key ideas or tells a story, and then later on tells the exact same story. You may fault the speaker for using unnecessary repetition. But, perhaps the speaker did this intentionally because he or she believed that you did not listen the first time. Listening feedback is crucial so that the speaker/sender can clarify the message or continue along the same path because you are "getting it." The way to show that you are listening comes from some basic phrases and nonverbal communication.

+ **"So, What You're Saying Is..."—Verbal Engagement**

While jumping in to take over the conversation or constantly interrupting to voice your own experiences will hinder listening, providing *small* verbal indications of listening will help you to focus. Bordone (2007) suggests three key skills to use when actively listening:

a. *Paraphrasing*: Restate what the other person has said in a genuine manner that does not condescend. This serves to give senders a chance to clarify, avoid misunderstandings, and show comprehension.

b. *Inquiring:* Get someone to elaborate on an idea by asking non-threatening questions, which is useful to keep the feedback loop moving effectively.

c. *Acknowledging:* By showing that you understand not just the facts but the feelings underlying the other person's message, you can convey that you have listened to the big picture. This may happen through the occasional "I know, I know" or a "That makes sense to me" verbal recognition. This should coincide with nonverbal signals of understanding, such as that sympathetic touch.

+ **"Look! I Am Listening"—Nonverbal Enacting**

Your nonverbal messages speak volumes. These signals let people know whether or not we are listening, understanding, or connecting This means that when you are listening, you should:

a. *Give appropriate eye gaze:* Do not stare, but make direct eye contact.

b. *Sit or stand in an engaging way:* Show attention in your nonverbal demeanor but do not be aggressively eager—leaning forward while others speak but keeping out of personal space.

c. *Avoid fidgeting or multitasking:* Pay attention to tapping or squirming, avoid reading computers or handheld devices, etc.

d. *Signal understanding:* Occasionally nod or show appropriate facial expressions or gestures (e.g., a sympathetic touch).

Practice

Understandably, listening does not come naturally, and sometimes it does not come easily. Lee and Hatesohl (1993) argue that good listening takes endurance. If done for a long period of time, it can leave you mentally (and physically!) exhausted. While it is tempting to give up listening efforts in frustration, dedicating some listening practice time will make the process easier and more rewarding. Zofi and Metzler (2007) suggest focusing on *mental rewards* for listening, such as reminding yourself that you are more likely to get a promotion because your boss sees you as the only one who pays attention or landing that new client because you asked the right question to understand their needs. It can be hard work but so worth it!

If everyone knew that listening was a choice then likely they would make the choice to do it, even though it is hard work. Another hard choice is asking good questions. If you are considering what good questions are a matter of "choice," consider the last time that you heard someone ask a question that was irrelevant. Did you think to yourself, "Why on earth did you ask that?!" You are questioning his or her *choice*. Strategic understanding of question choices helps us gather the best data and ask the best questions.

CHOOSING THE RIGHT QUESTIONS

"If I had an hour to solve a problem and my life depended on the solution, I would spend the first 55 minutes determining the proper question to ask, for once I know the proper question, I could solve the problem in less than five minutes."

—*Albert Einstein*

Effective and accurate message reception depends on the audience (which is the listeners) taking in the information and then getting any missing information through asking the best questions. Barker and his colleagues (1980) developed the connection between listening and communication one step further to argue that in order to *truly* listen, a receiver must take a message and provide feedback on three levels:

+ **Self-Feedback**—Did I get that?

+ **Listener-to-Listener Feedback**—Did you get that?

+ **Listener-to-Speaker Feedback**—Did you say that?

In order to utilize all of these forms of feedback, we must be skilled in the art of asking questions. No—it is not enough to just ask speakers to repeat themselves or just chime in with the first thing that comes to mind. You must be prepared to ask questions, choose the best questions, *and be open to the answers.*

Self-Feedback—"Did I Get That?"

Have you ever listened to an entire presentation from a professor (or your boss or even a co-worker) while enacting all listening behaviors such as nodding, smiling, and at the end felt completely informed—only to think back on the talk a few hours later and realize that you have no idea what you were supposed to have learned? You have not yet utilized self-feedback. We all have done this, but it is actually an illustration of poor message comprehension.

Message comprehension is the complete understanding of a message as it was intended by the sender. There are a number of reasons that we do not comprehend information but the most glaring reason is because we fail to stop during the interaction and ask ourselves if we really "get it." There are three strategies of self-feedback that can help to improve your listening and comprehension.

1. *Assume Speaker Expertise:* If selected appropriately, the person speaking should be an expert to some degree. Kevin Cashman (2012) suggests that we try to appreciate that others may know more than us, even if it is not to the degree to which we would like. We can be better listeners if we look for that expertise and should ask ourselves, "*What might this person understand better than I do?*"

2. *Listen for Content, Not Delivery:* We may be more caught up in how the message is presented than the message itself. Delivery is important but should not gain our attention more than the content of the message. Instead, look at how the content impacts the appeal to pathos. Cashman (2012) suggests that we ask ourselves about the emotional undertones of the speech or message that might alter receiver message comprehension: *"Is the speaker afraid, nervous, mad, etc.?"* and how does that change the message?

3. *See the Big Picture and Details:* Sometimes we understand (or agree with) part of a message but not other parts. Negotiations expert Michael Rosenthal (2012) prompts us to set aside our own position long enough to consider that even if the other person's overall analysis seems poor to us, that perhaps the individual facts offered are accurate and useful. Conversely, even if facts of another's argument are subpar, the overall idea could have merit. He says, "It's the ability to suspend your confidence in your own conclusions and consider a competing view that distinguishes the great leaders, managers, and salespeople from the average ones" (para. 8).

Once you have stepped back to evaluate these elements, it will be time to turn to the person next to you and see what additional help his or her perspective can be.

Listener-to-Listener Feedback—Did You Get That?

"Is everyone getting this but me?" If you have ever been a freshman in college, at a first meeting at your new place of employment, or even watched C-SPAN then you have wondered if everyone got what was being said but you—or if you were *all* just woefully lost.

Human beings were not meant to understand everything. If we were, we would all need to come from the same background and experience, and our heads would be considerably larger. Instead, allow yourself to benefit from the experience, expertise, and understanding of those around you.

Think of all of the times outside the office that you have done just this! If you have listened to a band and liked the music but still have gone online to read others' reviews before buying the album, you have reached out for listener-to-listener feedback. If you have gotten class notes from a friend to compare them with your own or waited to ask a question during orientation to see if others will ask it, you are looking to others. This is a regular behavior that should not suddenly be avoided in a professional context.

Daniel K. Oestreich (2009) suggests that we are hesitant to ask others not because it would not be helpful but due to emotional discomfort. He asks that we balance that discomfort with a clear understanding of the benefits.

Feedback leads to disclosure, which in turn builds trust, which means problem-solving can improve as stress in communications is reduced. We have a chance to deal with things the way they are, not just as we assume them to be. In a work place, these outcomes can be of particular value. The work place and the way we work together are changing greatly. (p. 1)

If you can move past your discomfort and into questions and answers with those around you then you can prepare to offer the speaker useful feedback.

Listener-to-Speaker Feedback—Did You Say That?

Once you have made smart choices to ask questions of yourself and of those around you, you should be able to direct your attention to the feedback loop. It is time to move to back and forth questions between senders and receivers. Good questions consider both the goal of the message and the direction of feedback, and are filtered by the tone of our questions.

Listener-to-Speaker Question Goals

Considering what questions you will need answered *before* listening to a presentation can help you to be prepared to ask questions. We refer to this as **goal-oriented listening**. If you expect the speaker to offer facts and hard data but she or he does not, you can then ask the speaker if these things exist, are important, or even if there is a reason that they were not included. Vogt, Brown, and Isaacs (2003) suggest that most people do not ask good questions of speeches because, "much of Western culture, and North American society in particular, focuses on having the 'right answer' rather than discovering the 'right question'" (p. 2). Figuring out good questions begins with knowing what you are seeking and selecting the right type of question to get that information. We can divide our question types into either closed-ended or open-ended.

A **closed-ended question** is one with a limited set of available answers (Air Force Negotiation Center of Excellence, 2004). Closed-ended questions can be answered with only the options that pre-exist. If you ask a person what month it is, this question only has twelve answers. If you ask a person the date on which he or she began work at a current company, this question must be answered with a specific date. Closed-ended questions serve to provide you with facts and details that may be missing from a message and are needed for comprehension. The concern about choosing to ask closed-ended questions is that they may encourage the answerer to limit his or her sharing (Air Force Negotiation Center of Excellence).

An **open-ended question** is one with an unlimited set of available answers. Open-ended questions cannot be answered simply, and encourage the speaker to talk and explain ideas in complete sentences (Air Force Negotiation Center of Excellence, 2004). These questions invite a person to open up, provide his or her personal perspective, or provide rich data—which sometimes is far more than is needed. Examples of open-ended questions include, "Can you tell me more about [the subject]?", "What happened next?", "How did you feel when that happened?", or "What would you like to see as an outcome?" Selecting either a closed- or open-ended question depends on the kind of data that you are hoping to get in return! Once you have this difference mastered, you can ask questions based on the role that you are assuming—speaker or audience.

Be an Audience Who Asks Questions of the Speaker

If you have listened to a speech and simply walked away silently at the end, then you are on your own in terms of grasping the speaker's intended meaning. If instead you decide to ask questions that have not been answered through the presentation itself then you may further your own comprehension while forming a bond with the speaker. Joe Takash (2010) argues that it is our responsibility to demonstrate that we (the receiver) are providing meaningful responses to issues raised by the speaker. He differentiates between vague and/or not related questions, such as, "Ok, so where do you want to go from here with the project?" and responses that search for solutions, such as, "How will it improve our odds of meeting our project deadline if we are able to get Bob to help with editing?" As an audience member your questions should be designed to produce more information, provide clarity, or introduce a different perspective (Ferarri, 2012) or summarize ideas (Pearce, 2011).

> "Sometimes listening itself may not be enough—some people must be prodded if you are to find out what they're thinking."
>
> —*Mary Kay Ash (1915–2001),*
> *U.S. entrepreneur, business executive,*
> *and founder of Mary Kay Cosmetics*

Ferarri (2012) recommends that, as speakers, we challenge our own assumptions. We should not be so narcissistic, as Maccoby (2000) calls it, as to allow ourselves to think that our idea is the only one or will always be the best one. Instead we must believe that our audience has the potential to have better ideas than we do. Some questions may include, "Have we asked for input from everyone with a stake in our issue?" or "If we had to completely change this product by next month, what would we do differently?" Whatever you ask, do so with a tone that encourages a response.

Watch Your Tone

Asking questions is a tricky business of emotional sensitivities. M. Neil Browne and Stuart M. Keeley (2006), authors of *Asking the Right Questions: A Guide to Critical Thinking*, remind us that,

> If you question in certain ways, others may very well become annoyed. Most human beings do not welcome being questioned by others with open arms. We think this is a very important issue for interpersonal relationships….we recommend that you try different approaches to questioning others until you find ones that are comfortable and do not seem to create too much resistance or defensiveness. But we also recommend that you work on tolerating some short-term annoyance from others. (para. 6)

It is a very valid, and business related, point that the desire to be liked often makes us avoid asking tough questions. That is, of course, understandable. The rub is fear that our question and tone will be ill-received results in no one asking questions and our inability to grow. Instead, try to (according to Browne & Keeley, 2006; Ferarri, 2012; Sharer, 2012; Takash, 2010):

+ *Pick Your Spots:* Avoid jumping in but wait until the appropriate time.

+ *Clarify Your Intention:* Try to convince others that you are asking questions to try to better understand their reasoning, not to put them on the spot.

+ *Be Respectful:* Use words and emphasis that show respect for the speaker regardless of your agreement.

+ *Work to Reveal—Not Criticize:* Remember that your purpose should be to come to a better understanding and not to make another look foolish.

+ *Endure SOME Annoyances:* Be tolerant of those who are intolerant of you but avoid putting yourself in a position to be humiliated or bullied.

Michael Rosenthal (2012) puts it well: "Everybody…seeks to be heard and understood. By providing that platform through sincere questioning, you will create valuable goodwill" (para. 7). So, follow the advice. Take some time to figure out *how* to ask questions but *do* ask them!

Being Open to Answers—As Either a Speaker or Receiver

Flip the above situation around—if you are the speaker who presents a message and does not ask for feedback then you have no idea if your audience has reached your intended meaning. Speakers who do not *ask* are doomed, at best, to not know if the presentation was effective and, at worst, to alienate audiences (Dewhurst, 2010). Even if your audience has been somewhat interactive throughout the presentation, you will never know if they are on the same page as you unless you ask!

The art of asking for and acting on feedback demands both patience and practice. Because people are not used to others seeking this sensitive data, they may be reluctant to immediately open up or may just comment that "there are no problems." So the irony is that to ultimately reduce tensions in a relationship, one may have to endure, even create, a little tension in order to get the ball rolling.

Is it ethical to imply to a speaker that we have received and understood a message when one or both are not true? If we choose to tune out a message because it goes against our existing ideas, are we doing to another what we would never want done to us? How should we evaluate someone who chooses not to ask about the consequences of his or her actions to avoid considering how those actions hurt others? Truly considering business choices necessitates evaluating the ethics of those choices.

MAKING ETHICAL CHOICES

All people in the workplace face on a daily basis the choices between optional courses of action. These choices, we hope, do the best for all those involved—but not always. Bernie Madoff took 50 billion dollars of other people's money and used it for his family and himself (Lenzer, 2008); Canada was attempting to overturn environmental guidelines in the U.S. in order to pump sand-oil over the border (Kunzig, 2009); former California Governor Arnold Schwarzenegger fathered a child with another woman while his wife was expecting their fourth baby (Chaney, 2011). It is hard

not to ask ourselves, "What were they thinking?" It is even harder to ask ourselves, "What would we do when faced with choices between ethical options?"

One of the most important choices that we place on our companies' leaders is to uphold the highest standards of ethical behavior. If we assume that only leaders are faced with these choices, then we likely have not been listening or asking good questions. The last part of our discussion on choices involves you looking at the information that you have and deciding what to do with it—these are choices of managing ethical dilemmas.

Defining Ethics

What does it mean to be ethical? This is a difficult question to answer. Ethics are not tied to a particular religion. Ethical behavior does not mean following specific or even all laws. Ethics is not what society tells us to do. At its most basic level, the *Oxford English Dictionary* (OED) defines ethics as, "the moral principles by which a person is guided; the rules of conduct recognized in certain associations or departments of human life; having or pertaining to ethos." Within a business context, the *OED* goes on to assert that, "in accordance with the principles of ethics; morally right; honorable; virtuous; decent; spec. conforming to the ethics of a profession, etc." If we look at these together, we can argue that **ethics** are standards of behavior or the study of how we develop standards of behavior. These standards typically come into play when business professionals face what are called ethical dilemmas.

When you view a choice with disgust or as despicable then you are viewing it through your own lens of appropriate standards of behavior. Many people, however, do not realize that others may view *their* behavior as sub-standard. Look to your own everyday decisions to see if you have faced what Rushworth Kidder (1995) defined as an **ethical dilemma**—not a choice between right and wrong, but a choice between two rights—and think about how your choice might look to others.

Foundational Ethical Perspectives

The idea of determining the best path for one's behavior did not start in the world of business. For thousands of years, philosophers have pondered what constitutes "moral behavior" and what should be deemed ethical or unethical. We see these concerns play out today—where organizations (e.g., executives, managers, employees, and other stakeholders) need ethical guidelines to help guide the decisions that they make every day. There are three long-standing philosophical positions that still guide many organizational leaders' decisions to this day: **universalism**, **utilitarianism**, and **virtue ethics**.

Kant: Universalism

Have you ever felt that it was your "duty" to do something? Maybe as part of being a good citizen (such as picking up trash on a trail you were hiking even though it wasn't yours) or being a good person (such as helping your parents move)? Do you believe that everyone has a *duty* to be a good employee? Is there any standard or rule that you think applies to everyone (such as "the Golden Rule")? The notion of duty is key to the philosophy of Immanuel Kant (1785). Those adhering to Kant's philosophy are called **deontologists,** or one who believes that all people in every situation have a duty and obligation to uphold the highest moral principles.

If you have ever uttered the words, "no matter what," then you have to some degree embraced a deontological position. Putting this into a professional context, you may have thought: "I will not stab my friend at work in the back, no matter what," or "I will not sell out, no matter what," or even, "You cannot get me to fire people during the holidays, no matter what." Each of these positions reflects a duty to which you feel bound. If you are having difficulty determining if this philosophical take on professional choices will work for you, consider looking at those choices through the criteria of deontologists—the categorical imperative.

The **categorical imperative** is a means by which we can evaluate our actions as being either moral or immoral. It is the rule that has us do unconditionally for any one person or any one individual the exact same thing that we would do for any other person or individual. This means that you would give the same pay to every person doing the same work no matter the person's gender, race, religion, etc. This means that if both your sister and a total stranger applied for the same job at your company then you would treat them absolutely equally. It is not as easy as you might think, but this is a sound means of evaluating all of your potential choices. Is this your only option? Certainly not. Another position through which you might be evaluating your professional choices is the idea of utilitarianism.

Mill: Utilitarianism

Most people think of utilitarianism as the effort to do the most good for the most amount of people. That is true to some extent but the actual philosophy is a bit bigger than this simple idea. John Stuart Mill (1972) came from the **consequentialist school of ethics**—which is to say that he believed that all of our actions have direct consequences. When evaluating any set of choices, Mill recommended that we look at all potential consequences to make the best decision. If we know (based on all of our information gathering) that a particular outcome is likely, we must ethically consider the impact of that outcome and choose to do the least harm for the largest number of people.

For example, if you are a manufacturing plant's safety supervisor and you come to work each day doing your best possible job but someone still gets hurt, you are not *ethically* responsible. If, however, you come to work drunk and do not watch for safety violations as your job dictates then, when someone gets hurt, you *are* ethically responsible. Why is this the case? It is because of our ability to predict consequences. In the first scenario, you could not rationally predict that a safety issue would occur. In the second scenario, you knew that you were impaired and doing your job at a less than ideal level so it was fairly predictable that something could slip through the cracks and that you would miss it. These rules actually are the basis of many laws and legal standards that we follow today.

As with Kant's (1785) universalism, utilitarians have a means by which we can evaluate our actions as being either moral or immoral—the Golden Rule. The **Golden Rule** is the position that we evaluate consequences and select consequences for others that we would choose for ourselves. In other words, do unto others as you would have them do to you. This means that if we opt to not tell a potential client about the shortcomings of our proposal which will impact how successful it will be (i.e., the consequences), it is because we would not want someone who was pitching an idea to us to reveal the shortcomings of their proposal. It sounds wonderful to say that we would treat others based on how we want to be treated but looking at every possible outcome is not easy. It requires amazing listening skills, asking every potential question, and weighing the answers with skill.

Aristotle: Virtue Ethics

Aristotle (in *Nicomachean Ethics*, trans. 1980) was not concerned with choice from a consequences perspective—those business leaders who follow his ethical perspective are not either; they are focused on moral virtue. Aristotle saw **moral virtue** as the possession of particular qualities (such as self-control, courage, generosity, high-mindedness, gentleness, friendliness, truthfulness, etc.). He did not believe that some people were born virtuous while others were not but saw people as spending their lives in an effort to live and grow in a virtuous way. If you have ever heard of a horrible businessman (or woman) who hurt others throughout life and then did one big nice thing for the world before dying—this person would not have, according to Aristotle, been ethical. Virtue is something that we aspire to accomplish. It is not a single act.

If you are unsure how to live an entire professional life that is ethical by virtuous standards, as with the other ethical philosophies, virtue ethics has a standard by which you can evaluate your actions as being either moral or immoral. The **Golden Mean** is about finding the middle ground between living a life of **vice by excess** (having way too much of something) and a life of **vice by default** (giving up too much of something). If you are debating how much of your company bonus to give to charity, the golden mean would neither suggest that you keep all of it or that you give it all away. There is a middle ground that is more appropriate.

Soule, Hedahl, and Dienhart (2009) propose in their article, "Principles of Managerial Moral Responsibility," a set of "managerial moral principles" around which business exchanges should be built. All of their principles were designed to answer the question, "What do we owe morally to others in the context of business?" (p. 538). This is a good question and a reflection on ethical choice. They suggest that leaders, managers, supervisors, and even employees should:

+ act in a non-coercive manner;

+ not subject others to uninvited risks;

- not build arbitrary barriers that would prevent access to the benefits and opportunities of commercial life;

- care for others' interests when they legitimately trust us to do so;

- rescue those in grave peril when we are qualified to solve the problem, there is a high probability of success, and the effort will not involve significant risks or compromise other moral responsibilities

These are good suggestions. You may start to think about the choices you have made so far and wonder if you have made the best decisions. If you think that you have already embraced an unethical choice, remember that Aristotle (in *Nicomachean Ethics*, trans. 1980) would not judge. He would suggest that we live our entire lives to be virtuous and that every day is the day to make better choices.

Knowing all of this, what will you do now when faced with a decision? What choice will you make? Viewing your professional life through **universalism**, **utilitarianism**, or **virtue ethics** can help you to see the outcomes of your choices from a larger perspective. You can then apply this perspective to your choices right now—and throughout your career.

Applying Ethics to the Business World

Early education becomes the foundation for later education and later education prepares us for life after school—our professional lives. This means that our ethical choices begin during our education. Unfortunately, many students have made choices that, regardless of ethical philosophy, would be considered to be poor decisions.

Harding, Finelli, and Passow's (2004) study found that 64% of students reported cheating a few times per term in high school, and nearly 80% reported cheating at least once in high school. Sims (1993) found that 91% of graduate students enrolled in two courses at an MBA program reported engaging in "some form of academic dishonesty" (para. 17). In a more technological age, Martin, Rao, and Sloan (2009) reported that 61% of the papers submitted to the website Turnitin.com demonstrated plagiarism.

What we know is that individuals who engage in academic dishonesty are likely to engage in unethical behaviors in the workplace (Harding, Carpenter, Finelli, & Passow, 2004; Martin, Rao, & Sloan, 2009; Nonis & Swift, 2001; Sims, 1993). This means that if we have begun to make bad choices already then we are more prone to carry those into our professional lives. Continuing to do so or starting a habit of small unethical choices (like taking just a few office supplies or making personal phone calls during work time) can easily become glaring abuses. For example, the human resources company Challenger, Gray & Christmas (2012) says that companies will lose *almost four million hours* of otherwise productive work time in 2012 just by following college basketball for March Madness™ (Ryssdal, 2012)! And, a study conducted at the 2007 NetQoS® annual network performance-management technology conference found that "instant messaging, downloading of music and video, and visiting social networking sites and news/sports sites" actually forced a dramatic drop in network speed and function to the point of severely impacting corporate function (p. 6). (That was in 2007, so we can imagine the impact of today's levels of social media use on companies!)

These are fragile times and it is not always easy to see how our small choices have big consequences. Remember that you will always and regularly encounter **ethical dilemmas**—not a choice between right and wrong, but a choice between two rights (Kidder, 1995). Think about how your choice might look to others. The point here is to view the choices that you are making now as they would be evaluated in the professional world, and in general through the eyes of the bigger picture.

REFLECTING ON CHOICE

No one can make our choices but us. Making a choice will feel better than living with indecision. People at the highest levels undoubtedly *chose* to be there. People who ignore the ethics of their actions are *choosing* to do so. Tuning out the ideas that we do not like or not listening to the ideas that we do not want to embrace… these are choices.

Take a moment to reflect right now on your performance on the LQ (*Listening Quotient*) Test. How did you do? Even if you were quite pleased with your score, had you ever before thought of listening as a choice? Does it change you at all now to think of it that way? How will your listening choices change when you consider the impact that they have on your ethical decisions? Perhaps you will be more apt to open your mind to a new perspective or you will more critically evaluate a business talk or speech.

You have all the choices—and all of the power. Move forward with a new (or renewed) sense of control over your professional path. What you have learned here is that choosing to take messages in is the key to becoming successful no matter what you do. *How* you take in these messages and what you do with them are matters of choice.

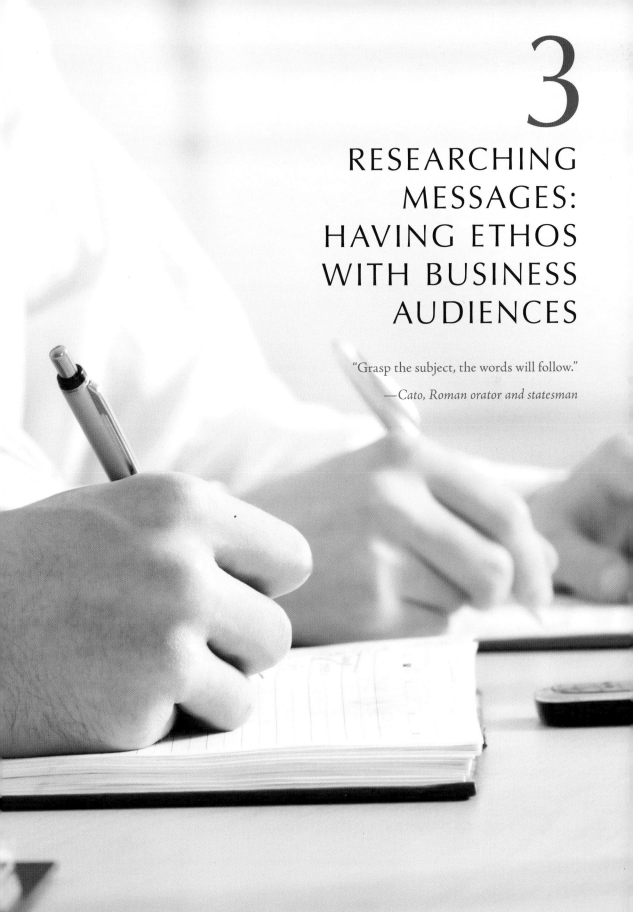

3
RESEARCHING MESSAGES: HAVING ETHOS WITH BUSINESS AUDIENCES

"Grasp the subject, the words will follow."
—*Cato, Roman orator and statesman*

BEING THE EXPERT

Early in your professional career, you may think that it is unlikely that anyone would ask you to give a presentation—after all, you are not an expert. The chairman of your company is an expert. The head of your department is an expert. The guy hired the month before is more of an expert than you are...at some things. These people are likely to be experts in their own particular subject matter or have expertise in particular areas beyond yours. You must realize that *you have expertise* that will result in you being asked to speak on particular subjects. When you ultimately are asked to provide a "business talk," your goal should be to grow this expertise into a substantial and comfortable foundation.

Let's start with the most basic question: *When* will you be asked to speak? Will your boss come to you to lead a discussion on information produced in another department? Likely not. This is not your area of expertise and businesses tend not to ask non-experts to present ideas. Will your co-workers ask you to take on the task of the presentation if you are clearly the least informed member of the team? Again, it is not likely that you would be the speaker of choice. In order to be asked to give a presentation, someone will have concluded that you have a level of expertise in the area. You do.

Expertise is a variable element. Everyone has a level of **expertise**, which is skill or knowledge in a *particular* field. Your boss (or co-workers, for that matter) may very well ask you to speak about an idea or plan where you know *more* than they do. Does that make you an expert? In this situation, it does! You know more than your audience. Even if you only know a marginal amount more, you are still in a position to offer valuable input. You, however, should not simply move into your business talk without having increased your expertise to the highest degree appropriate for that situation—this is where too many presenters fail (note there are many websites and even a Facebook page dedicated to "Speaking authoritatively about subjects in which I have no expertise").

Respectable presenters know that offering up information in a public setting must come with a level of investigation into the topic. (What if, after all, your audience is really listening and asks questions that you cannot answer? This is what your choice to investigate beyond your existing expertise will prevent.) The presentation of ideas in a business talk must involve diving head first into what you know, what others know, what you can prove, what you can support, and anything else that lets the audience know that you have done your very best to provide them with the best information possible. If you do this well then you are able to have **ethos** in the eyes of your audience—that high level of credibility gained from an honest attempt to present the highest credibility information.

This chapter explores how you can build a foundation for your talk using available resources—including you. You will learn how much research you will need to support your business talk, how to collect and evaluate evidence, as well as how and why to give proper credit to your support.

Why Start with Research?

Imagine being asked tomorrow to give a speech on your college major or degree plan. You would undoubtedly know something about it but perhaps not enough to cover all of your bases without checking a few facts. You would not want to tell your audience something that you assume about your major (such as how it is the most popular at your school or one of the most difficult degrees to complete) only to have them tell you that they have read otherwise. Having a foundation for your ideas, *before* you begin to organize or deliver them, ensures that you maintain credibility with those listening to you. Research gives us effective evidence on which to base our talks.

Evidence is any external verification that you cite as support for your ideas. Without evidence the ideas that you offer are simply assertions, which means that they are nothing more than stating your own personal opinion. Regardless of your personal dynamism and sparkling personality, most audiences are not willing to give your opinion any more weight than their own. What is worse is that if your audience disagrees with you then your opinion carries *even less* weight than it would otherwise. Evidence can clarify your ideas by taking abstract notions and developing them into *confirmed* information for your listeners. Different audiences are swayed by different types of evidence (Bryman, 1998; Firestone, 1987). What you will want to offer in your business talk is verification that establishes your ethos and meets the needs of the particular rhetorical situation.

Contemplating Your Rhetorical Situation

Most groups to whom you will be speaking will have gathered for a reason or an occasion. If you think back to our discussion of Lloyd Bitzer's (1968) **rhetorical situation** (the exigence, the audience, and the constraints of a given situation), you know to consider these elements before you move on to gather the evidence needed to have an impact on the occasion. Think of how all of the elements come together to tell you what *this* group needs from *this* message in *this* moment!

Consider, first, what needs to be said to address the particular issues of that moment. For example, your company might have had a sudden dive in sales for the past fiscal year. If no one at your company addressed this issue, the stockholders would be completely confused. In this case, someone *must* say something. But not all responses are appropriate. If you simply told the audience that things would get better but offered no foundation for how or in what way, your message would not improve the situation. You need to offer facts, statistics, and examples for your position! The need for these is the **exigence** (Bitzer's word for *urgency*) of the situation.

You must also consider the people who will hear your message—the audience. As you put together your business talk, you will want to provide a source for any information that did not come from you or is not common knowledge for *this* audience. The "this audience" part is the most important. What one group will know as fact, another will have never heard before and need to hear external support (for example, think of the difference between stockholders knowing that your company's advertising strategies are effective and potential clients needing to hear about the advertising awards you have won and the specific sales figures that resulted). Different audience—different evidence collection needs.

Finally, your need for support will be dictated by the constraints of your situation. It may seem odd to think that the time, place, and environment will determine the amount of foundation that you need but do not judge so quickly. Imagine that you are the third speaker in a group of five. You plan to offer evidence of three elements but the first speaker introduced one of them and touched on another. If you spend your time going over the same evidence again, your audience will wonder if you were listening to the earlier speaker or if perhaps you did not understand the earlier speech. By not adjusting your support to the constraints of the situation, you damage any potential effectiveness you could have (Hall & Robinson, 2012).

Speakers who ignore the rhetorical situation will not only waste time but often look foolish. An effective speaker adapts his or her evidence to the occasion because *your topic may stay the same, but your rhetorical situation does not*. Knowing this will help you to begin your evidence collection process.

HOW *MUCH* EVIDENCE SHOULD I COLLECT?

The very first question that is typically asked when speakers are told to offer source citation in a speech is, "How many sources do I need?" While some college professors will assign you a specific number of sources to include in a given presentation (e.g., "You must have six sources in this five-minute informative speech"), the world outside of a classroom is not like that. No one will tell you how much research to do or what will provide you with *enough* credibility to have established ethos with your audience. It will be up to you to figure out how to develop and deliver a strong foundation.

Your next question may be, "How will I know when I have developed a strong enough foundation?" or "What will make me trustworthy?" Your friends and family probably already know you as a trustworthy person, which is fantastic! This means that you are already making choices that they respect, find to be ethical, and they believe that you can back up what you say. Hopefully, your colleagues will feel the same way. If you continue to give presentations at work with no backing for your ideas then you should know that your wonderful personality and projection of confidence will eventually not be enough to keep people invested in your ideas. In a professional setting, you must prove that your ideas are trustworthy by showing that they are backed by outside experts from the most credible sources.

COLLECTING EVIDENCE

Evidence collection is the most malleable (meaning not set in stone) part of speech construction. You will be gathering data at every point of your business talk from the day you have your topic until moments before you begin. You will be revising both what you know and what you decide to relay to your audience; research is *not* one-stop shopping. You might collect a substantial amount of information only to find out later that you are missing key facts and need to do another search. You might do a run-through of your finished presentation with colleagues who suggest that some sources are not needed but others are. There are good steps to follow for collecting the information and critically selecting what to include as part of your talk.

A Good Place to Start

The best thing about research is that it is relatively straightforward. Think of your process as similar to lacing up shoes—there is a natural place to start and if you find that you have missed something, you can always go back and fill in the gap. When giving a business talk, you will need to: 1) have a topic, 2) broaden or narrow your focus, 3) outline what you already know, 4) set up a search record, 5) collect data, 6) strain the data, and 7) fill in holes. (Not to worry—once you have begun your research, the later searches are far easier and far more productive.)

Have a Topic

Having a topic seems like the easiest part of your speech but it is a good step to articulate. Ask yourself (or the person who asked you to speak), "What should my business talk be about?" In most cases, your position in the organization will dictate the topics on which you speak (Bass, 2010). For example, if you are a sales representative, you are likely to be selling a particular product that your company produces; if you are a CFO (Chief Financial Officer), you are likely to be offering internal and external updates on company finances; if you are an event planner, you are likely to be directing volunteers and coordinating efforts.

In some instances, you may have the freedom to select the topic on which you will speak. For instance, you might be asked to speak at your organization's annual retreat on a topic of your own choosing. You may be asked or even choose (as speech making becomes second nature) to make presentations at regional or national conferences based on your areas of expertise. In cases like this, you have a great deal of leeway in what you talk about. As you advance in the organization, the variety of occasions on which you might be asked to speak will broaden, both internally as well as to external groups—and your topic selection will become more autonomous (Bass, 2010; Gardner & Laskin, 2011). If you have the luxury of choosing your own topic for a presentation, your choice should be guided by two key considerations: 1) *your* knowledge and interests, and 2) *your audience's* knowledge and interests.

- **Your Knowledge and Interests**

  First and foremost, you should choose a topic that you care about—one that you find interesting and about which you are knowledgeable. As a professional in your field, you will accumulate a valuable body of knowledge (even from the day that you are hired, you will bring in your entire current education and experience). Let's be honest—not all of this knowledge, however, is fascinating stuff, even to you. An appropriate topic means one  that you know quite a bit about and find interesting enough to want to find out more. If your boss assigns you that topic then it will be your job to figure out why and to bring your own expertise to the forefront.

When asked to speak, this is likely not the best time to view the situation as an invitation to explore a completely new area of interest or a time to attempt to develop a new area of expertise. Talk about what you know. Of course, you will want to supplement your knowledge with information from other sources, but as an "expert," you should already have an initial working knowledge of your chosen topic…even if you have just recently acquired that knowledge through research.

- **Your Audience's Knowledge and Interests**

  Yes, the speech should reflect you but your choice in the topic or the span of the information should reflect the particular audience in this (rhetorical) situation. For instance, if you are invited to speak to a group of business students who are nearing graduation, you probably will not want to discuss how they can manage the initial stress of college (something that is long since not an issue for them) but you can discuss the same "stress management" topic in the scope of entering one's first job. Again, your topic remains the same but your focus shifts to reflect the audience.

Effective topics are located at that nexus between your knowledge and interests and your listeners' knowledge and interests (Gardner & Laskin, 2011). Consider both types of needs and the final result will be a topic that is both interesting to you and that your audience will want to hear.

Broaden or Narrow Your Focus

A clear topic is a necessity before moving on. Now that you have it, think about it. Are you attempting to detail every aspect of corporate mergers to a group of new employees during a 15-minute window in their orientation? Do you have only to give a quick tour of the new facility that should last no more than ten minutes but the schedule has asked you to be with the audience for 45 minutes? You are now at the step of matching the scope of your topic to your particular rhetorical situation.

Some topics are naturally quite broad, meaning that there is a vast amount to know about them, while others are relatively narrow, meaning that there is a limited amount of information about them. This is the difference between the broad topic of "biology careers" versus the more narrow topic of "legal cases won from evidence assessments made by chemical forensic biologists." As you begin to think about everything that you must know about your topic and the evidence that you will want to collect to satisfy the needs of the audience and the situation, you will want to broaden or narrow the scope of that topic to suit the needs of the situation.

Defining the scope of your topic will have particular organizational benefits (which are discussed in the next chapter of this text) and, more importantly, help you to conduct your research to find the best support for your ideas (Bass, 2010). This means that as you begin to gather data, you will discover that what you thought was a narrow topic really has much more information to it and will require much more research (and perhaps even a later narrowing of the scope of your topic to one element of what you ultimately found). Conversely, you might find very little evidence on your topic and realize that what you thought was a broad issue is really more of a limited one. Until you know how broad or specific to get, you will not be able to effectively look for research. Part of knowing this will be looking at the information that you already have.

Outline What You Already Know

You are the expert. We have already established that—but you do not know everything (hopefully, we do not need to establish this but as a gentle reminder, *no one knows everything*). Outlining what you already know will help you to plan a path for your research that will allow you to: 1) fill in holes or search for particular expert evidence, 2) know who to ask before taking the next step, or even 3) allow you to see how you as the speaker fit into the rhetorical situation (remember that your position will impact both what you say and your audience) (Bitzer, 1954).

The beginning of your process might look more like a brainstorming sheet than an outline (lots of clustered words, terms, names, and sources). You can start by laying out the groups of information that you have, putting them into main ideas and then adding support for each of those main ideas. You can also begin by looking at the timeline of events. What happened before what? What should or would come next in the series of events? Do you know everything that happened or do you need to fill in time gaps? Once you have put all of this information down on paper (or, let's be realistic, typed it all up on your computer or iPad®) then try and get those ideas into an order. If you have listed that you have good evidence for A, B, and D, start searching for C! (You get the idea.) Know that this version of your outline will change as your research better informs you about your topic and your audience's feelings and knowledge on the topic. Now...to begin the search.

Set Up a Search Record

Looking for information can seem like looking into a big void. Knowing the scope of your search is a great way to lessen that void. You need to give yourself some credit and start filling that space by documenting your process. Perhaps the most crucial part of your research will be to start and keep track of where you have searched and for what you have searched in each location. Since you likely will not be able to complete your research in one session, this record will become vital for saving you time, getting help, and in returning for subsequent searches.

For example, if you were exploring the idea of teaching, you might have an initial search chart that looks like this:

Source	Search Terms	Findings (+/ −)
NPR (National Public Radio)	• teachers • students • testing	• teachers (3 stories +) • students (nothing) • testing (assessment story)
Google™	• education • school • teachers • students • testing	• education (vague) • school (org websites) • teachers (individual stories; some strategies) • students (not useful) • testing (examples and types; some assessment)
EBSCOhost® databases • Academic Search Complete • Education Abstracts • Sociology Complete • Psychological Review	• education • school • teachers • students • testing	• education • school (vague) • teachers (LOTS—mostly teaching strategies) • students (not useful) • testing (lots on assessment)

Imagine going into a co-worker's office and saying that you are stuck in trying to find good evidence to support the merger that you will be presenting to your team. Your co-worker says, "Where have you looked?" and you say, "I don't know. A bunch of places." This does not encourage your co-worker to help you. It sounds like a project that needs to be started from the beginning (too daunting for anyone to want to help chip in). Alternatively, think how different the same scene would play out when you whip out a chart that tracks all of your research! Not only will you provide someone with a quick way to figure out a way to help, but you will have impressed the heck out of them!

This chart will be useful when a colleague, friend, or librarian (which is a person that you should still make use of even after college, such as at the local public library, your company records librarian, or even government recorders in the public sector) wants to know where you have *already* looked. Rather than guessing, you can detail exactly where you have searched and even document what you have found—and *not* found. You should also include anything that you already know from your brainstorming outline!

Before you think that such a process would only be useful in a classroom or academic setting, you should know that in the business world, your projects and even presentations may be taken over by someone else mid-stream (de Bony, 2010). This is common when your project workload becomes heavier or you get moved (or promoted!) to another division. That person will need to know the status of your research so have it ready rather than creating it from scratch.

Collect Data

Begin to collect data! The process by which you will collect data is the meat of this chapter. We will discuss in depth the best methods and techniques, how to evaluate what you find, various collection methods specific to environments, and how to increase ethos by giving credit to your sources. While you want to read on about those methods, always remember that collecting evidence is a continuous process. You will start then stop then start again as you develop your presentation. The more that you do of this, the better that you will be!

Strain the Data

As you go about your search for evidence to bolster your ideas and arguments, you will come across good evidence, bad evidence, and even useless evidence. For example, your boss may tell you to refer to the wrong annual report for summary data (not his fault—he just did not know better) or you might find a wonderful example only to later realize that it was from a questionable source. If you are doing your job well, know that you will and should find far more evidence than you will use in your business talk!

Excess sources and even bad sources are a great way to get a good understanding of an issue. If you know the ideas from your competitor and that they have been shown to be scientifically flawed, you can avoid using this information in your own talk. All evidence will help you with your foundational understanding of an issue—and to answer questions from your audience.

We have all read something that is fascinating and interesting, something that we know, if placed into our talk, would appeal to our audience's sense of **pathos** (that emotional connection). What is vital to remember is that even the most fascinating or inspiring evidence, if not relevant, does no more than distract our audiences. Never get so attached to a single piece of evidence that you are unwilling to see how it may not serve the purpose of the goal of your speech.

It is your job to strain (or filter) your evidence. As you collect and then after you have collected a mass of data, take some time to put it into categories. Your potential categories might include:

- useful

- potential for later use

- poor quality source or argument

- irrelevant evidence

Fill in the Holes

You will finish your presentation preparation only to realize that you need more research. Do not get discouraged! The best presenters are always open to knowing that they will need more data or different data to have the best ethos appeal for that particular audience. Once you have a completed draft of your speech then open yourself up to going back into research mode. Look to see where you have too much and what you are still missing. You might have six sources to support one idea but no sources at all to support another of your claims. Often these argument areas lacking support are the things that we "just know"; however, your audience will need more to accept your claim than your word on it. If your audience does not have firsthand knowledge and you do not offer evidence in your presentation, consider that a hole and go back to fill it.

We have talked about the steps that you will follow to make sure that you have enough research, but have barely touched on the most important part: how to gather the evidence itself.

Gathering Evidence

If you were looking to find the best places to visit in Rome, you would likely go online and put into a search engine, "best places to visit in Rome." You would, as we have all come to say in verb form, "Google it." You are likely to do the same thing when you want to find out how to insert a video into PowerPoint or see what you can find out about a company with whom you have an interview next week. We would be remiss to ignore the fact that search engines such as Google™, Ask®, or Dogpile® are typically one's initial tool for finding information (Fallows, 2008; Purcell, Brenner, & Rainie, 2012). You will not find any discouragement here about using those tools. What you *will* find here is a guide to other useful tools and a way to evaluate the evidence that you find.

It is your job to use as many resources as possible to ethically do your best for your audience. Remember that there is no order to collecting data. You should use each tool as it becomes available to you and go back to those same tools again and again, as often as possible.

How We Gather Evidence in Different Environments

The process of gathering evidence will depend on where you are in your career. Most students have a tried and true method of collecting information for papers and presentations. They will typically first look online then go to the library and then perhaps ask some smart people that they know (professors, parents, internship supervisors, etc.). There is nothing wrong with this sequence. If it works, keep working it!

In the business world, the progression of your research task will differ. Businessmen and women who are asked to deliver a business talk will typically first compile what they know and then ask others in the office for additional information or direction. That makes sense because these are the very same people who will be in your audience and have links to your organization—such as customers, company leaders, or invested community members. This is also a good example of audience analysis (a tactic covered in depth later in this chapter) and great relevant information gathering.

Turning to one's audience for information does not eliminate the need for external research. Yes, in the "real world," professionals still look for outside sources such as online or published documents. In this setting, however, that external information will only suit the needs of the audience if it is anchored with company- or industry-specific information. It is useful to keep in mind that co-workers and members of your professional network can be valuable sources of credible evidence if this information is carefully evaluated.

While each group (students and professionals) has their own method, neither is right or wrong. What is *right* is finding support for ideas and using it to meet the needs of your particular rhetorical situation. What is *wrong* is neglecting the full utility of any source simply because it would be easier to use another. Having ethos means utilizing every available and relevant source.

Types of Evidence

Evidence comes in more than one form and different audiences are swayed by different types of evidence (Bryman, 1998; Firestone, 1987). For example, think about the considerations that the CFO of a company must take into account when speaking at a shareholders meeting. She must communicate to all investors about the financial stability of the company including stock projections, investments, and any financials that will impact corporate growth. This is all numbers. However, when the speech is given, the CFO will not speak in all numbers. She will provide both numbers and give specific examples. Why? Effective speakers know that some audiences will only buy arguments that have facts and figures for support while other audiences will need to picture the information and hear about specific examples of impact. In other words, effective speakers understand how to incorporate both quantitative and qualitative evidence.

Quantitative vs. Qualitative

Quantitative evidence is the information you offer that demonstrates measurements or *quantities*. Generally speaking, if you are trying to *prove* a point (not something that you can do in the social sciences), you need to present factual numeric evidence. In fact, some experts believe that numeric data is more persuasive with audiences than data in the form of illustrative qualifications and examples (Allen & Preiss, 1997).

+ **Statistics:** facts or pieces of data from a large quantity of numerical data that provide a general understanding of an idea (such as: "Karen Lynne, director of accounting here at *Tri-Star*, informed me that as of Monday, sales are down by more than 20,000 units, which will result in a 4% drop in overall revenue for 2013").

+ **Numeric Comparisons:** similarities or equivalencies in amount measures (such as: "A *Post Intelligencer* study that found that 30% of all material recycled in Seattle, Washington was glass or plastic as compared to only 3% of those products in Austin, Texas—a city with generally the same demographic").

+ **Hard Data:** information provided on the basis of the reasoning or calculation of amounts (such as: "Given the spreadsheet analysis provided by our accounting department, for a 12 ounce latte with milk at $1.95 per gallon and espresso costing $12.78 per pound, it costs us $1.35 per serving for a profit of $2.31 per sale").

You may want to check with your audience about what kind of data they will need to be convinced of the argument that you are trying to make. Does your argument only work if you have a numeric measure to back it up? Are you saying that your company will have greater sales by changing their selling tactics? If so, how great? What is the percentage? What are the current sales figures and how will those compare to later sales figures? When considering the use of quantitative data, think about the options available along with their merit for grounding your claim.

Qualitative evidence is qualities or characteristics. Numbers can be daunting and confusing for some audiences who will be better convinced by imagining the effect of your ideas. They will want to visualize your arguments. In these instances, qualitative evidence is necessary. The kinds of qualitative evidence that you can offer are vast but consider some of the more well-known forms.

- **Definitions:** a statement of the exact meaning of a word as it would be in a trade publication or dictionary; an exact statement of the nature, scope, or meaning of something (such as: "To be more precise, what I mean by *accountant* is consistent with the *OED* dictionary definition of 'a person whose job is to keep or inspect financial accounts'").

- **Full Quotations or Paraphrased Testimony:** a group of words taken from a text, speech, or individual's statement and repeated by someone other than the original author or speaker (such as: "Geoff, our team manager, told me that we have only six months to turn around our sales or this department is looking at cuts").

- **Examples:** a single, typical case that is characteristic of its kind or illustrates a general rule; this can include the edited version of a story that does not include the progression but only communicates the gist of the events (such as: "When I was new to this industry, I had a boss who insisted on micro-managing every detail of my work. After a networking event, he asked me to do the simple task of writing brief 'thank you' cards to all of the participants. I then had to bring them up to his office and he went through with a red pen and corrected any words or language that he didn't like and had me rewrite them…three times! Now, that was micro-management").

- **Stories or Narratives:** a spoken account of a series of connected events with a beginning, middle, peak, and conclusion; this evidence can take on a long and sustained form as well as a brief narrative form; narrative illustrations may have greater impact than simple examples.

- **Analogies:** a comparison between two things, typically on the basis of their structure and for the purpose of explanation or clarification; may be either **figurative** (comparing two items of different categories, such as: "Geneva's office is sinking like the *Titanic* so we know that we do not want to embrace their measures") or **literal** (comparing things of the same category, such as: "As you can see, Generitek's advances in nano-technology will change the face of corporate processor usage and data storage much like touch-screen technology changed how we use computers today").

As you read through these types of evidence, you may be tempted to use the type, either quantitative or qualitative, that is most convincing for *you*. Remember that you are already convinced so your needs are not the primary ones here. Instead, consider the needs of *your audience*. Will they be most influenced by numbers? Are they in need of a strong illustration to drive the point home? If you do not know then you are best to choose liberally from both groups so that you are sure to target all reasoning requirements. The next step is understanding how to begin your evidence search.

Locations of Evidence

Now that you know what to look *for*, you will need to know *where* to look. Quantitative and qualitative evidence is all around us. As mentioned earlier, how you begin your search will depend on personal preferences and where you are in your career. However, you must give every evidence location a full shot at providing you with data (do not stop after only looking in one location just because you found tons of data there, or nothing at all). Utilize all of your resources.

Looking for Online Information

Information is literally at our fingertips. As more and more groups go digital to decrease their environmental footprints, online resources will include almost anything that you previously could only find in hard copy (note that this statement says "almost" and that you do not get points for having not tried to obtain hard copy sources; more information on this follows). You may be familiar with personal and company websites, blogs, YouTube, or Twitter, which can be useful in business presentations but should not cause you to ignore online versions of academic journals, trade magazines, news outlets, or government websites. As students, your access to these online sources is even greater.

University students have resources that go beyond those found in corporate settings (however, registered alumni and returning students may have access to these sources), including the database collections to which your university subscribes. For example, EBSCOhost® (a well-known "systematic collection of online databases") gives researchers the advantage of "one-stop shopping" by providing full text or location information on different types of sources such as newspaper stories, journal articles, magazine stories, and government reports. (If you are familiar with it—use it!) You do, however, have other online resources that do not require a college affiliation to search. Find the most credible sources and use them in tandem with one another:

- **Google Scholar™** (provides a search of scholarly literature across many disciplines and sources, including theses, books, abstracts, and articles)

- **The Directory of Open Access Journals** (maintained by Lund University and lists categorized, searchable links to free, full-text, quality-controlled scientific and scholarly journals)

- **Project Muse** (a provider of digital humanities and social sciences content since 1995; provides books and journals from leading university presses and scholarly societies)

- **JSTOR** (an archive of over one thousand full-text, searchable leading academic journals across the humanities, social sciences, and sciences, as well as select monographs and other materials valuable for academic work)

- **ipl2** [merged collections of resources from the Internet Public Library (IPL) and the Librarians' Internet Index (LII) websites]

- **The Library of Congress** (the largest library in the world with millions of books, recordings, photographs, maps, and manuscripts in its collections with a searchable online access system)

- **Oxford Journals** (a division of Oxford University Press, publishing over 230 academic and research journals covering a broad range of subject areas)

- **PMC (PubMed Central)** (a free full-text archive of biomedical and life sciences journal literature at the U.S. National Institutes of Health's National Library of Medicine)

As a side note, notice that YouTube and Wikipedia® are not on this list. These websites are good for getting general understandings and examples but the information on either, as well as many other websites, is not verified by an external source on any reliable and regular basis (Traphagan, Traphagan, Dickens, & Resta, 2012). We do not want to get ourselves into trouble by relying on questionable sources for ethos. Evaluating the online information that we hope to use for support is the only way to determine if it is worthy of inclusion in our presentation.

To avoid being fooled by a source that seems accurate just because it gave you the data that you wanted, double-check the credibility of the evidence from your source just as much as your audience will be evaluating you as a source of their evidence!

Evaluating Online Information

"I found it online" is the worst rationale for using any piece of evidence. Online publication is no guarantee of credibility. In fact, even credible and well-intentioned sources can post biased or flawed information either by mistake or design. Websites bring on their own unique set of verification challenges. Using the below checklist can help you to make sure that you did not stumble upon the perfect information, only to find out that the information was perfectly wrong!

3

> **The Website Credibility List**
>
> + **Author:** Examine the ethos of the person or people who wrote the material. By searching for that person's training to provide such information, you can understand how credible the information itself might be. Many websites (for example, About.com, LIVESTRONG.org, suite101.com, wiseGEEK.com, etc.) hire authors, regardless of training in the topic area, to create material.
>
> + **Date of Publication:** Current publication dates do not always mean that the information is credible but older dates often indicate that the website has not maintained current changes related to the topic. Information moves at the speed of the internet. If the information has not changed (such as the writings of Aristotle), the interpretation may have.
>
> + **Publisher:** The organization or individual that has selected to put information on a website should also be evaluated for credibility. What is their motivation for putting up this information? For example, is the Corn Refiner Association the one telling you that corn sugar is not bad for you? Could there be bias in that reporting? How do others evaluate this publisher? (Consider how often this publisher is cited by others.)
>
> + **Evaluative Reviews:** Just like print materials, websites can have experts who review their information. For example, organizations that publish research (e.g., the Centers for Disease Control), many nonprofit organizations (e.g., Planned Parenthood), and even corporations (e.g., Microsoft®) will have an individual or teams of professionals who evaluate all information before it is posted. Check websites to see if there is a review board—who is on it, what are their processes, do they have credibility, etc.?
>
> + **Argument Bias:** Bias is an unfair prejudice in favor of or against someone or something. Bias in a source means that you are likely not getting all of the information or it is problematically (which might mean only a little bit or a whole lot) skewed in one direction. Ask yourself—does the information clearly take one side over another? Does it ignore obvious arguments or counterarguments?
>
> + **Tone:** If you were to cite the satirical website *Funny or Die* as a realistic source of information then your audience would wonder if you knew that the information was meant as a joke. Similarly, you must evaluate information postings to see if the tone implies that the information was not intended to be used as a credible source.

Professionals, and even students, often believe that a quick internet or Google search will result in an easy answer for their research questions. Indeed, this can be an easy process; however, as we learned above, the information can be invalid, unreliable, deceptive, or weak. Even if you have credible evidence from online searches, do not ignore the print resources that are not available through technology.

Looking for Print and Publication Information

Books, government documents, annual reports, financial statements, historical papers, periodicals, and other print resources may be both in print and online—or only be available in hard copy through various departments at your company or at a library or a government office. Traveling outside of your personal workspace and getting offline can take more physical effort but produces results far better than what any other presenter will have—and, thus, will increase your ethos in the eyes of your colleagues and supervisors.

Some sources to include from the print world, as noted above, can include items that you might have access to online; however, consider every possible category so that you do not miss a key piece of evidence! Consider:

+ **Books**

+ **Journal Articles** (professional and trade journals often just get hard copies mailed out to individuals but can be requested for research purposes)

+ **Historical Documents** (understanding how an issue was viewed throughout time, such as through personal letters, contracts, corporate documents, out-of-print texts, or even medical records, can help the audience to understand the full merit of your arguments)

+ **Recent Publications** (some sources that will eventually end up online are not *immediately* available and the most current sources can only be found in hard copy)

+ **Subscription Periodicals** (some magazines and newspapers will only allow you to access them online if you are willing to pay, but often local and school libraries will have free hard copies of materials)

+ **Brochures and Marketing Materials** (companies almost always put out materials to market themselves or explain corporate practices and these products will likely never have online versions)

Evaluating Print and Publication Information

All published materials have some type of credibility. However, source integrity ranges from none to significant. (You, of course, will want the best for your audience!) Therefore, effective researchers strive for the highest level of credibility while knowing that some cases will require them to use the second or third best level of credibility in order to have access to particular topics and depth of information. For example, if you work for an architect who is scheduled to show the best options for constructing a local skateboarding park, it is unlikely that high quality journals or long-range research will exist. Instead, you will be looking to county surveys, newspaper articles, and even blogs from skateboarders talking about their personal needs and wants in such a facility. The important thing to remember is to know that you want the best review of any resources.

Published materials undergo a review process. **Resource review** means that someone other than the author reads the work to make sure that it is reliable, credible, and valid. Information that has survived layers of review from editors and experts with appropriate credentials has the strongest level of credibility but many levels exist. Those levels of review include:

+ **No Review**

   The lowest level of credibility comes from those sources that have been published without any review—in other words, no outside source has proofread or verified the information. This information could be credible or could simply be made up or an opinion. It may provide color and examples but should be used cautiously and with an understanding that the facts or details have not been checked. For example:

   ▪ blogs

   ▪ personal websites

   ▪ Twitter

   ▪ etc.

+ **Audience Review**

   The next level of credibility comes from sources where the *readers* determine the validity of evidence and edit the details. The idea of such websites, company marketing materials, social media, or other such resources is that if enough readers contribute then the information collected from a large group, the more likely it is to be correct. This can work or it can backfire. For example, if you wanted to know the history of President Obama and looked him up on Wikipedia, there are enough readers of information that incorrect details are quickly edited out. The problem is when you read something before it has been changed (or if you go to a topic where few visitors participate, such as the page on Western region banana slugs!) wrong information can be left up for quite some time before anyone notices and correct information can even be deleted. For example:

- Wikipedia (all wiki websites)

- The Internet Movie Database (IMDb)

- etc.

+ **Editor Review**

An **editor** is an expert in the field of the publication who determines the applicability of information for the publication and is sometimes also charged with evaluating the validity of the information. This person serves as a gatekeeper to keep out irrelevant materials and verify information; however, the effort editors devote to review varies as  does their training in this area (e.g., think of the résumé differences between the editor of the *New York Times* and your college newspaper!). Some will conduct a strict evaluation of details and sources, while others may only confirm that the topic is somewhat on task. In general, editors' jobs are to review each of the following before they are sent to print:

- *The Wall Street Journal*

- *The Chronicle of Higher Education*

- *Vogue*

- *People Magazine*

- *OK Magazine*

- etc.

You can see that not only does the merit of the review vary but so does the merit of the publications themselves. *Within the category of editor review, publications have their own hierarchy.* The *New York Times* is more credible than one's own local town paper because of the strictness of the editorial review. Additionally, some publications just work better than others (for example: *The Christian Science Monitor* and *Vogue* are both credible but if you are speaking about industry changes in fashion then the latter is a far better choice).

✦ **Peer Review**

The highest level of credibility in published materials comes from sources that have multiple experts in the field who pre-screen an article before it is printed. These are called **peer-reviewed** (or **refereed**) sources and contain articles specific to a topic or industry. The process is that articles are submitted, sent out to numerous experts, revised based on their comments, and rejected if they do not meet the highest standards. Obviously, this takes time so peer-reviewed materials are not as up-to-date as other reviewed sources. Identifying these sources is easy if you know what you are looking for but remember that just because the title includes the term "journal" does not make it peer reviewed. Generally, you will see:

- "Submission Guidelines" or "Information for Authors" on the publisher's page

- the information will be an *article* (not everything that appears in a peer-reviewed journal is an article; these sources may also contain editorials or book reviews that are not subjected to the same level of critique)

- common formatting elements such as, 1) an abstract, 2) references or works cited, 3) discrete sections such as a literature review, methodology, and conclusion, 4) complex, formal language, 5) author job appointment

The support that you will need for your particular business talk is dependent on the talk—and the audience (of course, it's that ole rhetorical situation again!). When your boss asked you to find the most viable place for expansion of your company's production facility, she was likely not looking for you to offer a slew of peer-reviewed sources about the merits of expansion. *That* is not your topic. She is looking for you to summarize demographic studies from the area, find any news sources about neighborhood development, and government reports about crime statistics. She is looking for as many sources as possible in the highest level of credibility available appropriate to *that* topic, which may or may not include scholarly journals. The point is to do the best that you can for the situation that you have. This can also include looking beyond both online and print sources.

Looking for Information from People and Evaluating It

You are at work—you are surrounded by experts! You are at school—you are surrounded by experts! It is so easy when we see people every day to forget how smart, experienced, connected, or helpful they can be. We might throw ourselves into hours of online research only to find that Joe in the next cubicle has that information right on his desk. Your easiest form of research is simply to look around and *ask*. This is something that many professionals already do.

Professionals often turn to their colleagues or industry contacts for information or direction to guide research. These experts can offer advice or insights that are tailored to the needs of the topic and audience and simply asking them builds interpersonal relationships (Pullin, 2010). For example, if you are asked to give a presentation about the effectiveness of your company's new sales programs, ask the salespeople! Ask your accounting department what the revenue has been since implementing the program versus before implementation. Ask your clients how they feel about the sales techniques. These are valuable resources, but they also need to be evaluated for credibility.

Speakers should watch for red flags that come with gathering information from people. Individuals often, either intentionally or not, share *opinions* as facts (Bernard, 2000). Individuals are skewed by their own feelings and perceptions (recall the information on listening!) and can even be tempted to *over*state socially desirable behavior while *under*reporting undesirable behavior (e.g., "Of course I used the software suggested by the CEO!") (Bernard). A smart speaker looking for quality evidence knows that individual statements represent *one* piece of information, which should be taken seriously but checked against other sources for accuracy. One of those ways is through audience analysis.

Audience Analysis

As you collect evidence to convince or inform an audience, it might seem odd that you would collect evidence from your listeners and then give them their own ideas back during your speech. In fact, your audience will respond more favorably to you if you do show them that you are listening to their position *before* offering your own (O'Keefe, 2002). Audience analysis sounds rather formal but there are actually numerous ways of understanding and gathering data from your audience. You likely have completed audience analysis prior to previous speeches without even knowing it!

Informal audience analysis is a means of gathering information about your potential listeners without any predetermined and set procedures. These are the natural steps that we take on a regular basis to figure out who is in our audience and whether or not our information will be right for them in a given rhetorical situation. Think of it this way: have you ever told a joke to a group of friends where they howled with laughter but you decided later not to tell the same joke to family members or co-workers? This is likely because you had prior knowledge that the other groups would have a different response. You did an *informal analysis* of the rhetorical situation! Elements of informal analysis can include:

+ **Prior Knowledge** (if you have already interacted with the audience then you will already know something about them)

+ **Common Experience** (if you know that everyone in your audience has read the same newspaper article, experienced the same cultural/historical event, or had a common encounter, then mentioning this will bind you together)

+ **Asking Around** (contacting business insiders or others who work closely with your audience can help you to understand the needs of that *specific* group)

+ **Observation** (you can watch your audience before or even during your business talk to get information about what they know and how they feel; be careful, some observation can lead to **stereotyping**, which is an oversimplified image or idea of a particular type of something; stereotyping is often thought of negatively but can in this context be a useful—albeit, not always accurate—method of drawing conclusions about a group from a single or few times of observing them)

Informal audience analysis is likely the most common type of "investigation" that you will use before beginning communication with an audience of one or of many, and it should not be discounted. This is a valid and useful means of focusing your message and connecting with your audience without having gone through the more rigorous means of formal analysis. While you may see the ease of informal audience analysis, a more formal process can provide rich and generalizable details that will help to give a strong ethos foundation to your talk.

Formal audience analysis is a means of gathering information about your potential listeners by using predetermined and set procedures. These methods are the ones with which speakers tend to be more familiar, even if they are less often used. The reason that these methods are not typically used is that they are more time consuming than informal means (or doing nothing). Yet, if you have ever had a salesperson try to pitch you something and wondered how they knew you so well, it is because that person's company has invested time and significant resources into substantial formal audience analysis!

Formal audience analysis methods range from ones that gather rich, detailed, nuanced (typically **qualitative**) information to those that are less individualistic and more generalizable (typically **quantitative**). The most common forms of formal audience analysis include:

- **Interviews** (*the most rich data*; conversations between two or three people, either face-to-face or mediated, for the purpose of a topic specific consultation)

- **Focus Groups** (gathering a demographically specific group such as people of all the same age, race, or gender to participate in a guided discussion about a particular product or idea is also a means of getting rich data, while not as rich as a personal interview)

- **Surveys** (measurement instruments that deliver *generalizable* data—something that you can show as applying to a larger group—but can be designed to produce some rich data; surveys can ask either quantitative or qualitative questions, such as understanding that an interview can tell you that one person in the audience had a horrible interaction with the new boss but survey results can tell you that 65% of your audience can't stand the new boss!)

Because you are the one asking the questions in any audience analysis, you must determine the credibility and validity of the answers that your information gathering strategies will be able to generate. Bad questions…bad answers! Good questions…better answers! There are strategies to get the best feedback.

The way to find out the best information is to ask the right type of question while avoiding questions that will inevitably push the audience to provide you with truly not useful information. In talking about feedback loops and listener-speaker feedback (remember Schramm?!), we began a discussion of question types: closed-ended or open-ended. To recap, a **closed-ended question** is one with a limited set of available answers. An **open-ended question** is one with an unlimited set of available answers. You will need to consider both when analyzing any audience. Think about what you want to know and how to ask so that you can include the best type of support in your business talk.

Closed-Ended Examples (for including basics and demographic information in your talk)

1. What is your gender? (circle one) Male Female
2. Who is your supervisor? (circle one)

    Krystal Kennedy Sandra Lawrence Mike Willis T.C. Winebrenner

Open-Ended Examples (for including detailed examples in your talk)

1. What questions do you have for management?
2. How many hours do you work per week?
3. Briefly explain your daily job duties.

It is not always good, however, to come right out and ask something; this can create barriers with your audience (the concept from our discussion of listening!). For instance, if you wanted to convince your audience to work an extra hour each day, you may not want to come right out and ask them: "Would you work an extra hour each day?" They might start to think of a million reasons why this is a bad idea. Questions should, instead, be directed toward every consideration that would impact the audience's position. For instance, you could ask questions about how much they like their work, how dedicated they are to the company, and what they might offer to save the company from going under. If you have this information then you would be able to talk (hopefully) about the high percentage of people who care enough to save the company by offering something as little as a change in work hours.

Knowing what type of question you will ask and the purpose of that question determines the kind of response that you will get back. This could be rich, generalizable, or inaccurate. Some questions, in fact, naturally lead to inaccurate responses, including **leading**, **bias**, and **double-barreled** questions.

Any question that pushes the respondent to a particular answer is a **leading question**. How an audience gets led to a response can be subtle or obvious but, if you intend to get a real understanding of your audience, be sure to avoid this common questioning issue. For instance, a leading question might include asking your colleagues, "Wouldn't you prefer to come in for training on Saturdays since the boss thinks it's such a good idea?" Do you honestly expect that your fellow employees are going to give you an honest response? None of them want to be cited in your presentation: "Everyone but Janet thought that coming in on Saturdays is a *great* idea!" Likely they will just tell you what you want to hear. The same thing happens in formal audience analysis.

Leading Question Example

> 1. It is incredibly important to vote regardless of how much information you have on the candidates. (select one)
>
>   ☐ Strongly Agree
>
>   ☐ Agree
>
>   ☐ Neutral
>
>   ☐ Disagree
>
>   ☐ Strongly Disagree
>
> *Leading Problem: pushes respondent to think favorably about voting rather than giving an honest assessment*

An equally problematic issue is audience analysis questions that assume that a respondent has a particular background or experience; these are questions of **bias**. New employees may feel pressured to say that they have expertise that they do not rather than feel unqualified. "Hey, newbee. Which did you learn in school: Keynote® or Prezi®?" This question assumes that you learned one or the other and does not give you the chance to have learned some other presentation software—or none at all. A bias question will skew your responses and hurt your ability to use the information that you gather.

Bias Question Example

1.   What was your favorite biology class at Avery University?

Bias Problem: assumes both that the respondent went to Avery University and has taken at least one biology class

Finally, questions that have more than one idea buried inside a single question are called **double barreled**. These questions mean that no matter what answer you get, you have no idea what it is really answering. If you asked your team if Product A and Product B were resolving client issues and they said yes, you would not know which product was actually having the beneficial impact. Is it A? Is it B? Is it both of them together? This question automatically creates a lack of clear answers. Better to ask the first question and then the second, so that you know what the answers mean.

Double-Barreled Question Example

1.   Have you had a friend or family member that has gone bankrupt?

　　☐ yes　　☐ no

Double-Barreled Problem: does not allow the respondent to differentiate between responses that are in regard to friends as opposed to family members, or vice versa

With such wonderful resources at our fingertips, we would be both foolish and remiss to collect bad data. We want to look online, find print materials, ask others, and even ask our audience. We do not want to be in the middle of our talks only to have the audience tell us that we have misquoted them or that they do not trust our evidence. We want ethos—and to be trusted. Part of that trust is from giving credit where it is due.

CITE IT...DON'T STEAL IT

As you go about your presentation utilizing information from online, printed, and people sources, you will be, as Isaac Newton said, "standing on the shoulders of giants." Being up that high is a great benefit to you as a speaker because your expertise increases when you put it on top of others. You lose that stature when you deceive others into thinking that the expertise of others is your own. You are stealing. That's right—stealing.

Stealing another's expertise is not only in bad form but unethical and *dangerous*. The ethical ramifications of using the information provided to you by Joe in the next cubicle and saying that you found the resources yourself are, hopefully, fairly obvious. It seems to be just a crummy thing to do! (After all, Joe might have been counting on that information for an ethos appeal of his own!) Also, from our earlier discussion on ethics, you learned that all ethical positions are *choices*. Whether you choose to follow the **categorical imperative** (employing high moral principles at all times regardless of the situation), the **Golden Rule** (doing to others what we want done to us), or the **Golden Mean** (having neither too much nor too little of any good), you make the *choice* to give or to not give Joe credit. This is not to say that all people who do not tell audiences where their information comes from have intentionally stolen another's intellectual property. Some people either forget to verbally cite their sources or did not realize that their choice not to would mislead audiences. If it was unintentional then there is not an issue, right? Sadly, no.

Copying another's work without citing that source is *dangerous*. One case in point is the copying of information and visuals from websites for presentations. **Fair Use Laws** (covered in detail in our later discussion of visual aids and the internet) state that all use of another's work is illegal unless it is for educational purposes—and even these have limits to five images per author and no more than 10% of a text or 1,000 words. If an educator violates this standard, "depending on the circumstances, educators may not be required to pay statutory damages (as high as $150,000 per instance), but they may still have to pay copyright owners actual damages caused by their illegal copying, plus legal fee" (Talab, 2001, p. 7). No one cares that you did not have ill intent or that you did not realize that using another's work was wrong; you still may end up in jail!

In sum, there are good reasons not to steal—it is not ethical, not citing makes you look bad while citing makes you look good, and the consequences are drastic when you get caught. From the classroom to the conference room, your ethos will increase when you verbally state out loud the sources from which you drew your information, and it vanishes when you do not. Take advantage of every chance that you can to show that you have done your legwork—cite. This leaves us with the important question: how do I cite?

When giving a speech (or writing a business memo, or engaging in any professional communication), you must make sure that your audience understands what information comes from you and what comes from another by stating this out loud. It is necessary that you "qualify" your source by advertising the source's credibility! (Think of the difference between, "I heard that we will be moving our headquarters to Rome next year" and "I spoke to all three vice-presidents and confirmed with Steve Gimber in our legal department that we will be moving our headquarters to Rome next year." One has far more ethos than the other!)

If you are trying to figure out how to verbally give credit to sources in the most engaging and effective manner, follow these decision-making guidelines:

+ **Known versus Unknown** (if there is any reason that your audience will not know the source; for example, no reason to qualify "President Obama" but, who the heck is "Smith 2012"?)

+ **Who versus What** (this means that you should state your source, then qualify it, and then tell us what the source said; if you wait until after the information is stated, you leave your audience wondering how far back the source applies—was it to the last sentence? The last two sentences? Farther back? Up front sources clarify before confusion can arise)

+ **Find It versus Follow Up** (when writing a report, you will want to give enough information that the reader could find and verify the citation on her own; conversely, in speaking, you want to provide enough information that a listener could make a mental note and follow up later; for example, "You said that you read a *New Yorker* article by Carly Timmons about changes in sales trends—when was that?")

There are many ways to place your sources into your business talk. As we move into a discussion of presentation delivery, you will want to give attention to being conversational rather than faltering as you give credit. This might involve a bit of rehearsal to get those name pronunciations right and have the details flow. Basically, introducing sources should be done purposefully. This means that you should organize your statements and use appropriate language based on the nature of the source and the idea that it is supporting. For example:

> "The editors of the *New York Times* just put out an article last Sunday where they argue that sleep is the least valued of our personal resources."
>
> "In a statement on the Tasty Cakes online homepage updated June of this year, it would be a travesty to have this institution leave the Philadelphia area."
>
> "I had a chance on August 17th of this year to speak with Tracey Holden, who is the inventor of fried ice cream, and I asked her about the mechanics of the process. She stated....."
>
> "Professor of Business Communication at Harvard University, Pamela Marshall, argued in a June 19th, 2012 lecture that it is nearly impossible to predict all of the outcomes of miscommunication in the workplace. She went on to say..."

While you want to have as large a breadth of sources as possible, you may have occasion to repeat (different or new) information from a previously cited source. Rather than giving the credibility statement again, and since the audience now knows this, abbreviate the verbal citation as follows: "Dr. Mary Wainwright, the Biochronologist at MIT that I mentioned earlier, goes on in the same book to state...."

It is worth emphasizing here that, whether you use a direct quotation or paraphrase the idea, you still must give credit to the source where you found the idea. If you do not, you are committing plagiarism, which is just as serious in a verbal form as a written one. This is an ethical violation, which carries grave penalties itself, and rocks your foundation.

ETHOS—SOME FINAL IDEAS

Your first day on the job might not result in your being asked to present for your company or boss. And...it might! When you are hired it is because you are already an expert. You have been trained in your schooling, your internships, and your experience. You come with a background that does give you an expert position, but you do not know everything and *evidence* is the means of appealing to ethos with your audience.

Evidence comes from a variety of sources in a variety of collection methods. You may look online for resources or to print sources or even to those around you. Each is a legitimate source, as long as you evaluate the information for accuracy! You will with time increase your expertise, confidence, and ability to answer questions. You will compile so much information that you will need to filter down to just the most useful data and then begin to structure it to meet your purpose.

4

IDEAL BUSINESS TALK ORGANIZATION

"Information is a source of learning. But unless it is organized, processed, and available to the right people in a format for decision making, it is a burden, not a benefit."

—*William Grosvenor Pollard,*
physicist and Episcopal priest

FRAMING WHAT YOU KNOW

Once upon a time, a girl lost a glass slipper. She had lost it at the ball that her Fairy Godmother transformed her for and where the prince had fallen in love with her. But, it all started when her father died and left her to live with her stepmother. That was ok because they all lived happily ever after and she found her shoe.

The End.

Most people know the story of Cinderella. However, even with a story so well known, the re-ordering of the story's elements means that the *message*—the moral, or the point to which the audience would otherwise be naturally led—is lost. Speeches and business talks work the same way. No matter how well you think that your audience knows the point of your message, the path must be clear.

Speeches' effectiveness hinges on the logos of the message. **Logos**, as discussed earlier, is the appeal to our audience's idea of what makes sense. Ideas should be presented through examples and evidence that support our arguments but these must be *organized* in a form that is easily grasped by our audience (Parra, Nalda, and Pereles, 2011). Logos asks the question, "Is this logical?" If your message is not logical to your audience then you have not properly selected and organized your arguments and support.

This chapter leads you through the steps of message organization so that you will make sense to your audience and achieve your purpose. You will learn to clarify your purpose, create your arguments, place your evidence, lure in your listeners and lead them along to a final appeal.

SPEECH PREPARATION

Ok. You have been asked to give a speech. Or, you have opted to speak in some professional setting. Some people would get up in front of the room and just begin to talk, having done no preparation whatsoever. This is called babbling. In the world of professional presentations (from interviews to meeting reports), effectiveness comes from preparation.

Before you begin to write a word (yes, speeches are written—but differently than you would write a paper or an essay with an outline that becomes your speaking notes...we will get to that), you must develop a plan. By articulating a clear action plan, you are able to best move your audience to the place that you would like them to be. (Think about the **rhetorical situation** and remember that speeches happen for a *reason*. If you know that reason and can figure out how your talk can lead your audience to a better place then you have a good plan.) Typically, presentation planning involves selecting your topic and then following specific steps. Before we get into those steps, we should remember the two key criteria to selecting a topic.

If you have the luxury of choosing your own topic for a presentation, you already know that your choice should be guided by two key considerations: 1) *your knowledge and interests*, and 2) *your **audience's** interests and needs*. Consider both needs, and the final result will be a topic that you find interesting and your audience will want to hear. Once you have done this you are ready to move into the steps of speech creation.

The details of the below steps are discussed in depth throughout this chapter. Are these steps set in stone? No. Of course not. There is no *single* approach to producing a presentation. In fact, the last three of the below steps are easily switched around and can really be completed in any order. These guidelines will give you an indication of the elements that you will need to include and complete. As you move forward, a logical progression is:

1. General Purpose

2. Specific Purpose

3. Thesis

4. Main Points

5. Claims

6. Evidence and Support

7. Rephrased Thesis

8. Introduction and Conclusion

9. Transitions

The most important part of presentation creation is that you do not leave an element out of your talk and, thus, become less effective. The best way to approach these steps is to first consider the purpose of your speech.

Determine Your Purpose

Once you have selected your topic, your next step in this process is to determine your purposes—indeed, more than one. This means that you will need to craft both your *general* purpose as well as your *specific* purpose. These are critical decisions because they will help you ensure that your presentation stays focused. (If a piece of information does not help you advance one of these purposes, then it does not go into the presentation.)

A **general purpose** is the overall aim of your presentation. If you have ever responded to a presentation with, *"What the heck was that about?"* or *"What **was** her point?"* or even *"Now what are we supposed to do?"* then you have heard a speech without understanding its general purpose. Every speech has a primary general purpose: to inform, to persuade, or to entertain. Many speeches have a secondary purpose (e.g., I want to *persuade* my audience to adopt this business strategy so I must first *inform* them of all of its elements so that they can appreciate its merits). You will need to select your general purpose to keep you on track.

+ **To Inform: Speeches that aim to inform** lay out a new understanding of the topic for the audience. If you are giving a presentation with this general purpose then your talk should not sway an audience or have them change to see a topic in a new way. A speech to inform simply gives the audience new knowledge (from a little to a significant amount, or from nothing to some). There are several good instances of business talks with an informative general purpose, but be careful that you do not stray off course. If you are, for example, training your peers (or subordinates) then you can provide them with instruction on how to manage company software. This is an informative speech. If the group, however, already knows how to use this software then the *information does not inform*; no new knowledge is gained. That being said, if your company is about to drop its existing software in search for another, your presentation purpose could be to provide employees with a *new understanding* about the existing software—such as recognizing the glitches and limitations of the existing software. This way the group will follow the reasoning when management makes the change.

+ **To Persuade: Speeches that aim to persuade** are designed to change the perspective of your audience on some particular topic. *Change* is the key aspect to any persuasive speech and there are specific elements of the audience that a speaker can change. They are:

    a. *Beliefs*: what one considers true or not true (most difficult to change)

    b. *Attitudes*: a positive or negative association

    c. *Values*: socially set regard for something

    d. *Feelings*: one's emotional state or reaction

    e. *Existing actions*: particular behavior or the absence of particular behavior

    Persuasion will aim to either **strengthen or weaken a listener's commitment to the topic**. For example, a salesman of a particular product can worry that existing clients are thinking of going to a competitor and, thus, must strengthen commitment to the current product. Conversely, you may not be able to get a new client to purchase your product instead of a competitor's. However, through speech to weaken commitment to the product they currently use, you have planted a seed that will create an opening for a future sales pitch.

As you can imagine, it is more difficult to change a person's belief system than an attitude. After all, beliefs are *truths* in the mind of the audience. This is much like trying to convince the audience that they do not need to breathe to live. Easy? Perhaps not. It will take quite a bit of evidence and solid argumentation! So, should you avoid attempting to change something that is difficult? Absolutely not.

Similar to a speech with the general purpose of informing, you can alter your take on the topic without changing the topic or your position (e.g., asking an audience who is not ready to *act* on voting to have a good *attitude* on the topic instead). Promoting a set of beliefs and urging action are two distinctly different goals; because of this, they place different demands on your presentation.

+ **To Entertain:** Organizations are far more amenable to comedy than you might expect. Retirement parties are great places for humorous looks back and even a CEO presenting the annual report to stockholders might ask someone to do a quick entertaining presentation beforehand to ready the group for the longer discussion. **Speeches that aim to entertain** are largely ceremonial and primarily designed to amuse an audience on a special occasion. Their chief purpose is *not* to either lay out new information or change the perspective of the audience even if they secondarily do either or both of these.

Once you have determined the overall aim or general purpose of your business talk, you need to focus on what you want your listeners to get out of your presentation. In other words, you need to construct a specific purpose.

Specific Purpose

Any presentation you give should have a **specific purpose** that *focuses* the direction of your talk into a single central goal. (If you have multiple goals you want to pursue, you probably should be giving multiple presentations!) Consider this scenario: if you were to give a speech on the topic accounting and knew that you wanted to solely inform your audience, what would you talk about? Some options may include:

a. Tests required to become a CPA

b. Currency differences between countries

c.   The financial workings of the American Cancer Society®

d.   How recession affects the USA

e.   Tax tips

If you tried to give a speech on all of these topics, then your speech (besides being painfully long) would have little focus and not have the logos that your audience craves. What your specific purpose will do is allow you to clearly articulate what your speech is about—and what it is not about.

The Application of General and Specific Purposes

It is one thing to think about a general purpose and a specific purpose in the academic setting but another to apply them to your actual professional presentation. If you work with a speech trainer who does not have you articulate these then you are likely with someone who does not know the foundations of presentation crafting or, more likely, does this unconsciously. Regardless, utilizing these two elements will keep you from confusing your audience. To show this, consider the construction of an actual speech on the topic of accounting.

When first selecting your topic, you will begin to research the topic in order to become more of an expert. You will look at literature, look online, and even ask others in the office or in your non-work life. You might find some rather discouraging stories in the paper about poor accounting practices (e.g., Bernie Madoff's multi-billion dollar Ponzi scheme!). This leads you to think about your rhetorical situation. You know that as you begin to talk about accounting, your audience will already have an idea about how accounting practices can be deceitful. You know that there will be a level of urgency—the **exigence**—for information about how to avoid being caught in one of those schemes. In reaction to that, you can decide to use the following purposes:

> *Topic:* Accounting
>
> *General purpose:* To inform
>
> *Specific purpose:* To teach my audience how to avoid financial fraud through strict accounting strategies

As you can see, once you have established your specific purpose, you have a clear and concise gate-keeping device to help you determine which evidence and ideas to allow into the presentation and which ones to keep out. This can help you to move into articulating the argument that you will make. These steps will also direct your subsequent research, help you to craft strong logos in your speech, and have the audience say, "*Wow…that makes sense!*" Now that you have completed the preparation steps, turn your attention to the crafting of the speech itself.

YOUR PRIMARY ARGUMENT: CRAFTING THE THESIS

It may seem that once you have focused your topic well enough that you are in a good place to begin ordering your ideas and placing your qualitative and quantitative evidence. Not quite. *Speech preparation is for you*—it is not for your audience. Thus far, all you have done is make sure that you know the direction that your speech will take. Now that you have that purpose planned, you need to begin to craft the parts of your speech that will be shared with your audience. Now is the time for speech creation.

Speech creation begins with your most important speech element, which is, undoubtedly, the thesis. Your **thesis** is the primary argument of your speech. Without knowing what it is that you wish to argue, you are not in a position to select what types of evidence you will use, how you will organize your presentation, or make any other crucial decisions about your speech. Should all speeches have an *argument*? They should!

Why Argue?

Whether it is your task to offer an informative presentation or a persuasive speech or even one to entertain, you must offer an initial argument. Some people are uncomfortable with the notion of putting arguments into informative speeches; after all, "Don't arguments ask for a change?" "Aren't arguments specific to persuasion?" For our purposes here, arguments are offerings of specification. Think of arguments as saying to your audience, "Hey, *think about this (rather than thinking about something else)*."

Like much of speech creation, your business talk thesis will differ from the thesis that you may have composed for a paper or other written material. Verbal communication differs from written communication because of how the audience can receive it. (If you have ever read a mystery novel and gotten to the chapter where the detective says, "If you were at the meeting last week then you are the killer!"— do you flip back to see if the suspect was there? Many readers do!) *Written communication allows the reader to take in information at his or her own pace and to review and to skip ahead. Verbal communication cannot provide these options.* Therefore, speeches must be structured so that the audience can absorb the information the first time and, subsequently, retain it. Consequently, a simplified structure is key.

A **simplified structure** is the verbal act of limiting the complexity of major arguments—not the complexity of the evidence or support. We use a simplified structure in verbal communication so that the audience can: a) follow and b) recall.

This does not mean that verbal communication is simple. Hardly! Crafting an excellent speech is an intense task providing a great deal of evidence and intentionally intricate details. Only the *structural* elements use this type of simplified design. Structure begins with the crafting of your thesis. The thesis statement must follow three basic rules in order to maintain a simplified structure.

Basic Rules of the Verbal Thesis (Primary Argument)

1. **From You:** A thesis statement is the verbalized idea that expresses conclusions that *you* have drawn from what you know and have learned from your research. It is *your* idea. This is not a place for quotations, statistics, or evidence from another. Rather, develop your thesis on your perception of all that you have come to know. (Remember from our earlier discussion that much of what you know comes from other sources. That's ok. You cannot be an expert in everything. You can and should be the person who draws conclusions from all that you have read and who offers your *own* position statement.)

2. **A Single Idea:** Unlike a written thesis, multiple ideas and concepts in your verbalized argument create confusion or can be mistaken for a presentation preview. However, a single idea will actually direct your talk. It can be difficult to specify just one idea but do not overthink it. If you come up with your thesis before trying to imagine all of the claims, ideas, and evidence that you will add, the thesis will be far easier to create. If you look too far ahead and try to pick the main ideas first (for example, "I know that I want to talk about A, B, and C...what thesis might tie them together?") then you will be playing a logical game of *Twister*®. (That's the old game with colored spots on a mat and someone would say, "Left foot—yellow! Right hand—blue!") In other words, you would be trying to pull together ideas that are difficult to connect without some serious stretching. If it is easier, eliminate any terms in your verbal thesis that connect more than one idea.

   a. Some common "connector" terms to avoid include:

      i. and

      ii. which

      iii. that

      iv. "," (the comma—or any other punctuation)

3. **No Questions:** Having no questions as part of your thesis is another crucial means of making yourself clear and understandable to your audience. As such, it consists of two elements:

a. **Your Thesis Should Not *Be* a Question:** *"How should our sales staff work to find the best results?"* (The audience would think…"Er, uh, I don't know. Shouldn't you? You're the one talking!") Remember that you are the one in charge of your talk. When you are asking questions of the audience as your primary argument then you cannot know how they will answer these questions and what expectations that they will form from their own answers. You put yourself in a position to not be able to meet the needs of your rhetorical situation. (Avoid that!)

b. **Your Thesis Should Not *Lead* to Questions:** "Sales is about the many aspects of relationship maintenance." How many? What exactly is "relationship maintenance"? With a thesis like this, before you even have a chance to launch into your speech, your audience is perplexed. If your thesis does not provide clarity then you are off to a rocky start; you must avoid ambiguous terms, unknown jargon, or ideas that will leave them scratching their heads.

These might seem like rigid rules for just the creation of one simple sentence, but they are the rules that will help you make your verbal thesis effective in your rhetorical situation. They will work together with your general and specific purposes to guide the remainder of your speech creation. For example, if we build on the example above, we get:

Topic: Accounting

General purpose: To inform

Specific purpose: To teach my audience how to avoid financial fraud through strict accounting strategies

Thesis: Strict accounting strategies can help you to avoid being taken in by financial fraud schemes.

Managing Common Thesis Issues

This thesis will guide your audience! They know what is coming in your talk and are ready to receive the information. Sometimes, however, we craft thesis statements that do not effectively guide our audience. There are common problems that you will want to avoid in your thesis construction. Each of the following thesis statements for the topic *management* fail to effectively guide the audience.

Thesis: I will talk about management.
(Problem: no argument here)

Thesis: My topic is management.
(Problem: a topic statement—not a thesis)

Thesis: Management styles help leaders to guide and control their employees.
(Problem: more than one idea—as indicated by the word "and")

Thesis: Contingency theory is the effective management style, which lets leaders change according to need.
(Problem: more than one idea—indicated by the word "which" that connects the two parts)

Thesis: Carter McNamara shows how management decision-making is contingent on managers' ways of thinking.
(Problem: evidence needing a citation—not from the speaker)

Thesis: How can managerial sense-making help you to become a more effective leader?
(Problem: this is a question rather than an argument)

Thesis: Post-modern management styles are true forms of effectiveness.
(Problem: leads to a question—what are "true forms of effectiveness"? and for that matter, does anyone really know what "postmodern" actually is?!)

Avoiding these common issues will help you to make more sense to your audience (which is what good logos is all about!). You can then achieve your purpose of informing, persuading, or entertaining. To clarify, notice how removing issues from the problematic thesis statements below serves as a better guide to the speech that would follow.

Problematic Thesis: Let me tell you about Product X.
Better: Product X is on the leading edge of information storage.

Problematic Thesis: There are two kinds of salespeople in this world: aggressive and poor.
Better: Aggressive salesmanship is your key to career success.

Problematic Thesis: Who was 'Mary Kay' Ash?
Better: Mary Kay Ash's frustrations with male favoritism in the workplace led to an empire of female empowerment.

Problematic Thesis: You must put your business information on LinkedIn.
Better: LinkedIn widens your existing network of trusted contacts.

As you can see, once you have established your general and then your specific purpose, you can easily lead yourself, and subsequently your audience, to the clear and concise primary argument. It is this argument that will guide the remaining organizational elements of your talk.

ORGANIZATIONAL PATTERNS TO MATCH YOUR THESIS AND GENERAL PURPOSE

Determine purpose—check!

Understand rhetorical situation—check!

Craft thesis—check!

Organize my thoughts—getting there!

If you have come this far then you have a superb foundation for an effective business presentation. Your diligence in completing the initial groundwork is about to pay off. From here on out you are in a position to organize your arguments as appropriate to your *purpose* and *audience*. You will begin to fill in the elements of your speech like coloring inside the lines of a picture. The structure is the lines and the way that you color is your own unique spin on your topic. This process begins with selecting an overall organizational pattern to match your general purpose and thesis and then filling in your evidence.

Patterns of Content Organization

Patterns of organization are more than just how you group ideas together as they make the most sense to you. Instead, these patterns are the sequence of your ideas so that they bring your audience to the informed, persuaded, or entertained position where you want them. Yes, the sequencing of your ideas and evidence actually helps you to *realize* your specific purpose. It has a reason! While there are numerous ways to pattern your talk, you should realize that certain patterns fit with particular general purposes and only a few overlap. In other words, if you wish to inform, then certain organizational patterns will work for you and others will not. The same goes for persuasive speeches. Speeches to entertain may employ either informative or persuasive purposes and, therefore, adopt the pattern that best suits that secondary goal.

4

Informative Patterns of Organization

Informative speeches lay out knowledge for the audience. They do not lead audiences to a *new* belief, help them to make a change, or to take an action. Since this is the case, you want to choose organizational patterns that simply present ideas and are not structurally designed to sway an audience. There are many such patterns but the most common include:

+ **Chronological**

   Chronological organization is the time sequencing of information that offers ideas or events *building* from the past to the present—or can deconstruct how time brought something from its most recent position to the least recent (**reverse chronological order**).

   ▪ *Example:* New employees can be curious about promotion processes. It might be your job to take them through the timeline from new employee to company CEO from the start of what they must do through the subsequent steps.

   ▪ *Example:* Many companies have a corporate narrative that traces the history of the company and you may tell this narrative to visitors or new employees from where the company is now back to where it all began (this is reverse chronological order).

+ **Spatial**

   Spatial speaking structures deal with relationships between physical parts or elements like geography, anatomy (parts of the whole), or magnitude (large to small, small to large).

   ▪ *Example:* You might give a presentation indicating regions to which your company has grown and expanded from one and then to the next that takes listeners from the East Coast to the middle of the U.S. and then out to the West Coast.

+ **Categorical (or Topical)**

   Categorical structures are sometimes called topical structures because they focus on key groupings or linked concepts within the main topic.

   ▪ *Example:* A speech on the key criteria for a successful career in sales could group concepts of building relationships, remembering to "close," and knowing the product (these could go in any order within the speech).

◆ **Causal**

Causal structures look at the *relationship* between catalysts and consequences (effect to cause or cause to effect). This is the pattern to be used when showing how one thing led to another or how something could not have occurred without some other previous or simultaneous element.

■ *Example:* BP, Halliburton, and Transocean were all trying to explain the reasons why the U.S. had a catastrophic failure at the *Deepwater Horizon* oil rig in the Gulf of Mexico in April 2010. Each showed how their particular acts did (or did not) *lead* to the disastrous results.

◆ **Contrast (Compare and Contrast)**

Using a **contrast** (also known as a **compare and contrast**) structure helps to present the differences (and/or similarities) between ideas or items. You may select to look at two items to contrast numerous different characteristics that the two either share or on which they differ (e.g., how two cars differ on cost, fuel economy, and safety); you might look at numerous items and contrast them on the basis of one or a few characteristics; the options are endless.

Regardless of how you organize your contrast speech, you must be sure that you are doing it ethically. You cannot ethically compare two cars by looking at the fuel economy of one and the safety of another. That would be comparing apples to oranges! You must ensure that you are not offering manipulative or deceptive arguments. Therefore, you must contrast all ideas or items on the same elements.

■ *Example:* Coke Zero™ must differentiate between its product and the previously developed Pepsi Free™ by showing key differences between the two products in elements of taste, calories, nutrition, and cost. This speech may be organized with: a) the product being a main focus and the elements being the points of comparison, or b) the elements of comparison being the main areas and the two products as the elements of comparison for each.

Contrast Organization A	Contrast Organization B
I. **Coke**	I. **Taste**
—taste	—Coke
—calories	—Pepsi
—nutrition	II. **Calories**
—cost	—Coke
II. **Pepsi**	III. **Nutrition**
—taste	—Coke
—calories	—Pepsi
—nutrition	IV. **Cost**
—cost	—Coke
	—Pepsi

Informative speeches are relatively straightforward—they aim to inform. Persuasive speeches are a different beast. If you will recall from above, persuasive speeches aim to change—but change what? Selecting an organizational pattern for the content of your persuasive speech means first identifying what it is that you want to change and in what setting.

Considerations for Selecting an Organization Pattern for a Persuasive Speech

Speeches that aim to persuade are designed to change the perspective of your audience on some particular topic such as beliefs or actions (see full list earlier in the chapter).

Your research will have uncovered information about your audience's current state of any of these changeable elements. Do they currently believe in an equal tax payment for all? Do they have negative attitudes about the idea of moving offices into the new space? Will some folks always value money over customer service while others will always feel exactly the opposite? Knowing this information will help you choose how to structure your content. Therefore, speakers must first identify the audience type. There are three **types of audiences** that you might encounter when delivering a speech in a persuasive situation.

+ **Types of Audiences**

   Hostile audiences will primarily include listeners who are *firmly set against* your topic. To be clear, they are usually not against you, but rather the topic or position included in your speech. For example, if you are speaking to new employees about the benefit of giving up annual bonuses and vacation time to help the expansion of facilities, the group may love you but are "hostile" to the idea.

   Supportive audiences primarily include those who are *firmly for* your topic. You might wonder how one can persuade a supportive audience if they already are on your side. Remember that their positive attitudes may not yet have resulted in action. Or, that your audience may hold two different conflicting values, and they need you to help them select which one to embrace. This might happen when you are speaking to accountants about the benefits of strict financial policies. They are already on your side but just need to be pushed into doing something about it.

   Wavering audiences can be a bit more difficult both to persuade and to identify. You will need to do some thorough audience analysis. In general, **wavering audiences** include either:

a. Those who have not yet developed a position on your topic (e.g., speaking to new employees about a potential change in the existing sales software).

b. A group who is divided on their positions (some hostile and some supportive) (e.g., speaking to existing employees about a potential change in the existing sales software).

Different audiences will have different needs. In fact, research states that the effectiveness of your arguments made to each of these groups is dependent on meeting the specific needs of the audience type (Perloff, 2003). For instance, a hostile audience that is simply told what to do without having their needs or position considered is likely to become more hostile. You do not want that! Similarly, a supportive audience that listens to you drone on and on about the other side of a case might become less supportive and start to take that other side. You now have a wavering or even hostile audience! To make the best choice, you will need to understand whether or not to present one or all sides of a given position.

◆ **Message-Sidedness**

Most literature on persuasion will tell you to choose your organizational pattern based on your type of audience because of the *message-sidedness* of that pattern. In other words, particular audiences need to hear either one-sided or two-sided arguments (Perloff, 2003). A **one-sided argument** provides only one view on the topic and is generally better suited to a group that shares your idea. A **two-sided argument** provides more than one perspective on the topic and is best suited for those who are hostile to your position (and, therefore, want to see that you recognize or do not discount their position) as well as those who are undecided on a position. The pros and cons of one-sided arguments versus two-sided arguments have been heavily researched and discussed. While we may assume that one-sided arguments *always* have a greater effect on audiences who share your ideas while two-sided arguments are *always* better suited for audiences who oppose our ideas, there is a bit more to the issue.

Two-sided arguments have been found to have better persuasive effects on all types of audiences in comparison to just giving one side of an argument; however, be aware—there are two types of two-sided message arguments (O'Keefe, 2002, p. 220).

a. **Two-Sided Refutational:** A message that presents two varying opinions but attempts to *refute* one of them.

b. **Two-Sided Non-Refutational:** A message that presents two varying opinions but does not actually try to refute one of them (just tries to make it look pretty bad!).

If you know that your audience is of a particular type and would best be persuaded by an organizational pattern that gives them the necessary argument sides that they need to adopt your position, then all you have to do is see which pattern best suits you!

Persuasive Patterns of Organization

As informative organizational patterns lay out ideas, persuasive organizational patterns are aimed at leading an audience along. Some lead using a one-sided argument and some lead using a two-sided argument. Some are more appropriate for one type of audience and others for a different type of audience. While this might seem complicated, picking a persuasive organization is an easy process of looking for the obvious fit. See below for the clear links between speech structure, audience type, and message-sidedness.

- **Problem/Solution/(Action):** The **PSA structure** defines a problem and offers a way (or ways) to solve it. In addition, the structure can sometimes suggest action to the audience when they are prepared to take an action; this pattern often includes the action step as the last main idea. As we get into our discussion of speech conclusions, you will realize that an initial appeal to action should never be put in your conclusion.

  - *Appropriate for this audience:* Supportive (only!)

  - *Sidedness of this structure:* One-sided

  - *Example:* A presentation to discuss the revenue problems your company faces due to an economic downturn and ways to attract new business in a more austere economic environment.

- **Option Elimination:** An **elimination structure** (also sometimes called a **residue structure**) helps lead the audience through any available options in a situation and eliminate each until they are left with the best option; hence the name—a "residue" speech because it is what we are left with at the end (not a pleasant image, but quite vivid!). The difference between this and a comparison speech is that the speaker is helping the audience to evaluate and then eliminate ideas rather than simply looking at how two or more ideas are similar and different.

  - *Appropriate for this audience:* Wavering or hostile

  - *Sidedness of this structure:* Two-sided

- **Example:** If your company is trying to determine if they should do a company-wide retreat this year in such financial uncertainty, you can help them to decide by looking at the viability of having the retreat, then what position the company would be in without the retreat, then also looking at options such as limited departmental retreats or even outsourcing some of the training.

+ **Monroe's Motivated Sequence:** The Monroe's Motivated Sequence (MMS) structure is the only organizational pattern that is named to acknowledge the person who changed persuasive formats so that the *audience's perspective* is highlighted over the speaker's perspective. The structure has four main points that include: 1) highlighting an audience need, 2) clarifying what will satisfy that need, 3) offering a visualization of life with or without the need met, and then 4) directing the audience how to act to realize the visualization (Monroe, 1935).

  - *Appropriate for this audience:* Hostile or wavering

  - *Sidedness of this structure:* Two-sided

  - *Example:* Most sales pitches and commercials are motivational speeches (e.g., the need is to feel young and alive, the satisfaction is a new sports car that can make you feel fast and energized, the visualization is the picture of you zipping down the road with all admiring eyes on you, and the action is to visit the dealership!)

+ **Causal:** Unlike the previously covered persuasive structures, causal can be both persuasive and informative depending on the speaker's treatment of the speech's sub-points. Using a causal structure for a persuasive speech is not an excuse to be biased or *mis*leading but instead uses researched evidence to highlight the positive or negative relationship between catalysts and consequences.

  + *Appropriate for this audience:* Supportive

  + *Sidedness of this structure:* One-sided

  + *Example:* BP, Halliburton, and Transocean are all trying to show how the others were responsible for the catastrophic failure at the *Deepwater Horizon* oil rig.

+ **Contrast:** Again, you are in a position to use a structure from our informative list in a persuasive rhetorical situation. In a persuasive contrast speech, you are allowing the primary structure to remain the same as above but using supporting structure to illuminate the positive or negative differences and similarities between ideas or items.

- *Appropriate for this audience:* Wavering or hostile
- *Sidedness of this structure:* Two-sided
- *Example:* Coke Zero must show how their product is *superior* to Pepsi Free.

These are not the only patterns—just the most often used. Start with these as you begin your speaking career and then look for more options in communication research as you develop your skills and gain experience.

To make your path even more clear, we can put all of our ideas of topic and audience together. If you are, for instance, a strong advocate of pulling all of your company's manufacturing plants out of Asia and placing them in the United States' Midwest region, you must pattern your talk to the needs of the audience, not the topic.

Your topic: manufacturing plant relocation

Audience is supportive: Problem-solution-action structure

or

Audience is hostile: Contrast or Monroe's Motivated Sequence structure

Choose your pattern purposefully rather than just assuming that you should follow a certain pattern solely because of the type of speech you are giving. You must consider the audience (rhetorical situation), your goal, and your purpose. Once you have this pattern chosen, you are able to move on to crafting the content of your speech—the main points.

LAYING OUT YOUR MAIN POINTS

You have a superb argument (your thesis) and have collected all sorts of evidence to support that argument. You have figured out what type of audience you have and know your general purpose. Your next step is to develop your main points. **Main points** are the cluster of ideas, concepts, arguments, and evidence that are gathered together and organized to fit the pattern that you have selected for your speech. *These are organizational categories that the speaker lays out for her or himself but are not actually stated in the speech.*

The number of main points you have in your presentation should develop organically. There is no perfect number for how many main points to have except that there should be enough to support your thesis. If you need *seventeen* main points, so be it! If you need *two* main points, fantastic! If you do not have enough information or time to fill seventeen main points, or even two, then you must go back and reconsider what specific purpose you can meet in the time that is allotted to you along with the information that is available and revise the number of main points to meet that goal.

Matching Main Ideas with Organizational Patterns

You might hear that the ideal number of clusters (main points) that you should end up with is three to five. This is because research has shown that this range is the number of items that can be kept in our *working* memory, and the number of interrelationships between elements that can be kept active in reasoning out an idea (Halford, Cowan, & Andrews, 2007). If you want to maximize the likelihood of your audience processing your particular reasoning, three to five main points or arguments is one way to accomplish this goal. In reality, though, phenomena and experiences do not typically parse themselves neatly in three to five areas. *Remember to have as many (or as few) main points as are necessary to support your argument.*

As you may have guessed, some patterns of organization will predetermine a base number of main points for you. For example, if you are giving a chronological speech then you need at least two main points in order to show a movement in time. If you are giving a motivational speech then you will have exactly the four points of need, satisfaction, visualization, and action (some folks may have more than one main point for any given element such as two need main points and three visualization main points, but you cannot fully motivate if you *delete* any of Monroe's steps along the way).

Main Point Creation

To determine how to create main points, let us take a classic (albeit not necessarily business related) example: football! Football is something of which most U.S. citizens have at least a passing understanding (no pun intended). If your topic were football then you may have collected evidence about teams, rules, players, history, playoffs, college and professional differences, mascots, injuries...this list could go on and on. Your specific purpose will have allowed you to focus your ideas and, yet, you will still have much to consider. Apply the steps and guidelines discussed above to start laying out the major clusters of ideas appropriate to your situation. For example:

Topic: Football

General purpose: To inform

Specific purpose: To show the cultural impact of the Superbowl

Thesis: The NFL Superbowl has become an American cultural phenomenon.

Option 1

Organizational pattern: Categorical

Main point ideas:

+ definitions of culture

+ product advertising

+ jargon creation

Option 2

Organizational pattern: Chronological

Main point ideas:

+ history of the Superbowl

+ early sponsorship, viewership changes

+ later product advertising

+ modern-day viewer-product relationship

Option 3

Organizational pattern: Causal

(Alas, we would need to change our thesis to make this pattern work because there is no causal relationship shown in the current thesis)

New thesis: The NFL Superbowl has led to the celebration of sport as a pervasive part of American popular culture.

Main point ideas:

+ changes in advertising (before Superbowl/after Superbowl)

+ changes in viewership (before Superbowl/after Superbowl)

+ changes in popular behavior (before Superbowl/after Superbowl)

As you can see, you will develop your main points based upon your thesis, purpose, needs of the audience, and the evidence that you have collected. Begin to lay out your evidence (even on the floor with piles of printed research and notes from interviews or audience surveys) where you have significant information and, again, read through your evidence to see if you need more to support one idea. If we look at the previous examples above, you can see that you may have tons of research on the "changes in Superbowl advertising" but really only one interview source about popular behavior. Before moving on to the next step in speech creation—the creation of central arguments or claims per main point—go back and do a bit more research to see if you really can fully develop that main point. If not, you need to drop it from your talk!

Claims

Just like with your overall speech, your main points cannot just "start." They need to have some type of foundation that demonstrates that all of the evidence and ideas in this main point really do belong together. This is the central argument of the main point, or **claim**. If you are thinking that you already have a central argument in your thesis, you do! But that statement reflects how everything in the speech is tied together. The claim only reflects how that particular main point is tied together. (Still struggling? Think of the claim as a topic sentence to a paragraph for an essay.) You have already worked through crafting a thesis so developing your claims will be easy.

Because we are still working in a verbal and not a written format, the structure of your speech must be kept simple. This means that you must adhere in producing claims to the same guidelines that you used for writing your thesis. Each claim sentence should:

+ Be from you

+ Be a single idea

+ Produce no questions

After this, you will want to look at each main point and determine the central argument statement that will bring it all together. We can use our football speech as an example. As noted above, we already have completed the following parts:

Topic: Football

General purpose: To inform

Specific purpose: To show the cultural impact of the Superbowl

Thesis: The NFL Superbowl has become an American cultural phenomenon.

Organizational pattern: Categorical

Main points (not verbalized):

+ definitions of culture

+ product advertising

+ jargon creation

+ general population behavioral change

(This speech has *four* main points so it will have *four* claims that will be verbalized in the speech.)

Claims (said out loud):

+ Cultural definitions help us to understand how changes impact our society.

+ Product advertising during the Superbowl has become part of our cultural memory.

+ The jargon that we associate with the Superbowl is now engrained in the American culture.

+ We can trace a general population behavioral change related to the American Superbowl.

You may find that, like with a thesis, you run through five or ten or more attempts at each claim before you find just the right wording that will be the launching point for all of the wonderful evidence that you have collected. Do not feel the need to get it perfect the first time. Write one. Wait a day. Write two revisions. Work on the next point. Come back to it, and keep revising it until you love it. (Now you can see why you should never wait until the last minute to write your speech!)

Incorporating and Organizing Your Evidence

Your claims came *from* your evidence—so now you must match your evidence to those claims. You have already gathered and created piles of all the evidence (perhaps on your floor) so now it is just a matter of organizing what you have and filling in the holes. Take every element of your research (your statistics, interviews, examples, analogies, hard data/facts, etc.) that is separated *per main point* and begin placing them appropriately to support a specific claim. This evidence will help produce your **sub-points**, or the cluster of ideas that will "prove" your claims (ok—prove is not a term we use in social science but you get the idea). How many sub-points? Use as many as are needed to support your claim. (That same research as above suggests that 3–5 ideas are the easiest number to retain for most audiences—Halford, Cowan, & Andrews, 2007.) For example:

+ *Claim One:* Cultural definitions help us to understand how changes impact our society.
    + Defining "patterns of experience" (Yip, 2012)
    + Definition of culture (Derth, 2008)
    + 30% change based on observation (Jones, 2010)
    + My personal narrative
    + CEO Jim Kyle's example (Kyle, 2012)

At some point you may decide that a piece of evidence needs to be moved to a different main point or that an example should be removed from the speech or that a new idea, statistic, narrative, or piece of data needs to be added.

What you will see now is a cluster of ideas that all can support the claim. What this should bring you to is a question: *do my sub-points appeal to logos?* Just as your overall speech must have **logos**, or organization that makes sense to the audience, so must your sub-points! If they can be put in some order (chronological, PSA, spatial, etc.) then you must do that to create a strong sense of organization that can be followed. Notice in the example above that the two definitions are grouped together (qualitative data) with the statistic in the middle (quantitative) and that the narrative examples are then grouped at the end (qualitative data). You can clearly see that the sub-points are put into a categorical order. This will "make sense" to an audience. On the following page you will see how to connect these sub-points through the use of internal transitions.

You have just finished your speech! Congratulations. By the time that you have crafted your arguments and placed all of your evidence, you really are finished with most of your work. See? It was not as hard as you may have thought. What remains in speech organization are the parts of your talk that will make sure that the audience is able to follow as your structure moves along, which is the linking of ideas, and that they want to listen in the first place (the introduction)!

LINKING IDEAS

If you have ever heard a speaker and at the end wondered what the key elements of the talk had been, do not blame the structure. Too often, speakers have beautifully structured arguments and wonderfully organized evidence but still the audience cannot follow the key ideas or recall them. If the speech that you heard was a comedian on stage—no problem! You are not supposed to remember the details, just that you laughed. If your boss listens to your talk and at the end cannot recall the key ideas of your talk—well, now you are in trouble.

Providing a clear sense of logos through transitionary statements will help your audience follow you and recall your ideas. Statements that *link* as well as differentiate your main points or sub-points are called **transitionary statements**. These statements will help you not to sound like your speech with six main points was just one big idea where everything ran together.

There are several places within your speech that will need transitionary statements. In each place, you will use them to tell your audience what is to come and to remind them what has already passed. These connections should come between all main points (**external transitions**) and are effective within main points (**internal transitions/signposts**) so that the listener has a verbal guide for understanding the information.

Some folks think that their transitionary statements begin to stand out more than their facts, and this bums them out. Indeed, it should. Transitionary statements should not be the focus of your talk. Think of transitionary terms as the scaffolding that holds up the rest of your speech. Practicing clarity and fluidity will allow you to have effective (but not obnoxious) transitions.

Organization between Main Points—External Transitions

Your external transitions are the most needed by your audience in order to follow your overall speech. Your audience will use these as a mental checklist (*"she said she would talk about A, B, and C...ok, she just talked about A and should next get in to B!"*). Skipping these transitions will leave your audience wondering if they missed something or, worse, if you did. There are three kinds of external transitions that can create this mental checklist: 1) your preview, 2) your transitions between each main point, and 3) your review.

Your **preview** is the statement that sets up an expectation of the main points that you will cover in your speech and is delivered immediately after your thesis. Your **transitions between main points** are the statements (or single statement if you only have two main points) that show a natural move or connection between the two main point ideas. The statements made in between major concepts are transitions (yes, like in an English essay). Transitions mention the idea that was just discussed and provide a logical link between it and the next idea. *This notion of logical links is crucial.* If the preview is a checklist then the transitions allow the audience to put checks next to each item and remember to grab it off the metaphorical shelf.

Claims and transitions should never be the same statement in your business talk. First, remember that they serve different purposes. Claims provide arguments. Transitions do not. Transitions provide links and help the audience to follow and recall. You will need both statements in your speech but they should be clearly different to effectively serve their individual purposes. As you are creating these, be sure that you both practice (and remember to state aloud to your audience) each part.

If you have trouble crafting a transition between main points, you may wish to consider if you have selected the best organizational pattern for your information. If you have, then the transitions should come naturally (e.g., a problem leads naturally to the need for a solution). If you are struggling then consider whether or not you are trying to force a pattern to work that is not best for the content.

Finally, your **review** (or **summary statement**) is the counterpart to your preview. The idea here is that just as much as an audience needs to have a mental checklist for where you will go, they need that same mental checklist to see if indeed you went to all of the places promised. The review is the statement that shows that you have met the expectations that you have set up and it is delivered immediately before your conclusion. You will need to make sure that you use the same key words for the preview, review, and transitions so that the audience will not think that you are introducing new ideas.

Your external transitions will basically produce themselves once you have written your claims because they come from the key word or words of those claims. Unlike what you have written on your preparation outline, when you verbally deliver your transitions, you will turn the key words into one fluid and concise statement. The statement should never give any information that belongs in the main point, but only show a link between these areas. For example:

4

Claims (key words underlined for emphasis):

+ <u>Cultural definitions</u> help us to understand how changes impact our society.

+ <u>Product advertising</u> during the Superbowl has become part of our cultural memory.

+ The <u>jargon</u> that we associate with the Superbowl is now engrained in the American culture.

+ We can trace a general population <u>behavioral change</u> related to the American Superbowl.

External Transitions (for outline):

+ Preview: cultural definitions, product advertising, jargon, behavioral change

+ 1–2: cultural definitions, product advertising

+ 2–3: product advertising, jargon

+ 3–4: jargon, behavioral change

+ Review: cultural definitions, product advertising, jargon, behavioral change

External transition between main point 2 and 3 (would be said aloud):

+ *2–3: As you can see, we Americans have become so captivated by product advertising; in fact, this has partly led to a completely refined popular jargon.*

While this seems like an easy process, it can be easy to give too much, too little, no connection, or no clarity in a transition. You will need to practice crafting each of these a few times before you find the one that really shows a good connection and logical link. Note the following transition "problems" and how they have been fixed to add clarity.

Preview for Speech: In order to understand why you will want to own Product X, let's take a look at its storage capacity—both in terms of its volume as well as how it compares to similar products; we will also look at your ability to access information efficiently as the next area—from how user friendly the program is as well as how quickly it responds to your requests for information; and last, I want to zero in on savings—including both initial costs and then just savings accrued through using this system.

(Problem: No one is ever going to remember all of those details to stay on track during your presentation.)

Improved Preview for Speech: Product X has three advantages over the system that you are using now: capacity, efficiency, and savings. Let's look at how each can affect your bottom line.

Transition between Main Points: Now that I have talked about fraud, I will talk about audits.

(Problem: No logical link)

Improved Transition between Main Points: As you can see, financial fraud is crippling our company, but, with keen attention to details through regular audits, we can change our financial future.

Review for Speech: We have just looked at several reasons for you to adopt Product X, such as savings, capacity, and efficiency.

(Problem: Not the same order as the above preview)

Improved Review for Speech: You have spent the last ten minutes hearing about Product X in order to understand how it gives you greater capacity, increased efficiency, and substantial savings.

Organization within Main Points—Internal Transitions

You are sitting in your company's annual employee meeting. Your CEO is giving a presentation hoping to get folks on board with the corporate move from one location to another. First, she details the problem with the current location. Second, she was, you think, talking about some good things about the new location and some stories about something. Finally, she asks that you help in the process by giving details of…

that's it. You tuned out! Sure, you could grasp what the main points of her speech were, but after that, all of the details just ran together and, suddenly, you found yourself creating a grocery list in your head. (P.S. You're out of milk.)

One of the most forgotten notions of speech giving is that not only must we have patterns of organization for our entire presentation (the main points), but we must have organization *within* each main point. If not, the audience may lose focus and have difficulty listening, or they may think that we are just babbling. **Internal transitions** (also called **signposts**) help to maintain clear logos for each major concept/argument in your talk, which is accomplished by using simple terms to move along the flow of your evidence and support (e.g., first, next, leads, etc.). What makes internal organizational patterns so simple is that the patterns that you might use are the same that you will have used for your main points:

+ **Chronological signpost terms:** First, Second, Third, etc.

+ **Categorical signpost terms:** Next, In addition, Moreover

+ **Causal signpost terms:** A leads to B

+ **Contrast signpost terms:** By comparison, In contrast

+ **Spatial signpost terms:** Next to this, As we move to

+ **Problem–solution signpost terms:** The initial issue, Which was fixed by

You will know you are finished organizing the body of your speech if the ideas flow clearly and smoothly, and if your main points do not overlap but logically relate to one another. In addition, you will know you are finished if all key aspects of your topic are covered while your purpose is fulfilled. Even having gone this far, your speech is not finished. You must pull your audience in—and then send them on their way.

GETTING IN AND GETTING OUT

Imagine hearing a speech that began with, "Today, I will talk about (insert topic)." Are you intrigued? Fascinated? Of course not, and why would you be? Even if the topic is something about which you already have an interest (such as video games or breakfast cereals), this sentence does little to make you want to hear what this speaker has to say on the topic. You likely feel the same letdown when a speaker finishes a talk with, "That's it." (Can you feel the disappointment?) Beginning and ending your presentations can either engage or disengage your colleagues. The great thing is that you get to decide which they will do.

Opening Your Talk

The reason to create your introduction *after* the speech content is complete is so that you can tailor your opening remarks to the content of the speech. If you develop the introduction first (prior to the body of your talk) then you will tend to try to force the speech to follow the path set by the introduction rather than the argument or the thesis. The body of your speech should not serve your introduction; it's the other way around. Opening your speech begins by grabbing the audience's attention in a way that effectively draws them into your thesis.

Grabbing Attention

A CEO walks into the auditorium full of 400 employees. He moves to the lectern, picks up a stack of the company's annual report, and proceeds to hurl them at the audience. The idea: that we are "throwing out the past and moving to the future!" Good idea? This really depends. Having something thrown at you may get your attention, but if you are hit in the face or fear that you will be, are you really paying attention to the message? (Likely you are thinking about medical attention or how not to get hurt if this guy tries that same theatrical trick again.)

Contrary to popular belief, *gaining attention is NOT the sole purpose of your introduction!* Grabbing attention is a good idea but it is not about shock value or drama for drama's sake. It is about making your audience truly believe that what you are about to say is of value to them. While most listeners will look at you as you get up to speak, they will typically be preoccupied with other issues (e.g., planning their dinner, wondering if the kids got home from school yet, or thinking "Wow, what on earth is that speaker wearing!?"). A myriad of thoughts can distract audiences from speakers. You want everyone to refocus their attention on *your* message, so you need to give them a reason to redirect their thoughts toward you. **The purpose of your introduction** is to draw your audience into your thesis, or primary argument.

You may wish to use a **quantitative introduction** (shock them with the numbers that impact their lives) or a **qualitative introduction** (pull on their heart strings with a narrative that could happen to them) or both. However, your introduction should be focused so be aware that using numerous ideas will actually work against you. Consider the following useful techniques:

- **Audience Identification:** Audience members can connect to speakers with whom they share an experience, which includes acknowledgement of the particular occasion ("We are together in these troubled times"), past experience ("So, I've talked to each of you individually and know that we have all lost someone to cancer"), or even shared reading ("Who remembers reading *The Catcher in the Rye* when they were in school?").

- **Story/Narrative:** The telling of an amusing or powerful story that relates to your purpose can bring life to hard data or basic information.

- **Analogy:** Relating current circumstances or data to similar and perhaps more well known or other significant scenarios can enhance understanding ("We all know that we are on the same path that led to the oil spill off the Gulf Coast last year...").

- **Rhetorical Question:** This type of question does not expect an answer but serves the same purpose as a persuasive statement (e.g., "How many of you want to reach your sales goals for this year?!"); however, it is only effective when you truly know your audience well.

- **Significant Quotation:** Sometimes others are better able to say what we mean ("Isaac Newton said that we become great by 'standing on the shoulders of giants.' I come here today as your CEO not on my own but humbly and appreciatively because of your great shoulders.").

- **Humor:** Telling jokes and amusing stories is a great way to produce an emotional response from an audience but *must be used with caution!* Humor can engage but it can also offend, not be understood, or just not be funny.

- **Demonstration or Visual Aid:** Showing images, actual models, and even providing a brief demonstration of your topic or something associated to your topic produces instant audience buy-in. However, you must keep these elements brief, focused, and introductory rather than visuals that are best developed and used to support claims.

- **Hard Data:** Numbers and facts can be dramatic and work best to involve quantitatively oriented audiences ("70% of you here today are at risk of losing your jobs; 10% actually will and 100% of those who follow the process that I outline here today will be able to remain with our company in a successful capacity.").

Demonstrating the Significance of Your Attention-Getter to the Audience

After grabbing your audience's attention (*not* by throwing things at them), listeners tend to wonder why your topic is important to *them*. You may have begun with an intriguing story of a lone man working long hours to make the vision of his dream company come true—this company. You may tell your audience that this man was your grandfather! Now your audience sees why the speech information is important to you, but not to them. Connecting the attention-getter to the audience and then to the thesis together will make a *full* introduction, which includes an attention-getter followed by a link to the audience and then to the thesis.

Significant Quotation Attention-Getter:

"Isaac Newton said that we become great by 'standing on the shoulders of giants.' I come here today as your CEO not on my own but humbly and appreciatively because of your great shoulders…

Significance to the Audience…:

We, Acme, Inc., are not a company that could have grown by 25% in two years without this sales force. We are not a company that could have surpassed our competitor's product turnout timelines by over 17% without the best manufacturing team out there. And, we are not a company that ignores the impact of each employee at every level. That means that what I have to say here today is about every person in this room! What we must do today is stand on the shoulders of others to keep our company growing.

(…Leads to) Thesis:

Acme, Inc. will expand into South America by purchasing our competitor's four biggest South American manufacturing facilities.

Two Main Points Speech Preview:

If you give me your attention for just a short time, I can help all of us move seamlessly into a bright future through, first, a quick integration and, second, a continuation of all existing corporate policies."

4

You will be amazed at the level of attention you get from your audience with this type of opening. They will want to hear what you have to say because it ties to them, and they will feel drawn into your thesis because your attention-getter led them to it. You will easily move through your claims, transitions, and evidence, all the way until you are ready to conclude your speech.

Closing Your Talk

How many times have you heard speakers end with, "I'm done; any questions?" This can be abrupt and does nothing to make a positive final impression on your audience. An effective conclusion should pull the key ideas of your speech back together and refocus your listeners' attention on your specific purpose. Finally, to give your speech a sense of unity (and your listeners a clear sense that they are fully and comprehensively empowered), you will want to employ a clincher that ties directly back to your attention-getter.

The Purpose of Rephrasing Your Thesis

Your conclusion should begin with a **rephrased thesis statement**. Speeches take time and, even in the shortest speeches with the most attuned audiences, listeners can forget the primary argument of your talk. Reminding your audience of why you are addressing *this* moment and *this* rhetorical situation occurs when you reflect back on the thesis of your speech. Rather than simply restate the same words, you will want to rephrase the idea. Why not just say the exact same thing? On the one hand, your audience may think that you have just had a mental hiccup ("Uh…didn't she already say that?"), and, on the other hand, while **redundancy** (the repeating of ideas in new words) is great in verbal communication for those people who did not completely understand the idea the first time, **repetition** (the exact and word-for-word restatement of language) can result in *less* understanding for those in the audience who did not understand the initial thesis and also confusion from those who think that you are making a verbal error. So, after you have reviewed and before you conclude, *rephrase*!

Style Matching with a Clincher

The last stop in creating your speech is to close it. Speeches that just end leave audiences feeling abandoned and ill-prepared. Consider every time that you have watched the last episode in a season of a television series where they used a cliffhanger. Something was said or done, but you would not find out the consequences until painfully waiting months until the next show. Imagine that your CEO did the same thing—finished up a speech by introducing something new and not finishing the thought. You would be confused, irritated, or anxious. This is not the way to leave your audience.

Your final words to the audience should serve the function of a last appeal to accept your information or be persuaded. **Clinchers** are verbal moments in your speech that inspire. They are an appeal to **pathos**, or the emotional connection that you have tried to inspire in the audience and are well suited to the last moments of your speech. Such as, if you have given a persuasive speech that asks for someone to buy your product, a clincher would deliver an idea or sentence just before you wrap up that encapsulates their newfound reason to buy that product. Think of this not only as a clincher but as a verbal zinger. You do this just before referencing your introduction and wrapping up.

A **style match** ties your conclusion directly back to how you began (Sprague and Stuart, p. 166). If you began with a story, return to that story by giving them the positive (or negative) result. If you started with a reference to the listener's or audience's identification, refer back to that statement and leave the audience knowing that you truly do *get* them. If you begin with a demonstration, return to it (or at least say something about it). *The most effective presentations end where they began.*

4

A FINAL FRAME ON ORGANIZATION

Once upon a time, a little girl lost her father. She then lived her life as a poor and ragged servant to her scary stepmother with no hopes of a bright future. But, when the prince of the land threw a ball looking to take a bride, her Fairy Godmother appeared and transformed her! She went to the ball, fell in love with the prince, and, even when she slipped away at the stroke of midnight losing one of her beautiful glass slippers and transforming back to her former self, the prince found her and they lived happily ever after!

Ideas that have order make more sense. We know it in our fairy tales and we know that the same ideas are true in business presentations. However, just as in fairy tales where we are captivated by engaging and descriptive language (and likely the comforting, familiar or great voices of those who used to tell these stories), how you say your message will be just as important as what you say in your message. It is with this in mind that we will next turn our attention to the words, voice, and movement of presentation delivery.

AIDING BUSINESS
TALKS WITH VISUALS

"It's a visual world and people respond to visuals."

—Joe Sacco,
award-winning international journalist

THE RATIONALE FOR USING VISUALS

"I have a presentation so I will need to create slides." There is a common misconception in the business world that presentations and visuals are somehow synonymous (just Google "giving a professional presentation" and see if you can find one result that does not tell you how to use slides!). In fact, many business people will tell you that when they know that they have a business talk to deliver, they will create a presentation slideshow and, when the slideshow is finished, then their presentation preparation is finished as well. If there is anything that you have learned in the last few chapters it is that giving a business talk is far more than having visual support! Many business professionals have forgotten this. If you remember it then you will deliver better business talks and make superior choices about visual support.

When you give a presentation in any business setting, it is not only likely that you will *use* visual support for your ideas but that it will be *expected*. We have become a society that is both drawn and attached to visual evidence (Genard, 2005). We want handouts, PowerPoint slides, graphs, charts—anything that impresses and wows our audience! The problem, of course, is that using visuals is not *always* a good choice. Almost every expert in public speaking will tell you tell that visual aids can distract the audience (Collins, 2004; Reynolds, 2008), hurt audience connections (Bumiller, 2010; Tufte, 2003, 2006), or even inhibit your audiences' abilities to understand or retain your messages (Carroll, 2007). Given the risks of using visuals, why would speakers use them? Good question.

Visuals are powerful. Visual aids have the ability to engage our audiences while increasing both listener comprehension and retention (Heap, Burill, Dewey, & MacDonald, 1994; Levasseur & Sawyer, 2006; Rotman, 2009). Using visuals can be an effective tool when your role is to *present* information in a formal way, such as a CEO giving annual report information to stockholders, a saleswoman outlining product benefits to a potential client, or even an in-house demonstration of your team's current work product. However, visuals are also useful when you are simply trying to help a small group understand your argument in an informal setting. Professional speech trainer Ethan Rotman (2009) reminds us, "The potential of visual aids is great, yet we often ignore this tool with small groups such as at staff meetings" (p. 32). Effective speakers find a good balance between the negatives and positives of visual use, which comes from an understanding of how visuals are used in particular settings!

This chapter is not intended to describe every single possible visual aid element of content and all potential mediums, to train you in all uses, or help you to become an expert of design. Instead, this chapter is an introduction to the most regularly used visual aid elements with an overview that will help you to understand what choices to make and not to make. Once you have made those choices, you will find some general guidelines of what to do and what *not* to do! Consider this your first step but do not stop your research here. As with your business talk, find every available resource to make you the best expert that you can be!

Defining Visual Aids

Visual aids are just that—they are *visuals* that *aid* a verbal presentation. If we were to send out our slides on their own, then these would not be visual aids—they would be the actual presentation (and some visual aid software can be used to create printed or emailed stand-alone graphic information). Images or visuals that go out alone would need to convey all of the necessary ideas and arguments without relying on a speaker to explain, verbalize, make audience appeals, or connect listeners to an idea. Instead of helping to clarify your argument, they would have to both make it and explain it.

The choice and use of visual aids is dependent on your industry. Every industry has distinct norms about the appropriateness of visual aids (for clarification on your own industry, do a quick search of the internet—e.g., health care visual aids). For years, lawyers and those in advertising typically avoided the slideshow approach of PowerPoint. According to the American Bar Association (see Unger & Jenson, 2009), sudden adoption of this visual in the courtroom led to a backlash of poor outcomes due to misguided visual design and lawyers are again cautious of the technology. Financiers, teachers, and sales people, however, still tend to actively employ this medium. The traditions of use for each industry change often and you should make every attempt to keep up with the specific visual expectations (as you later will read about informative interviews…questions about visuals can be asked in those talks). In your talk, you do not always need to supply your audience with visual support but, when you do, it is your job to ensure that you have selected the appropriate type of visual aid as well as that you are using it both in the correct setting and manner, and for the right type of audience. It is a tricky *business* (pun intended), but appropriate visual aid use requires strategic knowledge.

Because our focus here is on business talks, we will want to look at how visuals can aid your *talk*. There are other texts that will focus on how to create stand-alone visuals and graphics for sending through email or putting on websites, etc. In doing so, it is important to answer the question: *which comes first, the slide or the talk?*

The Slide or the Talk: Which Came First?

If you are to clearly embrace the definition of visual aids then you know that visuals should be the last element of your speech preparation and not your first. After all, what is there to *aid* if you do not yet know your argument? Too often, however, this is not how it works. In many industries, such as academics (Gurrie & Fair,

5

2010) as well as professional settings (Tufte, 2003, 2006), slide creation often begins the presentation process and, subsequently, structures it as well. In fact, when being asked to speak individually or in a group, the first question you may get asked is, "Who is doing the slides?" This means that others have the focus of your preparation turned around. If you go down this path, what will come next is likely to be a set of pre-packaged slides that may or may not be on target with your message. You are then in a position to rework either your talk or your slides through several revisions and then significant practice in order to get the whole package in sync. Do not let this happen. Save yourself some work. You know better!

You will begin to work on your slides after having completed your verbal message. At this point, it is important to know where to start and on what. You should become familiar with the difference between the choice of a visual and what goes on it—medium versus content!

Medium versus Content

The work that you will do to create your visuals will be in two parts: to create the content and to select and/or construct the medium. The **content** of your message is the substance, such as the words, charts, diagrams, and images that convey ideas. The **medium** of your message is the channel through which you send it. In the case of visual aids, this would include the type of visual that you select such as PowerPoint, handouts, models, etc. Selecting a medium/channel should not be a new concept to you; this is a crucial part of most communication models (see Berlo, 1960; Lasswell, 1948; Schramm, 1954). What we learn specifically here is that the audience and the environment will guide us in our selection of both visual aid mediums and content.

Speakers have many choices in both medium and content. You might be comfortable using PowerPoint slides but find that handouts work better in a new environment. You might be quite skilled at the creation of charts only to realize that a simple graphic is better suited to your needs. Do not make a selection because it best suits *you*—select because your choice best suits the audience and rhetorical situation! Also, open yourself up to using more than one medium and more than one type of content in any given situation…or none at all.

WHEN *NOT* TO USE VISUALS

All of us have been in a situation where the visual aid did more to annoy us than help understand a message (such as watching that person who puts every animation and every sound on all of his or her PowerPoint slides—we pay more attention to the fluff than to the ideas; do *not* be that person!). Just because you *can* provide a visual does not mean that you *should*!

Before even considering the visual aid to use, pull out your speech outline and determine what *needs* to have support from a visual. Ask yourself: would the audience better understand this idea if they could *see* it? Only think about using a visual aid if the answer is yes (Gieseke, 2010). If your answer is that you are not sure if a visual would help then it is important to examine the reasons to use or not use visuals. Consider the following.

All Visuals Distract

Visual aids are meant to grab attention. This is a good thing. If visual aids were meant to be ignored, what would be the purpose in using them at all? We want our audiences to look at them and, in some cases, touch them or interact with them (Smith & Woody, 2000). Remember, however, that while your audience is doing this that they are not paying attention to you. For most speakers, this works out fine. As you are using  your visuals, you will likely be talking about and interacting with them. There is no competition. The problem occurs when we try to compete with visual aids.

We compete with a visual aid when we show something that is supplementary to our argument rather than helping to support it. People do this all of the time (Atkinson, 2004). For example, imagine that you are in charge of showing a group of employees a new product and then helping them to sell it. If you put up an image of the product and then move on to discuss selling strategies, the audience is still looking at the image, asking questions to themselves or even others, and is not listening as you move on in your message. If you ask the audience, such as in this situation, to divide their attention between *the visual* and *the talk* then you have created problematic competition. To avoid such competition, follow these guidelines and avoid using a visual when that visual:

+ draws away from your point

+ becomes what is remembered (instead of the message)

+ disconnects you from your audience

The only way to avoid distractions is to not use visual support when these concerns arise or to alter the visual to better fit the needs of your situation. If you find that you do not need visual support, remember that you already have a great argument with fantastic evidence. You can have the appeals of ethos, pathos, and logos with or without visual support.

5

Avoiding the Boomerang Effect

We know that visual aids can distract but even worse, they can do more harm than good. In persuasion theory, we refer to the boomerang effect as the notion that ideas, arguments, or visuals can unintentionally encourage audience members to do the exact opposite of what you wanted them to do (Burgoon, 1999; see also Psychological Reactance Theory). Imagine that you wanted to encourage your company to move its shipping facilities to a Midwest facility. You showed pictures of the beautiful landscape, wonderful community, amazing waterways…and then someone in the audience says, "I'm not going to put a plant there—it will ruin that gorgeous environment!" Whoops. You have created a boomerang effect.

A reversal of desired impact can have drastic effects in business contexts. Man and Hill (1984) tried to understand these effects in visual advertising. How is it that we can watch and even love an advertisement but then not be compelled to buy the product? Their study reiterates the importance of the rhetorical situation. They found that context matters! Man and Hill showed that audiences view advertisements in context. If we see an advertisement and like the product but it conflicts with something else that we already like then we are less likely to buy either. The lesson? Never just show a visual without doing your homework on the audience. How will your visuals compete with their existing ideas? What other possible reactions could they trigger other than what you desire? How can this backfire?!

If you have decided that you have met the criteria for needing visual support and are now determining how to make the best choices for what medium and content to select, you must first turn to your audience. No visual is appropriate for all audiences at all times—no matter how great or effective it may have been in the past.

FOR *THIS* AUDIENCE AT *THIS* TIME

Have you ever been to a concert where the singer came out onto the stage and shouted, "What's up…" and then the wrong city?! Britney Spears, Lady Gaga, and Bruce Springsteen all did it in 2009. Kid Cudi got booed in 2010 for forgetting what city he was in when he performed at SXSW in Austin. The Alice in Chains lead singer got the city wrong *three times* during a concert in Alabama. And the list goes on. The response was the same each time. The audience feels like they are not meaningful to the performer. When you present with visuals that are not linked to your audience, you are that singer who hollers, "What's up, New York?!" when you are at a venue in Philly.

Before moving into the details of visual aid construction, we need to take a moment to discuss a foundational element of any visual construction—your audience. The visual aid type that you use as well as what you put on it must reflect the people or person to whom you are speaking. Keeping this in mind before making any visual choices will help you to select your visual elements strategically and selectively. It is just as essential for you to make a visual connection with your audience as well as a verbal one. How so? You must represent your actual audience, the one who will be sitting in front of you, on your visual aids (see Sawyer, 2010).

Say My Name, Say My Name—and Show It

While this line from the *Destiny's Child* Grammy-winning song may seem like a flippant reference (as well as from a song long before your time or interest), it is actually a great reminder of the importance of letting the entire room know just to whom it is that you are speaking. You will want to *verbalize* the name of your audience (e.g., "I would like to thank everyone at Octagon Research for having me here today, especially Mr. Willis who asked me to come talk about the benefits of using predetermined interviewing strategies for all new hires") as well as *show* it.

Showing your audience's name means that (whether it be handouts or a slideshow or even a model that you bring) you will want to display that name of the client/company/audience directly on your visuals to demonstrate that you are not recycling old materials (Reynolds, 2005; Sawyer, 2010). Some speakers might panic thinking that they would have to completely recreate a visual to sell the exact same product or service in the exact same way to only a slightly different group. In an ideal world, we would do that amount of work. In our realistic and limited-time worlds, it takes very little modification to remove the name, color scheme, and/or template focused on one group and replace it with visual ties to your new group. But, this step is important for audience buy-in even if all you are doing is making small modifications to an existing visual. Saying and showing a name pulls the audience into your speech by making it *their* speech.

Image Connections

Visual aids' content may be text, but it is even more likely to be an image (as you read on, you will get a full description of how to employ both). If a picture is worth a thousand words then you can make good use of your time by *showing* what you are arguing along with saying it. This means that you will have images, pictures, and graphics as part of your visual aids. Connecting these to your audience is a wonderful means of having your message resonate with that audience (Cyphert, 2007).

As a student in the past or even now, can you think of a classroom situation where the instructor showed a video that was seriously out of date? The clothing on the people is now considered "bad fashion" and the hairstyles are just laughable. And, what if they use phrases like "rad" and "fer sure"? You start to focus far more on the quality of the video than the message it wants to send. Now imagine that you are in that same college classroom and the professor shows a video that was clearly recorded at your school in the current semester—and you know some of the people in it! With this, you are captivated and trying to gather every piece of information because it directly connects to you.

Showing images from your audience to your audience is a wonderful bonding tool (Cyphert, 2007; Kay, 2011). You can typically take these off of their websites or the internet (be *very* careful about legality issues here and be sure to get permission!). You can ask for images, logos, and even candid photos from their marketing team or a liaison. If you cannot get images from the exact audience then making an effort to use relatable images is your next best option (e.g., not giving a handout with an old white guy in a suit on it to a group of young, Asian female new employees). In doing so, you walk the fine line of connecting your message to your visuals and the potential boomerang effect of them searching the images rather than listening to you. Connecting through imagery is important and can be accomplished without distraction only if you are sure to use images that you actually need to support your message.

Tone Connections

Businesses spend billions of dollars attempting to get just the right corporate image out to consumers. For example, according to Crain Communications Inc. and the Ad Age Group, Comcast spent 2.47 billion dollars on image management in 2011 (for a full list of company image investment, see Ad Age, "Database of 100 Leading National Advertisers," 2012).

Just like a political candidate must give voters a particular impression, companies craft and send their impressions out in calculated ways. If your client or your company has worked diligently to put across a fun and vibrant image and then you give a pitch to that client with visuals that are serious, somber, and rigid, you have failed to connect to that audience with tone.

Tone is a prevailing character of a message—especially with electronic messages in organizational contexts (Belkin, 2009). You should be sensitive to your audience's tone so that you can incorporate it into your visuals. For example, if your audience's corporate image is relaxed and laid-back like Disney or Ben & Jerry's, then have your visuals also show relaxed and amiable colors, images, and design.

> Note: A fun tone does not mean that either you or your visuals would ever negate the seriousness and professional responsibilities of a presentation; you are matching only the approach to the information and never altering the quality of the information itself!

Business professionals tied to their existing visual aids and wanting to avoid any extra work might argue with you that it is not necessary to have your visuals actually display the name of your audience on them. They might argue that you do not need to find images of your actual audience if your images are of the same general demographic of your audience. The validity of this position depends on your purpose. Similarly, a singer can walk out on stage and just perform without ever stating the name of the city. The performance may be fine and the audience may relate to the message but an opportunity for a more substantial connection has been missed. Even rock stars know that acknowledging the *exact audience in front of you* seals the deal.

Knowing that you must choose to use a visual aid or not, and that you can choose the extent to which you connect it to your audience, you are in a good position to begin working on any needed visual support. It is again at this time that you will need to fight your instincts to use what is familiar or what is expected (e.g., "everyone had a PowerPoint slideshow so I will have a PowerPoint slideshow") and focus on crafting what is *needed*. This begins with a focus on content over medium.

We already know that you would only display a visual when it helps the audience to better understand an idea, but what idea do you *need* to display?

Looking to the Outline

Your first step in determining your need for visual support comes from evaluating your outline. In the last chapters of this text you learned how to research your ideas and then put them together into an organized form. You may have found a fascinating picture or chart in your research and want desperately to show it. But do you need it? Does your audience  need to see a graph of dipping sales figures to make the decrease more evident to them? Would a picture of individual hungry residents sway investors to give more money to a women's shelter than simply describing them? Can you best depict the new strategies for effective product distribution with a map of production sites across the country? These are questions of content, which will ultimately drive your choice of medium. So, before moving on to how you will show your visuals, we must determine what needs to be shown.

Pull out your outline and imagine that you were to give your talk with no visual support. How would the audience react? If you believe that they would have full comprehension of your message and that you do not need visual support, stop reading this chapter now! You can move on to thinking about how to deliver your message and come back to this later. If, instead, you believe that your audience would not fully comprehend your message or that they would better grasp your ideas with visual support then we have a place to start. Look for the need to:

- demonstrate the organization of your ideas

- show vividness that cannot be expressed by words alone

- explain complicated numbers especially in relation to one another

- produce a 3-D representation

- present a comparison or make associations between images

- spend less time describing

- have a content element pop out as more important than other elements

- provide materials for the audience to take with them

While this list is not comprehensive, it will give you a start on when to include a visual and how to begin to design the correct one.

CONSIDERATIONS OF VISUAL DESIGN

Our discussion above should have put the issues of tone and audience at the forefront of your visual aid design mentality. Before launching into the details of what will go on your visuals and even the specifics of design for the type of visuals you will select, let us take a step back for a moment to consider overall design. You will be creating your visuals so that they link as closely as possible to your audience. The practical applications of this should be relatively easy but not so simple as to be ignored.

Design to the Audience...Legally

As noted above, the general look of your slides should have a clear visual link to your audience. It might seem easy to simply put relatable elements on your visuals (for example, if you are presenting to a school board, just have school images on the visual) but this diminishes your audience to a genre and not the public image that they have likely tried so hard to create. Think about your own time in school. If a speaker came to present an idea to you and put up crayons, a lined paper template, and a few pictures of computers on a visual, you might be a bit put off by their perception of you as juvenile. If you were to present to a pharmaceutical company and had a handout with clip art of vials and pill bottles, they would also think that you do not understand who they truly are. It is important that you do not make these same mistakes.

> Your audience expects a unique presentation with new (at least to them) content, otherwise why would they be attending your talk? No audience will be excited about a cookie-cutter presentation, and we must therefore shy away from any supporting visuals, such as the ubiquitous PowerPoint Design Template, that suggests your presentation is formulaic or pre-packaged. (Reynolds, para. 2)

Look to the audience's own marketing materials for cues on connection. Matching their own visual choices (layout, images, structure, and tone) is an indication that you are attuned to their specific needs.

Not Going to Jail

If at some point in your presentation you hand out materials that have taken the logo, design, the color, and even some of the company images to use as a marketing tool for your own product or service, watch out! You may find yourself dismissed, discredited, and even in jail. We have become far too comfortable in this digital age of gong to the web and simply taking whatever we need—because it is so easy to do so. When you are presenting in-house (meaning for your own company and to an audience of your own company), this is far less likely to be an issue. You might be training new employees and your PowerPoint slides are a direct copy of the company webpage. However, when your boss walks in and asks if you contacted the Legal Department about downloading the images and logos and you have not, prepare to cringe a bit. Something bad is about to happen—even if it is just your boss' loss of respect for you.

Information is not free or for public adoption just because we can freely and publically access it. Most material is copyrighted, protected, or simply unethical to take and use for your own purposes without direct author consent. If you have heard of the *Fair Use Law* and think it means that you may fairly use another's work, you have been misled. The rules of legal online content use are changing every year and even faster. The basics of these laws are this:

+ get written permission from the owner before using what is not yours

+ just because you used it in a classroom setting does not mean that it was legal to do so and likely you should not use it outside of the classroom

+ ignorance of copyright rules does not prevent you from the full penalties of the law including fines and jail time

+ pay for images when they are being sold

+ if you think it *may* be unethical (let alone illegal) think of the foundations of ethical actions and avoid actions that create an ethical dilemma

Text and Font

It may seem odd to include a discussion of text when describing visual aid *design*. Common experience, however, lets us know that it is rare to see a visual aid without some type of text (or words) on it. These words may just be the header on a PowerPoint slide or the title of your talk on a handout. For some reason, in fact, many creators of visual aids seem to believe that they cannot have visual support with no words. You can. Visuals can take on many forms that include no words whatsoever. (Some people even recommend this; see the U.S. Department of Labor OSHA guidelines, 1996, or even Toastmasters®.) Certainly, you can have visuals with words but you should use them sparingly and selectively as to not compete with your talk or distract from your message. Use these tools to help craft text visuals.

Typeface

Use of typeface refers to the style of the printed characters (Zaichkowsky, 2010). This means, in more simple terms, the font that you choose. You are likely familiar with all sorts of fonts from using a computer (e.g., Times, Garamond, Arial, etc.). The most basic difference between font typeface is the serif. A **serif** is a decorative line on a letter. If your font has this decorative line then it is a **serif font** (for example: Cambria on a Mac or Times New Roman on a PC). If it does not then it is without those lines, also known as sans serif (for example: Calibri on a Mac or Trebuchet on a PC).

The feet on serif fonts were originally intended to guide the eye from letter to letter in printed sources, supposedly making it easier for a reader to process the information. However, more current research suggests that using serif or sans serif fonts have actually quite small differences in terms of how easy they are to read. We know now that the difference in readability between these two styles on *printed* sources is quite small (Akhmadeeva, Tukhvatullin, & Veytsman, 2012); however, there are more pronounced readability differences in *electronic or virtual contexts* where sans serif is easier for audiences to process (Sheedy, Subbaram, Zimmerman, & Hayes,

Serif
Baskerville
Garamond
Century
Lucida
Sans Serif
Tahoma
Arial
Lucida Grande
Century Gothic

2005). In simpler terms, this means that you may consider using either font type in printed sources but that slide-show, web, or electronic visuals get a leg up in effectiveness when you select a sans serif font!

Research also indicates that there are good reasons to adopt particular font design types (such as Garamond versus Arial versus Calibri, etc.) in specific circumstances (Zaichkowsky, 2010). Fonts generate their own emotional meaning and have their own personalities (Li & Suen, 2010). For instance, Disney and Coca-Cola have crafted fonts that are now emblematic of the sentiment of each company. Similarly, particular fonts make readers feel a particular way about the speaker or designer (Shaikh, Chaparro, & Fox, 2006). For example,

- **Garamond**: classic, old fashioned, sophisticated, favorably judged
- **Times New Roman**: stable, mature, formal, efficient, not easily read, serious
- **Arial**: stable, formal, serious/less serious than serif, direct, friendly
- **Comic Sans**: fun, unreliable
- **Helvetica**: stable, generic, bold
- **Courier**: conformist, dull, unimaginative

Fonts are reflective of individual or corporate style. When selecting the font type-face for the text of your visuals, remember the impact that your choice will make.

Font Style

Once you have chosen your font typeface, you may be tempted to stylize it a bit. **Stylization** includes any use of bold, underline, capitalization, sizing, or other modes of *altering the appearance of a font to add emphasis*. In a visual context, you will want to use styles sparingly (and consistently) so that the style does not over-shadow the message. Think about how the simple use of formatting changes the look and feel of your text.

Style Distinctions

Visuals can be enhanced by the use of text. (century gothic, basic)

Visuals can be enhanced by the use of text. (bolded)

<u>Visuals can be enhanced by the use of text</u>. (underlined)

Visuals can be enhanced by the use of text. (italicized)

5

Similarly, the capitalization of a font can stylistically change its impact. If you have ever received an email and wondered why the person was so angry at you, go back and see what formatting choices the sender used. WERE ALL OF THE LETTERS CAPITALIZED SO IT FELT LIKE YOU WERE BEING YELLED AT? You are not alone (see Cumming, 2010). Avoiding "all caps" because of the tone it communicates is standard business etiquette but it can also just be hard to read (Winterstein & Kimberlin, 2010). In fact, the *New York Daily News* (September 20, 2010) reported that New York City will pay almost $27.5 million to change the lettering of its street signs from all capital letters to the more readable sentence case. In city government or in your own presentation, think wisely before CAPITALIZING!

Finally, you will need to consider the size of your text as an element of style. Many speakers want to put as much as possible on a visual aid (be it handouts or Prezi slides) as if the *more* information then the *better* the evidence. Given the fact that visuals compete with speakers, this is a poor choice. The smaller the text the more time your audience will spend trying to grasp all the details and not listening to you (Broadbent & Broadbent, 1980).

As a rule of thumb, you want the audience to be able to quickly glance at the text and get right back to listening to you. While appropriate font size will depend on the visual medium, in general, larger text size makes for an easier read.

Sizes

Visuals can use text. (font size 8)

Visuals can use text. (font size 10)

Visuals can use text. (font size 12)

Visuals can use text. (font size 14)

Visuals can use text. (font size 16)

Visuals can use text. (font size 18)

Visuals can use text. (font size 20)

Text Location within Slide Layout

Plopping your text on each visual wherever the cursor first lands or wherever the template tells you to put it leaves the decision of how to connect to your audience and captivate them visually up to chance. Much like a street sign has to be placed where it will draw the eye of a driver, text on a visual aid should be laid out such that it guides the eyes of the audience. Audiences should know where to look first and then in what direction to look after that. Awkwardly placed visuals, or text that is inconsistently laid out from visual to visual, takes too much time for audiences to process (Ruffini, 2009), which is less time for them to concentrate on your message.

Make strategic choices to guide your audience. For instance, English audiences read left to right. When showing visuals to this group, they should be laid out in this direction rather than justified from right to left. The key to any visual is to lay it out in the most accessible means for the audience and keep consistency as to not distract! Now that you know the basics of design, you are ready to determine what content belongs on your slides.

VISUAL CONTENT: THE STUFF THAT GOES ON THE AIDS

When we think of visual aids, it is easy to imagine presentation slideshows, handouts, or even flip charts (which, yes, are still used frequently in business and professional settings). But, before you even begin to think about how to visually display your support (the **medium**), it is crucial to consider what you will want to display (the **content**). There are two types of content that you will display based on the type of support that you need—quantitative and qualitative. This description of each area will not cover every single aspect of content but should give you a good introduction to consider just how to best support your idea!

Quantitative Content

It might seem odd to begin a discussion of visual content by first referencing something that we have already established as numeric based. How, after all, can numbers be visual, and aren't all visuals image based? No, not all visuals are image based. It is often incredibly useful to *show* a numeric value to your audience. **Quantitative content** includes the visual elements that allow us to demonstrate or represent numeric support. We can demonstrate quantitative content in a variety of means.

Numbers

Numbers are the reason that many visual aids exist. Salespeople or CFOs want to cram slides full of impressive sales figures in the hope that quantities and figures will give the impact of upward or downward trends. Yes, numbers belong on visuals but should be used with caution. A number, for example, can help make your point about a 28% drop in revenue simply by having a huge 28% drop from the top of a slide with a resounding "thud." The number alone verbally expressed in your talk may not resonate but seeing it can stick with an audience.

Visual aids are not the place, however, to number dump. Numbers may be the thing that disconnects you from your audience. In fact, some research suggests that a descriptive visual or image can actually explain numeric concepts without the need of the numbers themselves (Garcia-Retamero & Galesic, 2010). (Such as when your company is facing a 50% revenue loss, the same amount of money that could be used to build the on-site gym that your employees have begged for, and, rather than a number, you show a graphic of the plans for that gym exploding.) Consider a handout that you are given with columns of numbers that you are supposed to quickly process while listening to the speaker. This is difficult to do, especially since audiences take longer to comprehend quantitative data (which is a representation of a concept), so provide numbers sparingly and with time to stop and cover every detail.

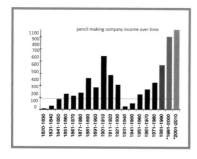

Too Much

More Appropriate

Because numbers used in visuals will be typed out, their use should follow all of the guidelines for text use previously discussed (e.g., make them big enough to be seen, in a legible font, and guide the eye from one number to another) but your initial focus should be on how a displayed number will *support* your argument.

Overall, it is important to consider when and how to use numbers. Most often you will not have a number on a visual aid all by itself but you will guide the audience's eyes by putting your numbers into a format such as a chart or table or other stylized format.

Table, Diagrams, and Charts

Do you need your audience to understand a large amount of data presented over time or between groups? Visual depictions of categories and quantities are often helpful for audiences to grasp relationships (Few, 2010). Quantitative relationships are typically found in the form of tables, charts, or diagrams. Whereas you may think of these elements as synonymous (and some graphic design software will not have a distinction between them), each has a distinct function.

+ **Table:** a set of facts or figures systematically displayed, especially in columns (e.g., an Excel® spreadsheet or a table of contents)

+ **Diagram:** a simplified drawing showing the appearance, structure, or workings of something; a schematic representation that shows connections (e.g., Schramm's feedback model diagram)

+ **Chart:** a simple graphical depiction of complex data (e.g., a map or pie/picture chart of categories of items); types include pie, line, bar, graph, flow, organizational, etc.

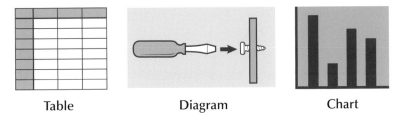

Table   Diagram   Chart

Determining what type of visual content you will use depends on what you are trying to demonstrate to the audience. **Tables** are used to demonstrate categories and allow for comparison. While you may wish to use a line graph to show decreasing sales over time, a table can allow you to list out those numbers next to each other so that we see actual figures and their relationship.

Have you ever tried to put together furniture that you bought at IKEA? Can you imagine trying to figure out what all those little metal pieces and wood blocks are for without the diagram of the stick figures putting them together? Scary! **Diagrams** are visual representations of an actual thing. These representations are useful when a verbal or written explanation will not capture the complexity and intricacies of the object; they also help when intercultural or language barriers may make the selection of terms difficult (Few, 2010).

Conversely, some industries even have **charts** that are specific to the type of work that they do and will expect that you show them data in this well-known form, such as open-high-low-close chart (investor and financial industries), stock (financial industries), Gantt chart (construction industry), and more. (*Note: Many industry-specific charts have standard settings in PowerPoint software, so be sure to ask or get training on this before attempting to create them from scratch!*)

5

Qualitative Content

If what you need to support your ideas is not the visual of a numeric, it might be that you will benefit from a qualitative representation of your support. **Qualitative content** on visuals allows us to depict or represent characteristic support. If images are worth a thousand words, using any of the available qualitative content options as visual aids can make you a real *wordsmith*!

Images

Images are a fantastic means of supporting ideas. In a study looking back at forty-six experiments of the impact of visuals on visual aids, Levie and Lentz (1982) found that picture-based visual communication improved learning and recall over text-alone visuals, in one case by 323%! This is impressive and may inspire you to put images on all of your visuals—but be cautious.

Most audiences have seen an image on a visual aid that is just…. bad. Maybe you did not know what the image even was? Or did you wonder how outdated the image was? Or perhaps you thought it was just ugly? Consider the audience appeal of this image.

Not liking this image? Sometimes graphic images, which are widely available with software programs or online—or even well-drawn objects—can have less appeal and less clarity than the real thing (Sawyer, 2010). Certainly a picture of an apple would leave no doubt as to the identity of the object whereas the fruit above may illustrate an apple…or is it a California holly, a red pear, or perhaps a quince? Actual pictures give the most professional appeal and clarity to your visuals with the least amount of room for interpretation.

Are image-based aids with *no* text a good idea? Absolutely. Showing people meaningful, content-based visuals, as opposed to text alone, lessens their cognitive exertion (how hard their brains have to work) and improves overall experience (Chabris & Kosslyn, 2005). Ideally, text should be used when it is the ideal support for your ideas, no text should be used when a stand-alone visual is the best evidence, and a combination of text and images should also be employed if that combination is appropriate.

Graphics and Illustrations

When you use the computer to draw or create visual depictions for you then you are using **graphics**. This might include architectural blueprints, representations of the characters for a Disney® Pixar animated film, or even webpage banner designs. Conversely, when you display a hand-rendering of an object, place, person, or thing then you are showing an **illustration**—such as on storyboards (very popular for art, media, and entertainment industries), artistic examples, or even your own drawing on a whiteboard of a product or idea.

Both graphics and illustrations can be useful to demonstrate a fully fleshed-out idea to an audience without having to take or find a picture of the item. For instance, if you are in the middle of a meeting with a beautiful PowerPoint slideshow depicting how your company will merge with another and someone asks about the new corporate structure, it would be silly to try and create a slide of this just because you have that technology up and running. No. Go over to the whiteboard or even grab a piece of paper and just draw the dang thing! This is the best choice for that particular rhetorical situation.

Color

As you are placing images, charts, numbers, and graphics on your visuals, consider how color can impact visual connections. Color is part of creating tone or mood, grabbing attention, engaging the viewer, and making the material legible. If you want your audience to clearly see your words or images, color contrast is a crucial element (Humar, Gradizar, & Turk, 2008). If you have ever seen how the cool colors of a spa's website make you want to ease in and spend the day, or how the primary colors associated with most high action sports get your heart racing, then you have felt the impact of color. If you have ever cringed seeing two colors together and wondered why anyone would ever create such a heinous display of visual conflict then you have realized how color can block our

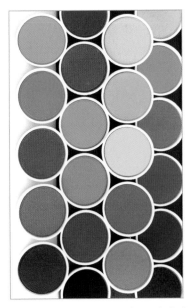

listening. In terms of visual aids, think along the lines of Greco, et al. (2008), "If the rule of thumb is 'What's beautiful is also legible,' this should be changed into 'What's legible is also beautiful'" (p. 824).

Select color that matches the tone of your message along with the color concept of your audience. If your talk will be a fun training or the company/audience is all about being fun and comfortable, use colors that show this tone. Remember, companies may spend millions on their image creation including the strategic choice of color (Ad Age, 2012). If you show up to give a presentation to a Virginia Tech audience with burgundy and carrot-colored visuals when they are emotionally committed to their Chicago maroon and burnt orange, you can do more to disconnect than connect. Be careful and specific so that you continue to appeal to pathos!

VISUAL MEDIUMS

If you now know what type of content your audience will need in order for them to best understand your argument then you can be *led* to the best choice of visual medium! Knowing if you need to show a number, that you need to have a high color display, or that the audience will not understand unless they can interact with a visual representation—this understanding is what will let you select your visual **medium** (or presentation device). Discussed below are several available options.

Types of Visual Aid Mediums

There are two types of visual aid mediums—low technology and high technology. Most people, when imagining visual aid mediums, will immediately think of high-tech mediums such as PowerPoint or Prezi or even the use of projected internet live websites with Flash™ videos. You might be surprised to find that you have had more exposure to low-tech mediums and will likely use these more than any other type (e.g., handouts, objects, people, etc.). The key is knowing which type is best suited for you, your audience, and your message.

Think of your visual choices in this way: what is better than walking into a class or a meeting and seeing a huge projection screen that suddenly has images scrolling by in a Flash movie slideshow, bright and colorful fast-moving graphics as well as booming sound? A handout! OK, this may have you a bit confused. Why on earth would anyone select a low-tech option when a high-tech visual option is available? By now, this should be an easy answer. It is because low- and high-technology visual aid mediums serve different purposes, and in many instances low-tech aids are more suited to your purpose. Selecting a visual medium is all about understanding the purpose of each type of medium and understanding what to do and not to do with it!

Low-Technology Visual Aid Mediums

Low-technology visual aids, for our purposes, refer to any visual that does not use computer-generated elements and/or modern computer-facilitated devices. In this list, the selected visual aids are non-electronic (although, if you are still using an overhead projector, you have a "low-tech" aid that is both electronic and quickly being phased out of regular use!).

Simply put, low-tech visuals include:

+ Handouts

+ Models and objects

+ Whiteboards

+ Flip charts/posters

The Benefits of Low-Tech Visual Aids

In general, low-tech visual aids have overall benefits for the user. First, low-tech is cheaper. Low-tech products are typically far less expensive than high-tech visual aids. Consider the costs of purchasing a computer or a slide projector or software or even access to technology. Some conference setups will charge hundreds of dollars for a few hours of web connectivity, and even more to hook you up to their in-house speakers or projector system. Low-tech visuals are typically created off-site and brought in with little expense. In addition, low-tech aids are often less attention-grabbing, which can be a good thing because they are less distracting (Collins, 2004). If the aid does not become the focus of your presentation, then your message has that focus—just as it should be.

Handouts (low-tech)

Handouts are detailed versions of visual information available to audiences at an individual level. Handouts can be created to contain images, text, or a combination of both. You may think that handouts are only for independent reading and, thus, do not fit into our description of visual aids. Not true. When your audience is *looking* at your handout, they are processing a visual message that must be constructed following particular presentation-centered guidelines.

Like any other visual support, handouts must be offered at the time when their support is needed or they serve only as a distraction to the spoken message

(Rotman, 2008). Some presenters (Heath, 2009) will tell you to never give handouts during your speech, and only to give them out after your talk, because this visual aid will interrupt your flow and draw audience attention away from your message. The choice for when to offer handouts is, ultimately, yours. If your handout serves to outline the information being discussed in the middle of your talk and would help the audience to follow along at that point, by all means, distribute away! If, however, your handouts summarize your talk to help audience members recall details at a later date, hold off on the handing out until the end.

Handout Hints

+ <u>Do</u> provide when audiences can refer to information at their own pace

+ <u>Do</u> include information referencing your specific talk (e.g., your name, topic, and contact info)

+ <u>Do</u> include significant white space

+ <u>Do</u> use for complex data

+ <u>Do not</u> hand out when the information can distract from the verbal message

+ <u>Do not</u> use cluttered layouts

+ <u>Do not</u> provide large visuals that can be shown at a single time and are not needed after the presentation

Models and Objects (low-tech)

In many instances (and in many industries), showing your audience the actual object about which you are talking is the best visual to offer (Atkinson, 2010). **Models** (or objects) are simply three-dimensional, scaled-down replicas of something you are talking about (like a building, a car, and so on) (Wyatt, n.d.). Models, if small enough, can be the actual item of discussion (think of a new cell phone proto-type shown to four researchers at a development meeting or the new Audi sports car revealed at an auto show). However, when you cannot get a full-size building into the room then a scaled-down version is the next best thing (and far more cost effective).

Models, however, are not always exact replicas. A model or object can also be used to represent something else. For instance, if you are explaining how time will move quickly on the proposed project, a ticking stopwatch set in the middle of the conference room table as you wrap up your talk makes for a strong visual reminder of that sense of urgency.

Model and Object Hints

+ <u>Do</u> use in very bright rooms

+ <u>Do</u> give audiences plenty of time to see and absorb the model

+ <u>Do</u> conceal models until they are relevant

+ <u>Do not</u> use with large audiences

+ <u>Do not</u> substitute for clear verbal information

+ <u>Do not</u> use models to conceal/make up for a poor presentation

Models or objects have the advantage of being interesting but have their own drawbacks (Atkinson, 2010). First, it can be difficult for a group of people to see the same object at the same time. Sure, you can hand something around and risk it getting broken or never making it to everyone in your audience before your talk moves on to a new idea. Additionally, models can be *too* interesting. As with all visual aids, you should be talking about the actual visual when it is shown and not allow it to be seen before. Models can be difficult to disguise before they are revealed and, thus, draw unnecessary attention. Be aware of your particular room and audience limitations and follow these basic dos and don'ts!

Whiteboards (low-tech)

Whiteboards are wipeable boards with a white surface used for teaching or presentations; these are the more business-friendly versions of **chalkboards** (also called blackboards, which are still regularly used in academic settings). Before you go dismissing what is likely affixed to the wall in almost any conference room as not being enough of a refined or captivating visual aid for your talk, think about how this resource is used regularly in the business world. Whiteboards serve as a collaborative medium (Perry & O'Hara, 2003; Xiao, et al., 2001), offer visual persistence, provide flexible interaction, are well-situated physically to help with project transitions (Tang, Lanir, Greenberg, & Fels, 2009), and are critical in a variety of industries including business, academic, and health/medicine (Chaboyer, Wallen, Wallis & McMurray, 2009). So, as you begin to think about this wonderful collaborative visual medium, remember the dos and don'ts of its use!

Whiteboard Hints
- <u>Do</u> use legible handwriting

- <u>Do</u> write in large, easy-to-see letters

- <u>Do</u> keep information visually organized and laid out

- <u>Do</u> regularly check in with audiences for clarity and comprehension

- <u>Do</u> prepare key/major notes ahead (write, then cover until relevant)

- <u>Do not</u> use cursive

- <u>Do not</u> use fingers to erase

- <u>Do not</u> have audiences sit to the side of whiteboards

Flip Charts/Posters (low-tech)

While technically two different breeds, flip charts and posters share enough of the same elements to have their merits and uses discussed simultaneously. What is the difference? First, a flip chart is…flipped. **Flip charts** are large paper tablets that are typically on easels and written on with markers. Conversely, a **poster** is normally one static display that is either shown or not shown and whose content is pre-prepared. Both overlap in construction, makeup, and utility.

According to the training website Speaking Tips (2004), "Unabashedly low tech, universally understood and easy to use, flip charts remain communication powerhouses. They continue to be popular because they are effective, portable, familiar, inexpensive and do not require electricity or telecommunications" (para. 1). All the same elements are true of the basic and low-tech poster (inexpensive, portable, etc.). With a sales pitch like that, you may think that flip charts and posters can be your new best friend. Allow them to be of good use to you but know how to use them.

Flip Chart and Poster Hints

+ <u>Do</u> have legible handwriting on flip charts and/or computer-generated or graphic posters

+ <u>Do</u> use along with other visual aids

+ <u>Do</u> pre-design elements (like with whiteboards)

+ <u>Do</u> use 2–3 colors with vivid contrast (no yellow)

+ <u>Do</u> put blank pages between written-on pages

+ <u>Do</u> bring tape or stands to hang

+ <u>Do not</u> set posters where they cannot be seen by all

+ <u>Do not</u> leave or put up when not being referenced

+ <u>Do not</u> use markers that smell too bad

+ <u>Do not</u> have your back to the audience (angle to be seen)

+ <u>Do not</u> use with large audiences (keep the group to approximately 20)

High-Technology Visual Aid Mediums

As you can see, low-tech visuals are easy to create and quite an effective means of connecting to your audience. If this is the case, why spend the time and money implementing high-tech visuals? Simple. As mentioned previously, all visuals have their own purpose with both benefits and detriments. If you have the skills, equipment, and the right rhetorical situation in which to use high-tech visuals, then these are a fantastic means of engaging your listeners!

Distracting or not, high-tech visuals have the pizzazz that low-tech visuals just do not. They offer color, movement, sound, and a capacity to change on the fly. You cannot distribute a handout and then have it magically become something else when the audience asks you to discuss the third idea before the first one. A high-tech visual can change and adapt as you go. On the other hand, high-tech visuals have their own set of complications. The trick is not to use them just because you can and to remember to avoid the pitfalls of too much unnecessary pizzazz. **High-technology aids**, for our purposes, refer to any visual that is generated through or delivered to an audience using contemporary computer equipment or machinery. These include:

+ Slideshow software

+ Web or internet use

+ Video/movie/audio visuals

+ SMART boards/IWBs

Slideshow Software

We would be remiss if we did not begin our discussion of high-tech visual aids without a nod to the darling (and devil) of all business visuals—PowerPoint. Microsoft PowerPoint, for those who have not yet experienced this pervasive visual medium, is an electronic slide presentation software program that offers word processing, outlining, drawing, graphing, and presentation management tools. According to Dale Cyphert (2004) in *Business Communication Quarterly*, "PowerPoint is the business community's primary tool for incorporating the imagery, narrative, and self-disclosure that are hallmarks of visual eloquence" (p. 80).

PowerPoint is the most debated visual aid of the modern-day business and academic contexts. Why? Perhaps it is because PowerPoint is the most used visual aid and yet it is still used so poorly (yes, even at the time of this publication, PowerPoint is used far more than similar softwares). Widespread and significant use of this visual has led to such poorly presented PowerPoint slides that scholars have made their living trying to convince others not to use this medium (see Tufte, 2003, 2006). **Keynote** is Apple computer's answer to the use of PowerPoint.

Critics of electronic slideshows would like us not to use them because:

1. they diminish a connection between audiences and speakers (Fried, 2004; Schwartz, 2003; Tufte, 2006),

2. they limit textual content (Buss, 2006; Carroll, 2007; Thompson, 2003; Tufte, 2003), and

3. they offer poor visual quality (Tufte, 2003).

Prezi is a spatial presentation software newbie but all three have basically the same function: to create and show slides using text, tables, charts, graphics, images, and other multimedia elements. If you are concerned that a single or set of slides is not useful to you, Duarte (2011) understands, "'But wait,' you say, 'the ideas I need to convey are genuinely complex. They can't be conveyed in a simple, airily conceptual image.' That's right, they can't. But complex ideas can be broken down into individual units of information. Think of each slide as a single word in a sentence" (para. 5). Slides are how you break down complex ideas into simple ideas and singular visuals.

To leave our discussion at this point might make you wonder why these aids are required in so many classes and expected at your office—*especially since all of the above critiques are true.* PowerPoint slides actually do have strong benefits when they are used appropriately, as best explained by Gallo (2010):

The enemy is not PowerPoint (or visual software). The enemy is a failure to understand how the brain processes information. Once you know how people learn best, almost any presentation software becomes a powerful complement to facilitating the transfer of knowledge. The key word is complement....The distinction is critical.

Knowing how to best give your audience what they need can help to increase audience understanding. What you must always do is consider your audience as the primary focus of your message and visuals. Some strategies for effective visual communication include:

+ designing visual elements that specifically connect to the presenter's audience (Beebe & Beebe, 2009; Foss & Kanengieter, 1992; Sawyer, 2011)

+ limiting slideshow effects and visual changes (Lowenthal, n.d.; Norman, 2004; Sawyer, 2011)

+ creating links between visual and verbal arguments (Cyphert, 2004; Foss & Kanengieter, 1992)

+ being as simple as possible (Beebe & Beebe, 2009; Sawyer, 2011)

Cyphert (2004) reminds us that presentational communication in an electronic age is better received by audiences in an electronic medium. The caution is not to allow those mediums to detract from the message.

Electronic Slideshow Hints
+ <u>Do</u> have the projection screen in a dim to dark area
+ <u>Do</u> make clear visual connections to your audience
+ <u>Do</u> have strong contrast between text and backgrounds
+ <u>Do</u> create a line for the eye (clean layout with lots of white space)
+ <u>Do not</u> allow visual animation to predominate
+ <u>Do not</u> rely on external connections (instead embed movie and sound files)
+ <u>Do not</u> use numerous types of animation

141

Numerous books and websites will tell you how to create any of these slides (take a look at the *For Dummies* series or even the *PowerPoint 2010 Bible*). However, few resources will teach you *design* elements. These resources, which explain *why* to use one design or *why not* to use another, are even more important than knowing how to make the software tools work. As a first step, use the guidelines earlier in this chapter. As a second step, consider such additional guides as: 1) *Save Our Slides* (second edition) by William Earnest, 2) *Presentation Zen* by Garr Reynolds, or 3) *PowerPoint Reality* by J. Kanan Sawyer.

Web/Internet Use (high-tech)

Web-based visual aids are more and more common in a day of ultimate connectivity. This may mean that videos are shown from an internet site or inserted into presentation slides, that search engines are explored as part of a researching process, or even that images are shown right from server databases. *Alone, the internet is not an effective visual aid* (in helping audiences to understand ideas, constructs, and arguments); however, paired up with a knowledgeable presenter, the internet is a highly effective and engaging visual medium (Eilks, Witteck, & Pietzner, 2009).

If your company has an existing website or if you can create one that will have all of the elements needed for your visual support then access to that website can help you to present visuals in three-dimensional views and reveal them as your audience needs them. The keys to making internet visual aids (and all moving visual elements) work in your presentation are to be sure that your webpage does not appear to be a generic page that you use for all presentations (i.e., you must show the visual connection to *this* audience and *this* presentation—see the previous discussion on image and tone connections to audiences) and to ensure that you are not revealing details that are unrelated to the specific moment of your talk (Sawyer, 2011).

As we will discuss more in later chapters, some speakers seem to have major difficulties when relying on server-based visuals (e.g., Apple's Steve Jobs attempting to show off features of the new iPhone 4 but the server would not connect) (Ogg, 2010). Most importantly, test your technology ahead of time and be prepared for technological failures.

Internet/Website Hints

- ❖ <u>Do</u> link websites to specific presentations

- ❖ <u>Do</u> embed hyperlinks in presentation slides as appropriate

- ❖ <u>Do</u> check connectivity before the audience arrives

- ❖ <u>Do</u> have a backup (e.g., handouts or screen captures)

- ❖ <u>Do not</u> wade through generic sites that are not audience specific

- ❖ <u>Do not</u> expect that audiences will all have technical or multimedia backgrounds to quickly follow along

- ❖ <u>Do not</u> become more engaged with maneuvering through the internet than with your audience

Videos/Movies/Audio Visuals (high-tech)

Today is no longer the day of VHS or Beta (ask someone over the age of 40 about that one). Today, we have DVDs and Blu-Ray and high-quality image movies. Even commercial 3-D players are starting to be just another typical video player option (Cieply, 2011). Movies or videos have the wonderful ability of helping audiences to see not just what something looks like but how it *moves*. A movie can show a process as it goes along or even a person who is part of a process as it progresses from beginning to end.

Movies and videos are now more accessible than ever before. From compelling political humorist shows (such as the *Colbert Report* or the *Daily Show*) to reality television (think of almost anything on Bravo), many programs provide entire online versions of their shows or even downloadable clips from their own network websites or YouTube. Whether you are accessing these shows from their online sources or have downloaded them into PowerPoint slides when internet connections are not available, remember that all *rules* of copyright still apply even if you are not selling the material or are just using a portion of it!

Deciding to use movies or videos in a presentation can be either the best or worst decision you as a speaker can make. The combined sight, sound, and movement can engage and inspire your audience, make them laugh, and connect them to the message and speaker. Movies can also distract, bore, or offend the very people you are trying to impress. Like all of the advice on visual aids, your decision to use a movie—as well as the type of movie—will depend on your rhetorical situation (so, no, sorry, there is no "one-size-fits-all" checklist that will keep you safe here).

Movie support should be visible no longer than is necessary to clarify an argument or illuminate an issue for an audience. Rather than have the video screen up and on pause so that your audience is fixated there while you talk, be sure to keep the movie under wraps until the moment you are ready to incorporate it into your talk and do make sure that these "clips" are fluid with the rest of a presentation.

Movie and Video Hints

+ <u>Do</u> offer clear verbal transitions into your video clip

+ <u>Do</u> embed videos into slideshow technology when using it (this may show your video in the slideshow or simply have a seamless link to open it)

+ <u>Do</u> be cautious with your content, knowing that humor is not universal and appropriateness is not speaker but *audience* determined

+ <u>Do not</u> make the clip any longer than is absolutely necessary to support your verbal argument

---

SMART Boards/IWBs (high-tech)

Have you heard of IWBs? If you are not a teacher or studying pedagogy (a fancy word for the art of effective instruction) then you likely do not know this jargon. An **IWB** is a short way of saying "interactive white boards" or **SMART boards**. And, while the terminology may not be important, the concept is vital for a business context:

The IWB enables presenters and audiences to interact with all the functions of a desktop computer through the board's large touch sensitive surface. The IWB acts as a port through which any computer-run ICT (Information and Communication Technologies) function can be displayed and interacted with. (Murcia & Sheffield, 2010, p. 418)

SMART boards or IWBs are visual aids that can integrate audiences into the creation of messages. Murcia and Sheffield (2010) discovered that IWBs used in a science classroom resulted in full audience participation—and not in just a casually engaged way but in a substantial and meaningful discourse about science. You might not have science as your topic, but imagine if you are an accountant who is trying to explain financial windfalls to employees with no financial background.

By involving the audience in the presentation through the use of a SMART board, you can help them to understand and engage in all types of material (Glover, Miller, Averis & Door, 2007; Schuck & Kearney, 2007, 2008).

Perhaps the most important aspect of this visual aid is...get training! The technology can be difficult to use and is certainly not something that you want to be testing out for the first time during the most important business talk of your career. There are numerous online tutorials and the IT department at your company may have an expert right in-house.

> **SMART Board Hints**
> + <u>Do</u> get training on the technology
>
> + <u>Do</u> use to explain technical data
>
> + <u>Do</u> ask audiences for help manipulating and designing visual elements of the presentation (the key benefit of SMART boards!)
>
> + <u>Do not</u> expect that all companies or all industries will provide or desire this technology

DELIVERING MESSAGES WITH VISUALS

Considering the chapter's focus on content and medium, you may have forgotten that the actual visual aid that your audience will spend the most time observing is you. You are your best visual aid! Whether or not you are modeling an idea or product—or you are speaking with no other visual support—you must learn to move comfortably in your space and maintain the audience's attention. Now, you must learn to coordinate your fantastic presentation delivery with the *delivery* of your visual aids.

Practice

First, you must practice using the visuals that you have developed for your presentation. Do a full practice run, preferably with someone you know well and simultaneously (or subsequently) with someone you do not know well. These two types of practice audiences will give you different feedback and even have different understandings of your message. You might find that your best friend at work who is also in your department thinks that your visuals are ideal while the guy you do not know very well from another department cannot understand why you would show the most complicated visual so quickly and spend so long on the more basic visual (a valid concern!).

No audience available? Use a video or audio tape recorder, or a mirror to practice. Then, review your presentation with a critical and detached perspective. Just seeing yourself present can give you an entirely new and incredibly useful outside perspective for making needed changes (Friend, Adams, & Curry, 2011). Identifying and fixing errors or issues with visual aids results in a smooth presentation on speech day.

Finally, whenever possible, scope out the place of your presentation early. Check the technical equipment and make sure your aids can be seen from all points of the room. Practice using your visuals with the equipment provided (sometimes differences between your machine and projector can throw you off your game and leave you attempting to adjust in the moment). Do things like: know where the on/off switch is, be able to have the lights dimmed, and, if necessary, know how to have your slides or images ready to go but not revealed until their time has come. (With PowerPoint, learn the "B" key!)

Presenting on Others' Machines

If you have worked hard on presentation slides or websites and then gone to show them at the venue only to find that they looked completely different from your original creation, then you may have had a compatibility issue. **Compatibility** means able to exist or occur together without conflict. Why might you not have compatibility? Perhaps the computer on which you were showing your slides had an older (or newer) version of the software. Or, the projecting computer has only basic fonts, which do not link to the ones you have selected. Any of these issues will create a last minute panic and we never want that! Achieving presentation effectiveness involves three things:

1. prior check of your space

2. prior check of your technology

3. prior check of your materials

Notice how all of these elements are about *prior* checks, which means that you cannot wait until the last minute. If you do wait to the last minute or you do not have access to these prior checks and something does not work, be sure to go with the flow when something fails. If you get flustered by an issue then you give your audience permission to focus on that issue rather than focusing on your message. If you believe in Murphy's Law (where the opposite of what you are ready for tends to happen) then bring backup visuals and you likely will not need them. If you do not bring them then you likely will need them!

Staying in Sync

He is talking—but not about what he is showing. It happens. We have all seen this with others (e.g., speakers whose PowerPoint slideshows end and then the slide sorter is on display until the speaker finishes or handouts that are given and being read long before the information is relevant to the discussion). Even worse, think of the speaker who shows an internet website and then forgets to turn off the screensaver of his vacation pictures that begin to scroll while he is making a dramatic point!

Syncing delivery issues make folks wish that speakers would just talk to us and not bring along any visuals at all. Certainly, a no-visual-aid speech is always an option, but if you need your visuals to support your argument, simply make sure that you have practiced enough to stay in sync with your slides.

Tips to staying in sync include:

- Practice both facing slides and facing away from slides

- Videotape yourself speaking with slides

- Avoid any type of auto-animation or auto-transitions

- Pay attention to audience feedback and look for concerned focus on visuals

- **Look at your visuals!**

A FINAL WORD ON VISUALS

At this point, you may be so inspired by the options right at your fingertips that you want to overwhelm your audience in visual support, but, be careful. Most research states that, in terms of audience engagement and retention, less is more (see Beaver, 2007).

Keep It Simple

Even after you have taken great pains to (legally) match the look of your audience and selected the font and design that best suit the tone of your message, you need to do a final check to make sure that what you are using will best suit your needs and that of your audience. The last part of visual design is to help your audience (and you!) to focus.

First, you will want to ensure a clean layout of any visual. Keep it professional. Handouts should not be crumpled or wrinkled and PowerPoint slides should not come up in slide sorter view. You want a clean delivery of your support. Second, remember the medium. Not everything is appropriate for every setting. If you have decided to mimic the visual design of a company's website, take a step back after you have finished. What works on a website may not work on a handout, model design, or slideshow. Do not sacrifice your *clarity* for visual connection. Give a nod to the audience's visual identity but be sure to clean things up when necessary to serve your own purposes. Cluttered visuals create potential for distraction. Third, look for any other potential distractions within the visual aids. Oddly enough, one distraction to visuals is sound!

Sounds Like…What?

Whizzzzzzz. Bang. Pop! Click-click-click. It is possible to have visual aids be also auditory aids—meaning that they would include sound. Of course! In fact, some visuals will naturally have sound such as movies and videos. Adding audio to your visuals allows audiences to get a more full experience. Like visuals themselves, however, sound can serve to distract when it is not crucial to the message. When your presentation begins with a soft rendition of Cee Lo Green's "Forget You," be sure that you have downloaded the correct version and not the one that subs in his favorite curse word instead. When you have downloaded an image from the internet, be sure to go through your entire presentation at home with your speakers on to be sure that the image did not come with an attached and not useful noise effect.

In addition, the decision to use audio comes with the responsibility to verify that your presentation room is equipped for sound and to check sound levels before the audience arrives. Too much or too little volume, the wrong sound, distracting or confusing sound, and those "noises" get the focus over your message and diminish your credibility.

Golden Rules

Without knowing the purpose of your talk, the audience, and the environment (basically, all of the components of your rhetorical situation), it is impossible to give any speaker specific details on what medium or content he or she should use for that exact presentation. Instead, the information here hopefully helps you to make good choices about visual aid use in general. What you should have learned by now is to never use visual aids to hide a poor verbal presentation. Too many speakers think that amazing visual supplements will *sell* the talk. They will not. If your presentation is lacking, the audience will notice and attribute you with low ethos or credibility. Spend most of your time on your talk and then look to see what *needs* visual support. This will help you to make strategic time choices and, ultimately, have better presentations. And, always follow the most important rules:

The four Golden Rules of visual aid use:

1. Only use what is needed

2. Keep visuals simple

3. Have someone else proofread your aids

4. Bring backups

Business presentations are the basic tool for sending messages in business contexts. Mastery of the verbal and the visual context allows you to be the most effective communicator possible. While you should spend the majority of your time crafting the verbal message, preparing visual support can be time well spent.

> Can you think of a way that a picture, chart, or real life object will help your listener better understand your point? Taking a few extra minutes up front to create this aid may save you time explaining and help you to be a more effective presenter. (Rotman, 2009, p. 32)

As you prepare any visual aids, remember that you are the expert on your subject matter. If you also become the master of your visuals then you will be well on your way toward effective business communication!

5

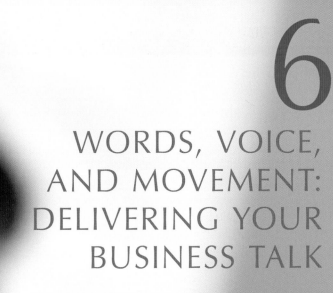

6

WORDS, VOICE, AND MOVEMENT: DELIVERING YOUR BUSINESS TALK

"The right word may be effective, but no word was ever as effective as a rightly timed pause."

—*Mark Twain, author*

TALKING THE TALK

Have you ever heard a presentation and thought to yourself, "Wow, that guy (or gal) is amazing!"? You likely have. We all have. Some presenters have a style or a flare that is captivating and intriguing. You might even be thinking about that person's dynamism days or weeks later. For the presenter, this is great. That person left an impression—and if his or her goal was to leave an impression then the presentation was effective. You might then be thinking that if you do not have an equally dynamic style that you cannot be effective, or that speaking is mostly about style. Neither is true. In fact, some of the most memorable public historic figures—the ones whose messages changed people, nations, laws, and social values—did not do so through any kind of flashy style.

Consider the styles of Mother Theresa, Mahatma Gandhi, the Dalai Lama, or Desmond Tutu. These are amazing communicators who affected the lives of their audiences, but none of them had *dynamic* (and by that we mean vibrant, energetic, and lively) speaking styles. They also may not have been the speakers that first came to your mind when you thought of amazing speakers. Your list may have included Malcolm X, Dr. Martin Luther King, Richard Branson, General Colin Powell, or even John Stewart of the *Daily Show*—a far livelier and vocally passionate group. The key here is that both groups have commonly used their own *individual* ability, style, and effective argumentation to influence audiences.

Message effectiveness is not dependent on a particular speaking style. Instead, many (both dynamic and reserved) speaking styles can effectively communicate messages. The task here is that speakers must be true to themselves, expressing their passion and appealing to ethos uniquely. Once you have compiled all of your evidence, ideas, support, visual aids, and organized it appropriately, you will still need to find the style that makes *you* successful!

In this chapter, you will learn how to embrace your own unique style by realistically assessing and managing your nerves, understanding the modes of delivery available to you, utilizing verbal and nonverbal delivery strategies, and (of course) seeing why and how practice will dramatically improve your speaking effectiveness.

ADDRESSING THE NERVES ISSUE

We must start any discussion of delivery style with the "elephant in the room" (the big, obvious issue that no one likes to talk about)…. the *nerves* issue. Because every speaking situation contains a level of uncertainty, it is natural to get nervous, at least to some degree, before giving a public speech. Speech anxiety is not only for those giving their first business talks but is common to most speakers. Even experienced professionals in high-powered positions can be anxious before a speech (Meyers & Nix, 2011).

This state of anxiety before engaging in public communication, no matter how large or how small, is referred to in academic literature as **communication apprehension** (Russ, 2012). Communication apprehension can come before, after, or during a speech; it can be those small butterflies in the stomach all the way to full-fledged panic (which is far more rare than you may have been told). In fact, Jerry Seinfeld once lamented, "According to most studies, people's number one fear is public speaking…if you go to a funeral, you're better off in the casket than doing the eulogy!" ("Jerry Seinfeld quotes," 2012). This simply is not true and it is a total misrepresentation of research in this area (see Garber, 2009, for how these rumors of "the number one fear" started).

Perpetuating these rumors actually hurts new speakers from becoming comfortable in a communication setting. People are subsequently less likely to get over these fears and also make a far bigger deal over their apprehension than is healthy. *This is the wrong mindset.*

The Right Mindset

The first step toward successful business talks is to develop a positive mindset about public speaking. So much of our ability to effectively reach our presentation goals depends on getting into the right *frame of mind*. For many folks (not quite as many as Jerry Seinfeld imagined), giving a speech can be anxiety provoking. *This is perfectly normal.* Giving ourselves permission to be nervous but still getting up to speak regardless of those feelings is an important part of overcoming our nerves (Bodie, 2010).

6

What creates much of that nervousness is the false belief that speeches must be perfect. In this pressurized condition, even the smallest mistake can feel like a monumental gaffe. It's no wonder Seinfeld's joke strikes a chord with so many people. You may believe that once your presentation is perfect then you will no longer be nervous. Instead of expecting perfection, we need to set a more realistic expectation. **No speech will ever be perfect—and that is ok.** The standard that we should strive to achieve is *effectiveness.* If you are effective in achieving your purpose (e.g., to inform or to persuade) then you are a success! There is no such thing in presenting as perfect. Practice makes…better! Changing your mindset from believing that others are perfect or that you must attempt to be perfect, and instead, striving to become better every day, will reduce nerves and there are practical steps to get there.

Practical Steps

It sounds easy to just "be positive" about giving a speech. But people cannot make that change from nerves to confidence with the flip of a switch. Changing your mindset can and will happen with time—but the first part of your change will be to take very practical (and sometimes even tangible) steps to ease any anxiety.

+ **Visualize the Bad and the Good:** The **self-fulfilling prophecy** simply means that if you believe *it*, that *it* is more likely to happen (Merton, 1948). Speakers too often picture all that can go wrong. This is a good idea but only as long as you picture how to *fix* those issues. Successful speakers tend to be those who visualize themselves being effective (Ayres & Hopf, 1999).

+ **Do a *Dress* Rehearsal:** The first time that you wear your new shoes should not be the day that you have your big speech. Some industries such as in the theater depend on dress rehearsals to ensure that the final product seen by the audience represents their best possible effort (Meyers & Nix, 2011). Business talks must work the same way. Skilled speakers (and skilled groups of speakers) practice their *entire* speeches while wearing exactly what they will wear on the day of the actual talk. Movement should be natural and your audience will know when you are uncomfortable in your attire—such as guys who do not regularly wear a sports coat and will be fidgeting or women who are struggling to walk confidently in high heels. Dress rehearsals will help you appear relaxed and natural.

+ **Examine the Nonverbal Impact:** Some speakers visually show when they are nervous with issues such as hands or knees shaking, red blotches, and sweating in usual (and unusual) places (Bodie, 2010). If you become aware of your individual "**tell**" (unconscious behavior that reveals feelings or thoughts) then you can work to mask these specific symptoms. The steps are as simple as no V-neck shirts for those who get blotches, a jacket to avoid showing sweating, not holding papers if your hands shake, etc. Know your own "tell" and how to manage it! (If you are not sure of yours then be sure to do your dress rehearsal in front of a spouse, friend, or colleagues who can point out your fixable issues.)

+ **Warm Up Your Vocal Chords:** It is not necessary to walk around outside of your presentation room saying "meee meee meee" or repeatedly verbalizing "rubber baby buggy bumpers." It is, however, important to have your vocal chords adequately stretched before you speak. Nothing is more telling of nerves than when your voice cracks as you attempt to speak. Vocal warm-ups are a practical step to help strengthen your verbal presentation (Bodie, 2010). If you have an early morning business talk, be sure to call your best friend even earlier that morning just to chat; if your talk is just before lunch and you have worked quietly all day, take your lunch break to go chat with the person in the cubicle next to you (you will be focused on something other than your speech or nerves and may even make a friend!).

+ **Bring Water:** Anticipating a dry throat may actually cause more issues than actually having a dry throat. If you believe that you will need water, then bring it! Having water will help you with dry mouth during a speech, not stain clothes if spilled (which inevitably will happen; no worries—water dries), and avoids coating your mouth or throat. Other liquids will work against you. Whether you wish to avoid the jitters or an unexpected burp, speakers should skip coffee, energy drinks, and carbonated beverages (Van Petten, 2007)! If you are cautious about having *permission* to bring water...why? The only person making this decision is you. If your mouth will get dry preventing you from clear speech then you need to put your needs ahead of what you believe to be expected of you or the trend of what anyone else is doing.

+ **Hold Something Small:** Your final practical step to managing your nerves should be taken just moments before you begin to speak. If you are someone whose hands shake or someone who gives no nonverbal signs of stress when you are shaking on the inside, a wonderful means of managing this is rather small! One of the great tools of anxiety management has no researched support but has significant anecdotal success (Ezenyimulu, 2010; UNC Speaking Center, 2009). Take a small piece of paper or item that cannot be seen by the audience and roll it up between your thumb and forefinger. As you begin to speak, just keep rolling it back and forth. No one will notice that it is there but you, and yet all that nervous energy suddenly has somewhere to go other than in your voice, shaking hands, or even running around in your brain. The article itself is not important (some people use a paper clip and others use a pebble or tiny object), but the strategy allows you to focus your nerves in a way that does not distract from your business talk!

While none of these tactics are life changing, they each have their own practical means of managing or masking nerves. Once you know that you are in the right mindset for your rhetorical situation, then you are ready to choose your mode of delivery and practice your individual style.

6

MODES OF DELIVERY

Most everyone has seen the president of the United States delivering the State of the Union address. Even if you have never seen the whole thing or just caught a moment of it on the news (or watched someone poking fun at it on a late night talk show) then you are well aware that the president does not take the time to memorize every single word and then practice for a stylized delivery. In your business life, it is unlikely that you as well will have the time to write out every speech word-for-word and then memorize it. Whether you give speeches for a living or just give one, you will need to determine the mode of delivery.

Modes of delivery are the methods by which presentations are expressed. There are four basic modes of delivering a speech: manuscript, memory, impromptu, and extemporaneous. It is your task to determine which mode of delivery is best suited to you, your environment, the constraints of that specific situation, and, of course, the audience...yes, these are the elements of the **rhetorical situation**. Some environments will call for a particular mode of delivery and some constraints or audiences will specifically call for you *not* to use a particular mode of delivery. Since you analyzed your rhetorical situation as part of your business talk research then you are in good shape to select your mode.

Speaking from Manuscript

Manuscript speaking is just as it sounds—a speech delivered from a completely written, word-for-word copy of your text. This type of speech is the one you see where the speaker is holding pages and reading directly from them, or in the case of the president, newscasters, or some actors, it means using a teleprompter to look directly at an audience or camera while being fed lines. Manuscript delivery has its advantages and its pitfalls.

First, if your presentation requires precise language to convey *exact* meanings then you may want to deliver a speech from a manuscript. For example, legal presentations—where even a one-word alteration can be detrimental—are strong candidates for manuscript speaking. However, most of us do not have to meet such stringent standards for our speech content. Demands for this precision are usually reserved for people who are in the upper echelons of management, criminal justice or legal industries, and politics. It may also be used simply during a portion of your talk to specify a definition or quotation but not an entire speech.

On the other hand, the manuscript mode of delivery can produce some painfully boring presentations! Manuscript speakers typically have limited eye contact, sound like they are reading a text (which they are!), which lends itself to an awkward pace and pausing, as well as low emotional connection to the text (Allen, 1989). This is certainly not to say that *all* legal or political speeches are boring (for example, Ronald Reagan's January 31, 1986 eulogy for the *Challenger* astronauts was heart-wrenching and inspiring, and after Representative Barbara Jordan's legal explanation of the articles of impeachment in the Nixon case on July 25, 1974, billboards were erected in her honor…yes, after a *legal* explanation!) (see Ou & Huang, 2008 and Kaylor, 2012).

To overcome the issues associated with manuscript speaking, you will need to spend a significant amount of time preparing your manuscript. Once it is prepared you will need to:

+ practice as much as time permits with the actual script format

+ *never* use note cards (Ellis, 2009) but opt for full-page notes or teleprompters

+ format your script or teleprompter with a font size and style that is large and very easy to read

+ space out ideas so that they are easy to see

+ mark up the manuscript in a way that highlights (sometimes literally) key ideas

+ gesture and add some animation to your delivery

Speaking from Memory

Similar to the manuscript speech is **memorized speaking**, which includes a word-for-word delivery of a speech but with no notes. At first, this mode seems similar to acting, but there are several key differences. First, actors memorize scripts written by another while a speaker memorizes a text that is typically written by him or herself (or a speech writer who composed the message for the specific speaker) and is directly connected to the rhetorical situation. Unlike an actor, a speaker changes the "script" based on the needs of the audience, situation, and constraints but an actor only portrays what is on the page regardless of rhetorical needs. Finally, while the actor can adopt a false sense of emotion, the speaker must use ethos, pathos, and logos to connect to the audience (Aristotle, in *Nicomachean Ethics*, trans. 1980).

Speaking from memory has all of the benefits of manuscript speaking but without the cumbersome and distracting notes in the way. This sounds fantastic! After all, you eliminate the need for a podium, lectern, or place for your notes (which helps to remove any physical and psychological barriers between you and the audience) and you still get the wording exactly right. Or do you?

Memorized speaking requires a skilled delivery ability and a monumental amount of time to both commit the words to memory and then practice for a natural

6

delivery. We have all seen bad acting on television or in a movie. We know that these people are just saying memorized words and we stop believing in what they have to say. Bad memorized speaking works the same way. If your audience knows that you are simply trying to recite a script in your head then they are far less likely to connect with you.

At some point, you may find yourself in a position in which you have to give essentially the same presentation on multiple occasions (e.g., if you are traveling around the country for your company to provide the same training for employees in various locations; if you are providing company status updates to multiple divisions one after the other; even teachers who give the same lecture numerous times!). Whether you have intended to do so or you have just repeated yourself so many times that you cannot help it, you may find that you have memorized your speech. You may, additionally, find that you are just going through the motions rather than working each time to try to *connect* to your specific audience and appealing to pathos. Just like actors with a script, memorized speeches still need to be connected in order to hold the interest of the audience. After all, if you begin to sound like you are giving directions to the same place for the millionth time, the audience can tell.

Even more problematic than sounding memorized is using a memorized speech as a crutch. If you have memorized your speech poorly then you can lose your place and not be able to move forward. The words become like links in a chain; drop a link and the chain is broken, and you cannot continue along the chain until you have repaired (recalled) the missing link. If you do not need to give the same presentation on numerous occasions, it is typically best to avoid memorizing your speech.

Impromptu Speaking

Impromptu speaking includes those speeches that are given with little to no preparation. (This does *not* mean little to no organization!) If you gave a business talk with no preparation and no organization then you would not be giving a speech as much as babbling out loud. Impromptu speakers do well when they know and use the basic speaking organizational structure (i.e., intro, thesis, preview, main points with transitions, review, rephrased thesis, and style match—the ideas that you learned in Chapter Three's discussion) to communicate ideas.

While it would be nice if you always knew well in advance when you would be expected to speak, unfortunately, you will not. If you are called on suddenly to give a presentation, you will want to use impromptu speaking rather than simply babble! For example, consider that you are sitting in a departmental staff meeting and your boss asks you to bring the group up to speed on your team's project. It

 is unlikely that this is a request that you can decline. Instead of saying, "Yeah...I"ll pass," you will need to gather your thoughts in that moment and then present a clear, coherent speech with only the arguments and support that you already have in your head. In the business world, these speaking requests will happen often and should not be avoided. View these events as opportunities to communicate the expertise that you have already gained! When should you not use impromptu speaking? You should always avoid impromptu speaking when you have an opportunity to do the research and preparation that comes from having more time.

Extemporaneous Speaking

Extemporaneous speeches are prepared well in advance and delivered from a speaking outline rather than word-for-word script. These speeches require less preparation than manuscript or memorized speaking but allow the speaker preparation time to fill in holes of evidence that did not come immediately to mind. For the most part, the professional presentations you will give will allow you a moderate amount of advance notice.

If you are having trouble imagining a scenario where this is the case then reflect on what your college professors do every day. Professors are well versed in their topics but are far too busy to write out their presentations word-for-word. If a professor does read from a script, you can imagine how disconnected the students would be—likely texting or reading materials from other classes. Audiences know when speakers are not responding to them in the moment. The extemporaneous mode allows the speaker the ability to spend most of their time connecting directly with their listeners (Henderson & Henderson, 2007). However, these speeches must be practiced extensively for delivery *clarity* and *fluency*.

Part of extemporaneous speech practice is the preparation of effective notes. Note cards tend to be something used in classrooms and for training, but how often do you see a professional speaker or a company CEO flipping through 3 × 5 cards? Not often (Ellis, 2009)! In the business world, you will typically use a typed single page, a teleprompter, or even PowerPoint slides to guide your presentation. Extemporaneous speaking notes must be brief and more easily handled than full manuscripts. These notes should include key arguments and evidence but avoid full sentence details. They should be a skeleton of your ideas where you can fill in examples and details distinctly for each specific audience. For example:

6

Project: ACME Human Resources Marketing Campaign

Introduction:
+ seeing catchy flyers in classrooms
+ not use this method for ACME

Thesis: Marketing Campaigns are the means to getting ACME's name out without using advertising.

Preview: company policy, marketing campaigns, our strategy

Claim One: It is ACME company policy not to use advertising.
1. company policy (ACME, 2005)
2. CEO rationale—need to be viewed as high class (Gunderbery, 2004; Grazer and Dohn, 2004)
3. other methods used by ACME (Trotman, 1999)
4. other methods used by other companies (AP Wire, 2004)

Transition 1–2: company policy, marketing campaigns

Claim Two: Marketing campaigns work to promote a name without using direct advertising.

1. marketing vs. advertising explanation (Stapleton, 1990)
2. marketing methods (Grazer and Dohn, 2004; Terrance, 2001)
   - pr
   - press
   - word of mouth
   - success rates per method (Terrance, 2001)

Transition 2–3: marketing campaigns, our strategy

Claim Three: Our strategy for this company involves using the most effective methods.
1. Public Relations with State Schools (PASCU, 2001)
2. Job Fairs (Donner, 2005)
   - on campus (PASCU, 2001; WCU, 2005)
   - off campus (Kelly, 2004)
3. Club Visits (PASCU, 2001; WCU, 2005)

Review: company policy, marketing campaigns, our strategy

Re-state Thesis: Marketing Campaigns are a feasible, non-advertising method to getting ACME's name out where you want it to be.

Conclusion:
+ seeing catchy flyers in classrooms
+ now use marketing campaigns

You can see here that notes are in the form of an outline rather than full sentences on note cards. These outlines provide "wiggle room" for tailoring examples to the moment and the audience. They allow you to gesture more regularly and focus eye contact. You can anticipate the need to refer to your notes and glance quickly at them. Once you grasp the idea, you can put your hand down and go on gesturing normally. Your notes should become totally unobtrusive, almost as if they disappear in the eyes of the audience.

Extemporaneous speaking has numerous benefits but should not be used on every occasion. The most basic reason to avoid extemporaneous speaking is if you have not adequately read through and understand your research. Extemporaneous speaking is not about faking it; it is about knowing your information and, because you do not need to, not getting bogged down in the words on a manuscript!

No one mode of speaking is inherently better than the others. The mode you should use depends on your specific rhetorical situation. In some instances, you will combine modes. You may be giving an impromptu speech only to pick up a page and read a report summary as part of your support. You may have memorized your introduction but give the remainder of the speech in an extemporaneous manner. The important thing here is to choose a mode or combination of modes *only* after you have thoroughly pondered the demands placed on you by your speaking situation. Once you have, you are in a position to work on the verbal and nonverbal parts of your talk.

VERBAL AND NONVERBAL CONSIDERATIONS

6

How you deliver your business talk will have a crucial impact on the effectiveness of your presentation. If you doubt the truth of this statement, consider a well-known instance of distracting delivery. On May 23, 2005, Tom Cruise jumped up and down on Oprah Winfrey's couch to declare his love for the woman who was soon to be the mother of his child—Katie Holmes (who is now his *ex*-wife). The passion was unmistakable. The jumping is unforgettable. The delivery of his message was…. perhaps unwise. Why? It is difficult to fault anyone for falling in love and being enthusiastic enough to show it publically. What was problematic in this public declaration was that the jumping became more memorable than the idea behind it. Tom Cruise made one of the crucial errors in public presentation—he let his verbal and nonverbal communication overshadow his message (Lynch, 2005).

If you think that such passionate and ineffective delivery does not happen in the refined business world, think again. Microsoft's Steve Ballmer screamed and ran back and forth on the stage (to the point of not being able to breathe when he began to speak) as he kicked off his company's 25th anniversary. His actions spawned several YouTube videos and earned him the nickname "Dance Monkeyboy" (Don,

2009). Apple's mega-presenter Steve Jobs was so unprepared for glitches while attempting to show off features of the new iPhone 4 that he stammered through the presentation with a series of "ah geez," "whoops," and nervous giggles (Ogg, 2010).

So, as you can see, even the best presenters sometimes fall victim to verbal and nonverbal gaffes. How do you avoid the delivery of your message overwhelming the message itself? You adopt effective tools of presentation. Remember that word—*tools*. Just like a hammer is a great tool, it does not work for every job. Not every tool mentioned in the following discussion will be useful to you in every single speaking situation and you will need to make your tool selections careful before making any choice part of your deliberate style.

Verbal Effectiveness

We all have different voices, vocal qualities, and even language choices. As a speaker, you must look to each verbal effectiveness tool to determine how to best use it with your natural style and in that rhetorical moment. (Remember, Gandhi and Dr. Martin Luther King were both highly effective but with vastly different verbal styles.) Think of using your voice in two ways—first, as a part of putting together effective *language strategies* and, second, as a means of communicating with strong *vocal qualities*.

Language Strategies

Any time that you give a presentation, you will want to choose language that both holds that audience's attention and clearly communicates your ideas. This means using an effective style of speech. Vocally, an effective presentation expresses your ideas in their full intellectual, aesthetic, and emotional dimensions. That's a mouthful, but it means that delivering a speech is more than getting the words out of your mouth in the right order. *Reciting* and *delivering* a speech are dramatically different. **Recitation** verbally expresses all of the ideas in the correct order, but robs them of their full meaning by reducing them to a mere arrangement of words. Strong verbal style means selecting language that expresses precise meanings so that your words engage your audience. Once you become a veteran speaker, your style will also become distinctive to you.

Just like fashion for how we look, verbal style is how we clothe our ideas in words. (Are you Nordstrom? Forever 21? Kate Spade? Burberry? Target? You decide!) Before you begin to think too much about how to stylize your speech to your personal taste, think about how personal style is altered for circumstances. You may be very fashion forward and cutting edge, but you would still not wear red to a funeral and you know the difference between what you would wear on a date versus to a job interview. These circumstances are like unique audiences and unique rhetorical situations. The core of who you are will never change, but you will modify that style for the specific occasion. Consider each of the following elements that contribute to your core while knowing that the exact details will be part of your speaking moment.

+ **Structural Simplicity**

  If you are reading a book and cannot remember an idea from an earlier chapter then you can simply flip a few pages back to remind yourself. Audiences of verbal messages do not have this luxury. If they do not "get it" the first time then it makes sense that they are more likely to tune out because there is no opportunity to go backwards. Part of the organization for your business talk, as noted earlier, is to keep your main arguments such as your thesis or claims simple and uncluttered. You may have done this when crafting your outline but be careful not to rephrase and complicate as you transfer your ideas to the spoken word. Certainly give yourself permission to paraphrase and stylize ideas and support once you begin to speak but practice primary arguments so that you can deliver them to the audience just as they were constructed.

+ **Word Economy**

  If you have ever told a story more than once then you know that as you re-tell it, you are likely to get either far more elaborate or cut to the chase. The style of your business talks works in the same way—what you have to say can be expressed in both the long and the short version. **Word economy**, or the skill of saying exactly what you want to say but in as few words as necessary, is the hallmark of good speaking style; however, *how* brief you will be is entirely up to you. In the 19th century, audiences were accustomed to speeches that lasted for hours but, today, lengthy speeches can create hostile audiences. Why? Digital media has given modern audiences a broad span of tolerance for the *kinds* of content we intake, but a short attention span for how *much* we take in (Hart, 1994). In other words, your audience will not be patient while you meander to your point. Elaboration is a luxury that should be reserved for only the instances that will captivate and require detail to be effective.

+ **Concreteness**

  If you tell an audience, "We have taken initial steps toward fixing the problem," this could mean just about anything. Admittedly, certain situations require a speaker to be purposefully vague, but be careful. Sometimes this fuzzy type of communication can backfire on the speaker.

  Concreteness is the opposite of abstraction—it means solid and real. Renowned semanticist (meaning *a guy who studies words*) S. I. Hayakawa

6

(1949) developed a concept called the **Rhetorical Ladder of Abstraction**. According to Hayakawa, all language can be described as going from some level of conceptual to extremely precise. If we speak in a manner that is strategically or accidentally incredibly abstract (e.g., "We have taken initial steps") then we have not attempted to provide our audiences with a clear understanding of reality. As we become more specific, we move up the ladder—a position of precision (e.g., "We called every stockholder and provided them with the information seen on your handout").

Individual speakers must decide where on the language ladder they want to be (both depending on their own personal style and rhetorical situation). As noted earlier, there will certainly be times in which being ambiguous will be to your advantage. After all, precision does not give you much wiggle room for backing out later. Being ambiguous, however, is rarely to the *audience's* advantage; if they want answers and you are vague then beware of the reaction! Choose your level of concreteness strategically and ethically.

+ **Jargon**

Words are specific to groups. **Jargon** is the specialized language particular to a specific profession, field of study, or distinct group. Jargon is a fantastic way to cut down on unnecessary terms or long descriptions with audiences who just need a reference to the larger idea, but it can also alienate speakers from audiences when overused. For example, if you were told to refer back to the TOC for outline information on this book, would you know that this meant the *Table of Contents*? If not, would you be annoyed that the author chose to be less than clear? Likely, you would!

Too often, speakers try to establish credibility by loading their speeches with acronyms and other specialized expressions that are not part of the ordinary language of their listeners (they are trying to *sound* smart). Unless this jargon is the "language" of your audience, you will be more effective if you use words that can be easily decoded. If you know that if Schramm (1954) were to hear your speech and know long before the feedback is offered that your audience could not comprehend the message...you have not been effective! Speakers should limit jargon and acronyms as well as explain any terms that might be new or could confuse an audience (Arnold, 2010).

However, not all jargon should be avoided. The art of rhetorical simplicity and the needs of your rhetorical situation might mean that a business talk full of jargon will save you time while meeting the needs of clarity. Jargon can be useful when (and only when) you and your audience know the same terminology and can process it efficiently. A good speaker will find the right balance between jargon and common language.

- **Qualifiers**

We use **qualifiers** to give scale or show magnitude in our speaking. This is something that anyone familiar with email or texting emoticons will know well. Have you ever attached a smiley face to a message? Are you skilled enough to show the emoticon of *very* happy versus just plain ole happy? These textual symbols are the same idea as the qualifiers that we use in our verbal speech. You can be "excited" about the new project or "SUPER EXCITED!!!" You can clarify the precise meaning of ideas by using terms that increase, decrease, or alter the nature of your verbal concepts.

Qualifying terminology can also unnecessarily overly complicate your ideas. Think back to your last trip to a restaurant for an example how tedious excessive qualifiers can get. Since when did a "bacon cheeseburger with fries" become:

> "A subtly seasoned, open fire-grilled, one-third pound Angus beef patty topped with aged baby Swiss cheese and a rasher of maple smoked pepper bacon served on an unbleached flour, sesame-seeded Kaiser roll, with locally grown heirloom tomato slices, shaved red onions, a leaf of romaine lettuce, with a dollop of fat-free mayonnaise, and accompanied by a generous side of Cajun batter-dipped, Idaho blue potatoes quick fried in canola oil"

Huh? This does sound yummy but an audience will never remember all these details and can likely miss the main idea. ("Oh, it's a hamburger?!") Like condiments, which are great in some conditions but too many will ruin a meal, use qualifiers selectively and strategically.

- **Repetition versus Redundancy**

Like many terms in this text, repetition and redundancy are discussed time and time again because they are crucial to so many aspects of a business talk. We know that audiences do not always get what we have to say the first time so speakers must be skilled in sending messages more than once—without sounding like they are having verbal hiccups (Arnold, 2010). Speakers who understand the differences in these definitions will see that one fits better in a verbally delivered presentation.

Repetition is the exact and word-for-word restatement of language previously used. **Redundancy** is the statement of previously expressed ideas in new language to help with retention. Repetition is a stylistic device that can help to drive home a point. Think of Martin Luther King's *I Have a Dream* speech. This catch phrase was repeated time and time again (nine times, to be exact!) for emphasis (Meyers & Nix, 2011). However, when the choice to include repetitive language is not made for style or emphasis, audiences will think, "Didn't the speaker already say that?" They may wonder if your mind has wandered and you have lost your focus on the moment! Repetition should be used to highlight or stress certain speech elements whereas redundancy should be used to help audiences absorb or process messages (Arnold, 2010).

In looking back on language strategies, you will see that some are universal but most are individual to the speaker. You will make choices that are specific to you (such as being someone who uses a bit of repetition in all speeches for emphasis) but that also respect your rhetorical situation (such as using less concreteness in one speech and more in another). Vocal strategies, however, are critical in *all* occasions to ensure that your voice reaches and resonates with your audience.

Vocal Strategies

Have you ever seen a speaker in a large room who chose not to use a microphone and, therefore, could not be heard? Have you ever been in a small room with a co-worker, boss, or friend whose voice not only fills the room but carries down the hallway? Have you ever been in a meeting or class where the person running the session had such a non-expressive voice that you have to fight every listening selection simply not to fall asleep?! We all have.

In each of these scenarios, the speaker chose not to respect the situational elements that called for specific vocal strategies. In some cases, the speaker's natural voice may have been difficult to control. In other cases, the speaker might not have had the training to know what tools to select to accommodate the setting. Understanding how to use your voice in various settings will ensure that your message has its best chance of effectiveness.

+ **Vocal Variety**

  Have you ever seen the movie *Ferris Bueller's Day Off* (or if not the full movie, the clip of teacher Ben Stein calling roll in the classroom? *Bueller? Bueller?*"). This is an example of having no vocal variety. What is commonly called **vocal variety** (or **vocal animation**) is the process of infusing your ideas with life and with energy. It is absent in the movie for comedic effect but the pain of an entire presentation with no variety is universal. (Can you imagine listening to that man give a 50-minute class lecture? Yikes.) Do you want that monotone speaker to be you? Absolutely not! Getting vocally expressive in your speech lets audiences get more out of what you have to say and increases your credibility in their eyes (Pearce & Conklin, 1971). For your business talk, this means bringing the full range of pathos-driven expressiveness to your voice. If the message is sad, we should *hear* that. If the message is inspiring, we should hear that as well. You will best be able to demonstrate appropriate vocal variety once you have embraced your message.

- **Limit Non-Fluencies**

As you become fully engaged in your business talk, you might find that you are falling back on some style elements that are more appropriate for chatting with friends than speaking to a professional audience. Speakers can clutter their verbal style and damage their credibility with **non-fluencies**, which are the verbal hesitancies or verbal fillers in our speech. These include terms such as "like," "you know," "um," and "uh." Non-fluencies hurt the fluidity of your presentation (thus, the name) and imply nervousness regardless of your actual level of confidence (Arnold, 2010). If you are prone to using these in your everyday speech and might be using them in your business talks, work to weed them out!

As you practice your speech, have a few catch phrases that you can insert instead of those fillers. When you begin to say "uh," change it to a more complete and coherent phrase such as "in other words" or "to clarify." The first few times that you try this, you will feel awkward and the catch phrase will seem to stand out more than the non-fluency. In time, two things will happen: 1) you will begin to naturally insert your catch phrase or, 2) the insertion will become such an interruption that you will start to phase it and the non-fluency out for more fluid speech. The only way to make this work is to take some time and practice.

- **Projection**

"Can you hear me now?" Noise in our feedback loop is not always message ambiguity but sometimes it is simply that the audience cannot hear us. (Remember the difference between hearing and listening!) Our speaking voices must be heard, but projection is not just about being loud.

Vocal projection means supporting your voice so that you are speaking with enough volume and strength to be heard easily by your entire audience. You should project your voice enough to both *fill the space* in which you are speaking as well as reflect the number of people in the room (e.g., if you are in a small but full conference room then you will raise your voice over the noise; however, if you are in a practically empty hotel ballroom speaking to one or two other people then you can drop down your volume to a more intimate level). None of this means that your voice should (or should not) boom to be heard down the hallway. We can again think of the difference between Dr. Martin Luther King and Gandhi—or even Jon Stewart and Rosa Parks. Each person represents a different verbal projection style but all are effective.

6

Too many speakers incorrectly believe that good delivery means being loud. Do you like to get yelled at? Do you want your boss to think that you are yelling at her? Certainly not. Too loud of a volume often wears your audience down or even makes them hostile (Reimold & Reimold, 2006). On the other hand, if you speak or project too softly, your voice can sound small and be easily ignored (Reimold & Reimold). To be sure you are striking a good balance, try to always talk in the space before you begin your presentation so you know how you sound in that environment and can adjust.

- **Articulation**

Articulation is another adjustment that you can make yourself. Are you an articulate person? Most folks do not actually know what this means. **Articulation** is the precision with which we say the words that we speak (see the *Oxford English Dictionary*). Slurring words, dropping syllables, or simply mumbling are some forms of poor articulation. Oddly enough, many associate being articulate with being smart. That association is a **connotation** (the sentiment attached to the word) rather than a **denotation** (the actual meaning of the word). Being articulate in both of these ways can establish ethos.

When we do not speak clearly, we force the audience to work harder to understand the ideas we are trying to communicate. Poor articulation, especially in some industries, can frustrate listeners who may opt to tune out rather than struggle to understand the speaker's words (Borrego, Gasparini, & Behlau, 2007). For instance, in the greater Philadelphia area, the expression "yanaamean?" is difficult to decipher for the person not well versed in "Philly-speak." (The translation: "Do you know what I mean?") Embracing a casual style in your everyday talk is fine, but no audience member should have to work hard to extract meaning from your words during a business talk. On the other hand, articulation does not mean overly distinctive verbalization (you certainly do not want to sound snobby or affect an accent or style that you do not own). Remember, as a speaker, your goals are to be understood and be perceived as credible by your audience. Saying words clearly helps achieve those goals.

- **Enunciation**

Articulation is often mistaken for enunciation. **Enunciation** in speech, according to the *Oxford English Dictionary*, is "the action of giving definite expression." In business talks, enunciation is the range that most of us experience when we are engaged in a lively conversation or friendly debate. Our inflection rises and falls, our pitch varies to reflect the emotional content, and we embrace verbal emphasis to stress key words or to convey different meanings. For example, all of the following phrases use the same words, but they do not *mean* the same thing:

- Key sales figures in the fourth quarter (strict information)

- *Key* sales figures in the fourth quarter (these figures are vital)

- Key *sales figures* in the fourth quarter (the figures are from sales and not another division)

- Key sales figures in the *fourth* quarter (the figures represent only one period of the financial statement)

You will want to emphasize words and phrases that result in your audience not just understanding your words but understanding your *meaning*.

+ **Pronunciation**

Let's face it…some words are simply difficult to say. This is either how they are spelled or their global origins or even that they simply look like they should be said another way. **Pronunciation** is saying a word using the accepted and recognized standard. Mispronunciation can lead an audience to discount your ideas because it may seem like you do not really know what you are saying (poor ethos!) (Hall, 1997). To avoid this, you will want to get your pronunciation practiced and accurate before you begin to talk. If you are ever in doubt of how to say a word, find options that absolutely do <u>not</u> include: "er, I think that's how you say it." This is not professional. If you are unsure:

- ask an expert (even in your company)

- check online (most online dictionaries will verbalize words so be sure to turn on your speakers and click on the icon; most smart phones can do this, too!)

- when possible and appropriate, select another word whose pronunciation you already know

+ **Pausing**

Making your ideas accessible requires silence as much as it requires words. While running sentences together robs both you and your listeners of needed reflection time, strategic **pausing**, or intentionally placed brief verbal hesitations, help speakers to emphasize ideas and help audiences to remember messages. In public speaking, pauses work best when they are *brief*. An effective pause gives an audience time to process a message and the speaker time to think, but an ill-placed or too long pause can be distracting (Miers, 2009). Dramatic pauses or loooooooooong pauses should be saved for finding out who was eliminated from *Top Chef* or *American Idol* but are not appropriate for business presentations.

◆ **Conversational Tone**

Incorporating the above strategies will take time and practice, especially if you are at the start of your public speaking career. Ultimately, you will want to blend these verbal and nonverbal techniques with a natural, conversational tone. After all, you are not giving directions on a Disneyland ride—you are making a professional statement to people who see you as an expert. **Conversational tone** simply means that the tone of your voice should sound natural and unrehearsed.

Your professional speaking style should be more informal than a written report or memo but still polished. You should avoid *performing*...leave that to the actors on stage! Instead, cultivate an authentic delivery style that shows your audience you intend to talk to—and not at—them.

Answering Questions

People want to engage with you and know what you have to say. You are likely to be interactive and should expect questions. "When given an option, most audiences want to be able to ask questions as they come up in your presentation...you will be interrupted," (Arnold, 2010, p. 100). While you gave significant attention to the nature of asking and answering questions when looking at business choices (see Chapter Two), there has been no considerable discussion of the *delivery* aspect of interactive questions.

Part of a good verbal delivery will be the style with which you answer questions. You know that a positive mindset helps ease nerves and this will transfer into your Q&A period. We know that questions are good. Approach them with a positive attitude! Thank your audience for their questions—even if they come at a time that is not ideal. If your audience asks you in the middle of your talk about an issue that you are not yet to, then let the questioner know that you will be getting to the information soon—ask if he or she is willing to wait a few moments. If questions come at the right time, appreciation of the question will develop a positive relationship with the questioner that can prime any answer.

Second, think before you speak. Some people are so uncomfortable with silence that they jump into an answer before having contemplated what would be best to say. Thank the person but then take a moment (not forever). Have a drink of water while you ponder. Now, launch into the most concise and descriptive reply possible. If the question is somewhat off topic, bridge it back to the issue at hand rather than being led astray (e.g., "That's an interesting point that actually helps us to understand the most critical element here, which is..." or "This is a good idea for our next step that we can only take by looking at the issue here of..."). These means of redirection are respectful without letting the audience take over. Practice a few that are comfortable to you and have them ready to go before you begin your presentation.

Finally, look the part. If a question comes up to which you have no answer or you do have the answer and would simply prefer not to share it (e.g., "Er, yes, Mr. President, I do know what our employees said about you on Twitter"), you will want to *show* confidence. Stand up straight. Look the person in the eye. Try to convey the nonverbal "tells" of expertise and ease. Now, speak with a clear, articulate, and audible voice and use the level of concreteness that is appropriate.

You will note that not all of this is a vocal exercise. When you speak in front of others, you must communicate with your entire self. Your whole body should work together with your voice and text to deliver your ideas to the audience. This comes from attention to your nonverbal communication.

Nonverbal Effectiveness

Do you know people who "talk with their hands"? Is this you? If so, try to sit on your hands. You might find that it becomes difficult to speak. Why? You are trying to fit into a mold that does not suit you. By embracing who you are as a physical speaker, you can fully realize your speaking style. If you have been told (or believe) that your nonverbal communication can hurt your effectiveness (such as having huge gestures or a tendency to meander), do not fret. These are not things that you must completely eliminate to be effective! They are part of you. You simply need to make small modifications so that your nonverbal communication helps to focus the audience on (rather than pull them from) your message.

Appearance and Attire

The first thing that will grab the audience's attention is…you. Before you even arrive at your speaking location, you will have already made a very important delivery choice—how to dress. Your appearance communicates volumes before you even open your mouth (Namhata, 2011). The rule of thumb for any interaction where you will be evaluated is that you avoid wearing any item that will distract the audience from the purpose of your presentation. These items may include very bright-colored clothing, "funny" ties, dangly earrings, squeaky or loud shoes, revealing hemlines, keys in your pockets, etc. While appearance and attire are culturally, regionally, and even industry specific, some general guidelines include:

- **Link to the Specific Industry:** A three-piece suit may work well for an attorney's office but will seem like an odd (and, therefore, distracting) choice in a construction office or hair salon; be sure to select appropriate attire that offers the *best* look (not everyday wear) for your speaking situation (Haefner, 2008).

- **Dress One Level Above Your Audience:** When you arrive for an interview or a presentation, your audience will assume that you are at your best (after all, isn't this what you assume of those who present to you?). If you show up to an office of folks who typically wear khakis and button-downs wearing khakis and a button-down shirt then the employer will assume that this is the *best* that you can do. They will not know if when a client comes in and your team is decked out in suits for the day whether or not you can make this adjustment. "In order to establish on sight that you are the authority, you must dress slightly better than the (audience) so that your attire supports the image that you have been successful as the result of your endeavors. Therefore, the most helpful rule of thumb is for you to dress 'one step up' from your (audience)" (Henderson & Henderson, 2007, p. 159). Keep in mind that the "one step up" advice refers to the audience's attire expectations, not yours.

- **Be Groomed:** If you look like you have not paid attention to the details of your appearance then your audience will assume that you will not pay attention to theirs. Again, this makes sense, right? To give a nonverbal indication that you have your act together, iron your clothes, bathe and lack body odor, shave or groom anything unkempt and visible, remove flashy or peeling nail polish, and generally look as if you care about your personal appearance.

- **Dress Like a First Interview, Not a First Date:** Today's television shows can give the indication that women's success is derived from their use of sex appeal in the office (for an older example, think *Ally McBeal*; for a newer example, think *Fairly Legal* on the USA network). Some popular television shows even indicate that men should use the same sexual prowess to achieve success. Unfortunately, provocative clothing in the real-world office is far more likely to distract than appeal (Field, 2000; Kiddie, 2009; Reddick, 2007). Keep the sexy at home during business talks and interviews. Avoid showing cleavage (or…plumber) in a business setting and consider what you want the audience to remember after you have left the room. While jeans may work once you are the CEO, when you are on your way up it is better to be overdressed rather than underdressed.

- **Avoid Distracting Colors/Patterns:** Just like your words and examples should draw in the audience and focus them on your message, so should your attire. If your tie is so fun and interesting that it is all that your audience remembers, then you have a problem. If you walk in and blind the audience with your outfit of hot pink, bright orange, bold stripes, or holiday patterns then they are certainly not focused on the important elements of your message. Therefore, if you thought about wearing that bright color to be memorable, know that research suggests that *warm* colors actually lead to stronger memories than cool, bright colors (Huchendorf, 2007). Toning things down can actually work in your favor.

- **Use Sparse Jewelry and Accessories:** Similar to those distracting colors and patterns, accessories can distract not only your audience but *you*. Avoid excessive, moving, attention-grabbing, or potential to "fidget with" jewelry whether you are a man or a woman. Understand that some industries and regions will expect limited and tasteful jewelry, if any at all (think Disneyland), and that men should be more selective than women. Accessories such as large earrings, bangles, cuffs, pins, belt buckles, or headbands can draw focus away from your message or can lend you to regularly touch the item and draw attention to that movement. If you are unsure, leave it at home.

- **Don't…Smell:** People have difficulty remembering a specific smell but the positive and negative associations that we match with scents are extremely long lasting (Keller, 2009). What this means for you is that if you have an odor that your audience does not finding instantly appealing, they can develop a long-term negative association *with you*. To be on the safe side, be clean and avoid having a distinctive odor. Know that odor lasts. Smoke becomes part of your attire, even if you did not smoke in that particular outfit, and perfume and cologne build up in our clothing and accessories over time so what we smell is far less than what others smell. Many strong, distinctive scents can be just fine in your personal life but are to be avoided on interview and presentation days…and in small elevators.

6

Movement and Walking

Have you ever looked at the United States flag for more than 30 seconds? *Really* looked? Try it. Now look away. What you will see is an optical imprint of the flag turned to black and green. Yes, the color image makes an impact on your eyes but there is no connection with the actual object (Simon, 1998). The same thing happens for speakers who select to stand in one place for an extended time.

Movement is a strong part of business interactions in both negative and positive ways. First, non-moving speakers have voice (and voice alone) to bring in the audience. That is a lot of pressure to put on just your voice! Second, non-moving speakers lose connection with an audience who is both mentally and physically engaged in following the presentation. *WAIT! Before you take this as an insinuation that you should wander aimlessly and never plant your feet, remember that movement should be used sparingly.* Indeed, moving into your audience's space and in sync with your verbal transitions can captivate a group (Clark & Greatbatch, 2011), but constant movement (even within a small area) will keep attention on your feet rather than your message.

Finally, movement includes changing your physical proximity to your audience. If you are far away then your voice must reach further and do more but it also indicates a discomfort with the audience (Clark & Greatbatch, 2011). Movement is like physical intimacy with new acquaintances. If you keep really far away, they may think that something is wrong with them (or you!). If you get too close then they may think that you are kind of creepy. There *is* a happy medium. (Hint: Take note of the location of the previous presenter; when you begin to present, take one step closer to the audience to help imply a greater level of intimacy and lack of nerves.)

Posture and Stance

One of the most basic distractions that a speaker will create during a presentation is poor posture. **Posture** refers to how you carry yourself from the waist up. Good posture implies confidence, trustworthiness, and persuasive appeal (Briñol & Petty, 2008). Many people have a very relaxed stance in their daily lives and might typically even rest their weight on one hip; this is too lax for being the center of an audience's attention and can give off an unprofessional impression. Keep your feet underneath your shoulders to have a solid base on which your strong posture will be grounded.

Stance refers to your leg position or way of standing. Some speakers will put their feet right up against each other. This stance alone is not a problem but what results from it can be. It is difficult not to lock one's knees in this stance. Locking knees after a bit of time can actually prevent blood from circulating in your body and make you light-headed or even pass out. Instead, keep your feet under your shoulders and your knees relaxed. (Guys: Be aware that your shoulders may not be as wide as you hope; sorry, but keep things realistic or else that "too wide" stance will come off as poor posture.)

Your posture and stance can alter dramatically if you are speaking from a podium or a lectern on a table. When asked to speak in this setting, stand close enough to be able to reach your notes while standing far enough back so that the lectern does not become your *excuse* to lean rather than stand up straight (White, 1964). Lecterns are so very irresistible but resist! When you have a choice, come out from behind any tangible barrier between you and your audience. If you have an ability to connect that other speakers ignore then you increase your chances to be the most effective speaker.

Gestures

Good physical delivery means incorporating meaningful gestures. **Gestures** are the movements of parts of the body, such as a hand or head, to express an idea or meaning. Some people have considered gestures so important that they have been called co-verbal, meaning that they are on equal footing with our use of words to communicate (Wachsmuth, 2006).

Yet, for some reason, when we get in front of an audience, these useful appendages that we have attached to our shoulders (our arms and hands!) become alien objects that we have no idea how to use. We try to hide them behind our backs, clasp them in front of us like a fig leaf, jam them into our pockets, turn them into hair rollers, or use them as fillers when we are searching for words. This game of charades changes the effectiveness of our message because our gestures alter how an audience interprets our message (McNeill, Cassell, & McCullough, 1994). If you think that this means that you should simply gesture at all times regardless of your comfort level, you may be in trouble as well. Gesturing constantly can be worse than not gesturing at all (Maricchiolo, et al., 2009). Therefore, you may want to follow a few basic guidelines:

+ **Keep It Simple** (a few gestures go a long way—they should emphasize *key* ideas, not every idea)

- **Avoid Repetitive Mannerisms** (an overused gesture will render all of your gestures meaningless and trivial)

- **Use Gestures to Clarify a Point** (consider what you would need to do to be clear if your audience could not hear you and use gestures to make proportions and emphasis more clear)

- **Do Not Gesture for the Sake of Gesturing** (eyes are drawn to movement so stay away from gestures that get more attention than your message)

For those who are not prone to natural gestures and do not know what to do with their hands while talking, remember that you should not force yourself to behave in a way that is foreign to you. (Gestures are a tool and you do not need to use every tool at your disposal!)

If you are comfortable gesturing, do it! If you are not, simply avoid doing anything distracting. Drop your hands to your sides, clasp them in a relaxed fashion at your waist level, even consider holding (not waving around) your note page with one hand. If you *will* be gesturing, set those notes down to keep the audience focus on you. Once their focus is on you, think about the expression that they will see.

Facial Expressions

As you stand in front of your audience, you are literally "facing" your listeners. Your face speaks volumes about both your message and how *you feel* about your message. What is on your face will also influence how your listeners feel about the message (Sato & Yoshikawa, 2007). Since this is the case, it is crucial that your facial expressions mirror the emotional content of what it is that you are saying.

If you are talking about something sad, do not smile...that would be weird (and even disturbing). If you are excitedly promoting a product then your face should *show* enthusiasm. If your face connects to the information, it is as if you are adding another visual aid to your talk that can help with audience understanding (Clark & Greatbatch, 2011). Importantly, you should attempt to avoid showing your nervousness on your face. Do not paste on a perma-grin that will have the audience wondering if you have something sinister in mind, but, also, do not look to be in physical pain (we have all seen speakers like this and cringe in sympathy). Practice your business talk in a mirror so that your facial expressions are connected to the content while still being natural to you.

Eye Contact

Strong eye contact, or the act of looking directly into another's eyes, is essential to an effective presentation (Clark & Greatbatch, 2011). In fact, some presentation scholars have suggested that you look at every individual in the eyes for 3 to 5 seconds per person (Zarefsky, 1998). Ok...so let's think about this. Try to go up to a person that you know and make direct eye contact for...one thousand one, one thousand two, one thousand three, etc. To be honest, this is just weird! The eye contact becomes a stare and, rather than connecting, it will make your audience members self-conscious. The key is to have sustained and substantial eye contact long enough to create a connection.

The best guideline for eye contact is to present a complete thought to an individual before moving on to someone else. Imagine Schramm's (1954) feedback loop. This is your time to send a complete thought and then wait for feedback. Because you are most likely, in a business setting, to be speaking extemporaneously, feedback will allow you to make changes as you move through your talk to suit the needs of the audience. If you are looking at your audience and they have the expression of "What the heck is she talking about?" on their faces, you can rephrase, clarify, and adjust as needed. Strong eye contact will help you (for examples, see Propp, 2008):

1. relax as a speaker

2. to have a series of "mini-conversations" with members of your audience

3. to build a bond with the audience

4. acquire feedback

It is often not possible to make eye contact with every single person in your audience. If you are speaking to a large audience (e.g., at a company retreat or a shareholders meeting with hundreds of investors) then eye contact with every person is simply not feasible. You do, however, still want to appear connected to as many people as possible. **Anchors** are select individuals spread out in a large space with whom you make eye contact (i.e., one person in the front middle, another person in the back left, a person in the back right). Mentally divide your audience up into clusters of perhaps ten to twenty people. Select one anchor in a cluster and connect with him or her. The people around that person will also feel as if you have connected with them (Bill Clinton uses this trick!) (Nash, 2010).

If you are speaking and you do not receive feedback from an audience member or anchor (in other words, you are getting the deadpan stare), do not belabor your point. Move on. Come back to that audience member for another idea and see if you connect. If you spend all of your time with one person then the rest of the audience will feel neglected and your ethos will diminish as they see you losing your mastery of the situation. Eye contact will often be dictated by the more tangible environmental aspects of the space in which you are presenting.

6

CONSIDERING YOUR SPACE

Much of your nonverbal communication will be dependent on the presentation's physical situation. What is the location? From where in the space are you speaking? Is it possible to see everyone in the room? Adapting to your space and (more importantly) adapting your space *to you* will help you best connect with your audience.

Every space is different, each offering its own set of opportunities that can be exploited as well as its own set of limitations that you must overcome. The more you know about the venue in which you will be speaking the better you can tailor your presentation to take full advantage. For example, consider what you would do if you were speaking in a room next to cheerleading tryouts for a local professional football team or in a room where the technology is only as fancy as a flip chart when you have painstakingly designed effective PowerPoint slides. Now that you have considered these issues, remember that perfection was never our goal. Effectiveness is our goal and *effective* speakers manipulate their presentations to meet the needs of each rhetorical situation (including the audience and the situational/environmental constraints). Therefore, you will do best when you consider (in no particular order):

- The size of the space
- The shape of the space
- Lighting and sound options
- Technology options
- Sources of ambient noise
- Room temperature (and ability to adjust that temperature)
- Seating arrangements and whether or not seating is flexible or stationary

- The acoustics of the space
- The accessibility of the space
- The amount of room you have for your presentation
- Whether or not there is a lectern
- Available storage (to stow items out of sight until you need them)

While this list is not all-inclusive, it gives you an idea of some of the variables that affect what is possible or not possible for your presentation in a particular venue. You will need to make sure that you *arrive at the room early* enough to adjust your speech to the constraints of your specific environment. If you arrange your room and then the speaker or group before you changes it to what he or she needs, do NOT let their arrangements stand. Own your room! Move their notes out of the way (courteously) and reset the room as you need or your group needs it. You will be more comfortable and the audience will recognize your control of the situation.

PRESENTING WITH A GROUP

In almost all business settings, there will come a time when you are presenting in a group. Some speakers hate this while others find it to be by far the best speaking situation. If we were alone all of the time with no one off whom we could bounce ideas, share the workload, brainstorm, and bond then all the pressure would be on our shoulders. Yes, group work can have its problems but it also has numerous benefits (see Chapter Nine for more details). And, whether you love them or hate them, group work and group presentations are an almost inevitable part of business.

When you are presenting in a group, coordination is the key. You will need to pay special attention to details in order to make sure that your presentation is cohesive—not just a series of individual presentations that happen to be on related topics and are given back to back. To make this happen, in addition to practicing separately (yes, still do this!), you should also run through the entire presentation as a group to make sure the individual parts flow together smoothly.

Group Organization

Group speeches are still speeches. This means that you are all working from a single outline and with a single purpose. Unfortunately, many business presentations are put together by third parties (for example, the Business Development office might organize a presentation that the Programming Team will actually deliver). When you do not have control over your own group then you are going to feel less confident and will be less of an expert even if your company is attempting to share leadership roles (Pearce, Manz, & Sims Jr., 2009).

Take control. First, create your own content whenever possible. If it is not possible then edit content so that it matches the expertise of your particular group. Second, assign roles. Designate one person in the delivery team to be the presentation's coordinator. (It can be tough in our careers to give power over to another person, especially to an equal, but this is necessary to make sure that you *all* look good in the end.) While the details of meeting with and leading a team are important for a business talk, take a moment to simply think of your team as a *presentation unit*. How will you deliver this group message?

Group delivery is about focus. Know who needs to speak when and be sure that the audience focus is on that person rather than on another. No fidgeting or drawing attention, or even zoning out when someone else speaks! One person may be assigned to be the emcee of the presentation by opening and closing the talk and perhaps introducing each element and presenter as they come up as well. After this, each part of the presentation should have an "expert" assigned to that specific area. Be sure to take your own personal preferences out of this part and assign the best person to do the job in the particular area. To show cohesion, all presenters should be assigned generally the same speaking time.

Group Language

If you handed your speech to a colleague and asked that he or she deliver the second main point, the audience might wonder who this person is and why he or she is jumping up in the middle. Audiences need clarity, and group presentations ask for additional verbal clarity. Offer it to them! Include all of the following language in your presentations with others:

+ **Offer Full Names** (After your introduction, be sure to tell folks who is standing there with you before moving along. Give full names and areas of specialty or position titles as part of the preview or the opening.)

+ **Give a "Group" Preview and Review** (When previewing your talk, you will want to tell the audience the person with whom each coverage area is associated; for example, "John, head of marketing, will lay out the needs that you have identified for us; our tech team, Marcy and myself, John, will then go over possible options to satisfy those needs, and, finally, Tom from programming will introduce our product.")

+ **Speech and Group-Oriented Transitions** (Group speeches are no different than singular speeches; you individually would not, in between main ideas, state to your audience that you plan to "hand over" the first idea to the second. Yet, groups tend to think that "hand it over to (name here)" is an acceptable group transition—it is not; keep transitions effective and professional. For example, "As you can see, the financial fraud that Karen discussed is crippling our company, but, with keen attention to details through regular audits, we can change our financial future. Lynn will tell us how.")

+ **Q&A** (While one person should run your Question and Answer session, it is important for ethos that each team member be able to interject answers and speak to his or her own expertise; the coordinator should ask those people to do so as appropriate. For example, "Pamela is our sales executive. Pamela, would you like to address that question?")

Group Look and Movement

You should also be aware of how you *appear* as a unit. Indeed, this means coordinating your attire (not matching; after all, you are not the Rockettes or a boy band). You are professionals who should all appear to have the same level of professional appearance without wearing the same outfits (i.e., all black pants and red button-down shirts is perhaps a bit over the top and distracting, but agreeing to all appear in business casual attire with warm tones can work). It also means coordinating all elements of group visual appeals.

Spread Out, Select, and Move to Speaking Areas

Many groups will come into a room and flank either side of the PowerPoint projector screen. This looks awkward and ill planned. They then will walk up in front of the slides when speaking and back to their designated spot when finished. You might be wondering, "Where else should we stand?" Good question. Consider your space. Would it work to have the first main point speaker begin while in the back of the large auditorium and have the audience turn to become physically involved? If you can be unique without distraction then you stand out. Some presenters might wish to sit until it is their time to speak. Again, figure out if this will work and not distract.

Give One Another Full Attention and Control Distractions

Your audience is only as interested in your team members as you are. Reviewing your notes to make sure that you are prepared is important, so do it before the presentation starts. If group members look inattentive during one another's presentations, why should the audience be attentive? When not presenting, hold your notes to the side or set them down (or do not have any at all) and be sure to give your full attention to either the audience or the speaker. Avoid fidgeting or drawing attention away from the speaker and *never* talk to one another during a presenter's speaking time.

Be Polite with Necessary Interruptions

Someone messed up—and we all know it because your face looks so appalled that you might actually pass out. This is not a good strategy for a group presentation. Your expression just works to distress and distract the audience. You may be thinking, "Oh no! He just gave them the wrong sales figures!!" but your face should be as calm as if things had gone perfectly.

Do not panic, but also do not just let it go. If you let an error pass uncorrected, you may have lost the client because they know that your group was wrong in its analysis. When someone messes up, help the person out by having a coordinated and pre-planned way to step in. Do it with a calm and pleasant facial expression. For example, "Tom, I do apologize for interrupting, but just noticed that we may have pulled up the wrong figures for last year. Can I just shift the slides for you?" Notice the use of "we" rather than the blame of "you." If you do not work together, you will all end up looking bad. This tactic also works well with nervous speakers who tend to go over time (e.g., "Mary, I'm so sorry to interrupt but noticed that we are limited in time. Can I distribute those handouts for you?").

Ultimately, your physical and verbal delivery, whether it is individually or in a group, should be relaxed and engaged. It should connect to the audience and show that you are comfortable enough to have an organized conversation but informed enough to have strong ideas that you express well and without distraction. To get there, practice, practice, practice.

PRACTICING FOR EFFECTIVENESS

Practice makes better (not perfect—remember?). If someone told you that practice makes perfect then they were both wrong and setting you up for failure. We have already talked about the notion of perfection, and you know that you can be extremely effective without being perfect. So, let that idea go and get down to practicing for effectiveness! When you practice your speech you should have two key goals in mind.

Become One with the Ideas

Because you are speaking extemporaneously, you will not memorize your speech word for word. However, you will need to practice to make sure you are comfortable with phrasing ideas in the moment. Your business talk should sound like a conversation that you are having with a peer about a subject that you know like the back of your hand. Try out different language choices as you practice. As you practice, you will settle into wording that is vivid and fluent without having to commit to specific words or completely depend on notes.

Ultimately, you will reduce your notes as you become comfortable with the flow of the ideas in the speech. As you move from session to session, cut your notes down. By your final practice (yes, there should be more than one and even more than three practice sessions!), you should be able to use just a key word outline to jog your memory to the order of stories and data that you do not know without the notes. If you find that you are bound to your notes, you need to keep practicing.

GO BEYOND VISUALIZATION

As you started this speech, you visualized the outcomes. You thought of yourself doing everything right and of any issues that could go wrong and how you would fix them. This was the self-fulfilling prophecy that means that if you believe it, that it is more likely to happen (Merton, 1948). Now that you have crafted every element of your presentation, you need to see how it actually is done and adjust to those discovered needs.

Final sessions of practice are best done in front of an audience rather than in isolation (Smith & Frymier, 2006). You should, as you know, run full dress rehearsals and practice every element of your technical presentation. Your actual day-of presentation is not the time to discover you have technical difficulties. The visual aids chapter (see Chapter Five) talked you through the elements of visual aid creation and delivery, but if you have not practiced that delivery then you may as well guess as to what will happen. Your audience will not care why your planned presentation went sour. They will simply assume that you are not capable.

Practicing your speech fully can let you know where the potential glitches are so you can avoid them, or, if they are unavoidable, you can develop a contingency plan. While no presentation ever goes exactly as planned, some go better! What matters is how you handle whatever happens *during* your presentation. By using every delivery tool that you can then you are in the best shape to make your message count! Remember, we do not have to be perfect but we do strive to be effective.

6

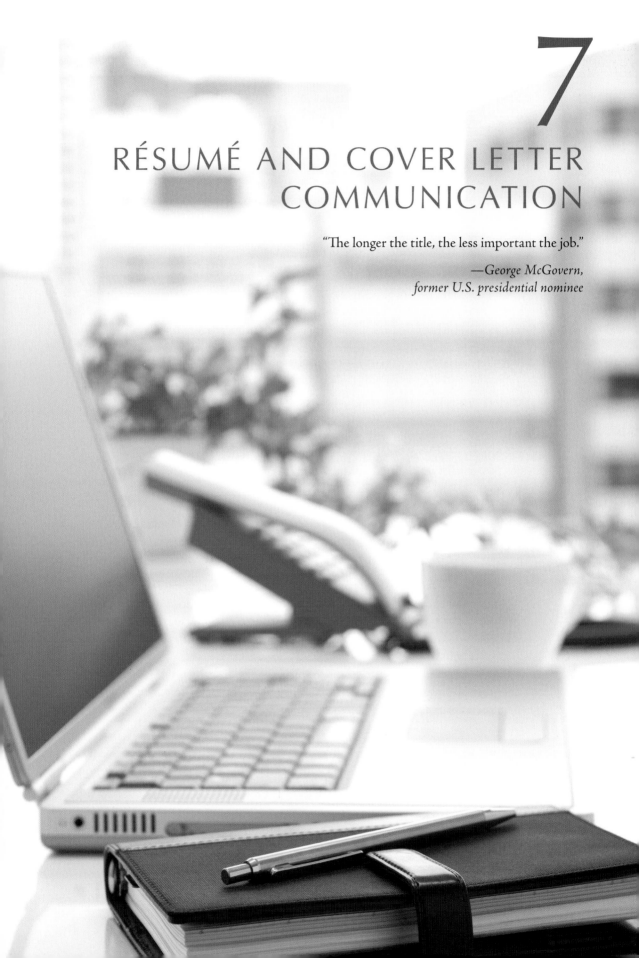

RÉSUMÉ AND COVER LETTER COMMUNICATION

"The longer the title, the less important the job."

—George McGovern,
former U.S. presidential nominee

THE RÉSUMÉ AND COVER LETTER EXPERIENCE

So…you speak Finnish? Graduated top in your class? Were responsible for 100% of your last company's profits, *and* you planned an initiative to create world peace?! Wow! Or, actually, whoa! Why do people think that lying on a résumé or cover letter will somehow impress? (This only works in the movies!) Neither of these documents should be your attempt to craft an identity of who you *want* to be; they should be a representation of the best version of your *real* self applicable to a particular job, company, and industry.

Let's start here: you do not need to lie. Aside from the ethical ramifications of this (which you should already have in your mind from our earlier discussion), it is better to start by re-evaluating what *you* have to offer. First, you are unique. No one has the experience that you do and no one has the characteristics that you have. Second, you *do* have something to offer. The reason that most people lie on a résumé or in a cover letter is because they believe that they do not have enough of what a company wants to get a job. In fact, you don't have the experience to get *all* jobs—but would you really want them? If you are a sophomore in college and applying for a CEO position with only experience of babysitting on your résumé, you will not get that job. More importantly, you should not want it. When people get jobs for which they are not qualified then they spend their time panicking, playing catch-up, and typically failing to effectively communicate (for the limited time that they have the jobs). That being said, if you have babysitting in your experience then you have the skills of multitasking, crisis management, maintaining a safe working environment, and organizing group activities along with a calm, amiable personality. Wow! Now, that is impressive and it comes without a lie.

The goals of résumés and cover letters are simple: to get you the interview. This being said, the notion of encapsulating all of your skills, accomplishments, talents, and potential for career success into a crisp, concise form can be daunting. Do not be intimidated! Whether you already have a great résumé but would like some expert thoughts on it, you feel ill-prepared to write a résumé, or you have a résumé but are still mastering the craft of cover letter "talk," then this chapter will help you with the strategic business communication to use for these specialized mediums. Job seekers who demonstrate credibility and choose a format that showcases their content as well as a connection with an employer are far more likely to catch a recruiter's eye than those depending on tricks such as paper style, color, or scent. This chapter will give you clear guidelines for preparing a professional résumé as well as an excellent cover letter.

WHAT IS A RÉSUMÉ?

A résumé is more than a piece of paper that lists all the jobs that you have had. A **résumé** is a mechanism for articulating your skills, experience, personal style, and accomplishments specific to a job or industry. Your résumé is a vital tool in business communication because it is your first connection to potential employers or clients. If delivered well, your résumé can showcase your experience and land you that desired interview for that sought-after job. Without a solid résumé, you will rarely have an opportunity to engage in business talk with an employer to show him or her that you are the ideal candidate (Thoms, McMasters, Roberts, & Dombkowski, 1999). In order to fit the needs of this rhetorical situation, consider what makes a *good* résumé.

First, good résumés, from the viewpoint of employers and recruiters, are a *concise*, written summary of skills, knowledge, and experience that is relevant to the position to which you are applying (Hornsby & Smith, 1995; Praetorius & Lawson, 2004). Résumés are not an autobiography, so do not feel the need to cram in every one of your experiences and skills. View it as a sales brochure where you will highlight your most relevant and impressive attributes.

Your résumé will best *sell* you if it:

+ is clear, succinct, and easy for employers to quickly scan,

+ stands out from the others,

+ is inviting to look at (not distracting), and

+ is persuasive (clearly showing that you are qualified, competent, and can deliver results).

Important: *Persuasive does not mean inaccurate.* The element of résumé credibility is becoming more crucial every day, especially in a technologically advancing age.

7

Résumé Credibility

What do former Yahoo CEO Scott Thompson, former RadioShack® CEO Dave Edmonson, and former Notre Dame head football coach George O'Leary all have in common? They are all *former*, which means that they were all fired from their jobs for, in these cases, being caught padding or fudging information on their résumés (Jacobs, 2012; Kidwell, 2004).

Despite these high profile examples of the results of résumé padding, many job seekers still risk lying. In fact, 49% of hiring managers have caught a lie on a candidate's résumé (Career Builder, 2008). Even those who swear they would never lie on a résumé can be tempted to embellish or stretch résumé content. For example, a writer may claim she is fluent in French, when really her knowledge of the language is limited to one semester abroad. It could be that somehow that 2.9 grade point average got rounded to a 3.2. Your résumé is an amazing tactic for creating a connection between you and a potential employer; it is also a fantastic hard copy of any lie that you offered, which can subsequently be evidence to get you fired (the folks above learned that lesson the hard way!). Be cautious. If you struggle with résumé ethics or have taken outrageous poetic license with the titles and responsibilities listed on your document, you may not even get an interview for the job at all. Remember—you do not need to lie. Detailed and descriptive (but accurate) explanations of who you truly are will be the most effective communication that you can use to obtain your ideal career!

Résumé Tailoring

As you read through the discussion in this chapter, you will be advised time and time again to tailor the information on your résumé specifically to a single job. It may seem daunting to draft dozens of documents. You actually will not. Begin your process by creating one document and then altering the details of that document to fit specific positions. For those who have ever lost a document (and haven't we all!), be sure to save each one on your computer under the name of the job (e.g., "Tri-State Public Relations Res.docx" and "Vernon Advertising Res.docx").

This process of tailoring is an appropriate act of audience analysis followed by message customization. You did this when crafting your business talks so that every message would be accurately decoded (see Schramm, 1954). But all of this tailoring might lend you to receive some conflicting advice. You might go online to Monster.com or TheLadders or another résumé source and find very different recommendations for the format or content of your document. There is a reason for this that you already know: résumé creation is very specific to the industry, personal experience, style, and, yes, preference.

Like all forms of communication, résumé (and cover letter) crafting starts by considering the needs of the audience. In this case, the audience is employers and recruiters. This means that both documents must place the needs of the audience above your own needs and preferences as well as be crafted to suit the medium where they will be read. What works for one employer may not work for another and it will be your job to research which one will work best in a given setting. Employers and even your most trusted resources will provide contradictory recommendations. With all of the contradicting "advice," it is no wonder that many first-time résumé writers are bewildered. Do not fret. All you are hearing is that message receivers would like their messages encoded in a way that is easiest for them to decode. You are already a skilled expert in this tactic and the remainder of our discussion here will help you to place your skill in a résumé/cover letter context!

Part of the context of résumé creation is knowing that the channel by which you will send your résumé has dramatically changed in the last few years. Today, we are going digital! In the quest to put all information into an online format, you may have even heard that paper résumés are no longer necessary because of electronic submission requirements or career networking websites such as LinkedIn. This is not actually true. The majority of human resources directors surveyed by Robert Half (2012) in their Resourcing and Talent study argued that online résumés and profiles will never make traditional methods obsolete. Instead, you must know how to submit résumés in both the traditional sense (which simply means printing it and handing it over) as well as in a digital medium.

Digital Résumés and Portfolios

Job seekers who know the intricacies of the online job application process have a far more likely chance of success than those who do not. Unfortunately, current academic literature does not provide a consensus on the requirements for résumé content for digital recruiting (Furtmueller & Wilderom, 2001). What we know instead is that the crafting of a "hire me" message in any medium must be clear and articulate. The crafting of a clear message online requires a moderate mastery of the nature by which employers use online resources.

Online Locations and Practices

Where do employers look for potential employees? These days, that answer is less and less in the traditional sense or even electronic "job boards" such as Monster or CareerBuilder. McGregor (2010) found that only 13% of external hires at Fortune 500 companies are filled using job boards and that senior positions tend to ignore job boards all together, valuing instead referrals and personal recommendations. The Wharton School's Cappelli (Knowledge@Wharton, 2012b) explains this phenomenon by arguing that these systems are not as efficient as they once were in part because of the explosion of users. Companies are receiving too many résumés to process and users sense (not incorrectly) that their applications are ending up in "a black hole" (para. 4).

So, if posting your résumé on a basic online job board is not the answer, where should a job seeker post their résumés and profiles? Today, that answer is LinkedIn and other social media job websites. Jobvite's annual survey of recruiters who hire online showed that 87% plan to use LinkedIn, 55% plan to use Facebook, and 49% plan to use Twitter (see Russo, 2011). To increase your chances of a hiring manager actually seeing your résumé, you will need to adapt your strategies to the needs of this new era but also use social media appropriately in your professional setting. Job seekers should invest in polishing their online presence—as well as creating one that reflects their professionalism and potential.

You may have had it beaten into your head (figuratively) that your online presence must be kept to professional standards. Let us beat that in a bit more! Whether we like it or not, Facebook and other social media websites do influence hiring or even interview contact decisions (Knowledge@Wharton, 2012a). You may have a wonderful LinkedIn page and hope that potential employers will only go there but, do not be fooled; they will also be looking to see if that same professional image is shown on your Facebook page, your Twitter account, Pinterest, or any other online version of yourself. The task of being professional must cut across all of these mediums. If your goal is to have a professional online presence then start with these basics.

First, make sure your profile has a recent and professional picture. LinkedIn profiles that show pictures are viewed *seven times more often* than profiles with a blank box, and, unfortunately, the absence of a picture can even lead the recruiter to not trust the profile (Casserly, 2012). Second, unlike traditional résumés where less is more, your social media website is the place to communicate as much about yourself as you can. Let employers know who you are by completing all aspects of your profile, uploading examples of writing work, and even linking to blogs or websites. This does not mean that your LinkedIn profile should list twenty or even forty "skills;" what you show online is a brand of yourself. If you show that you know everything then an employer might think that you are compensating for knowing nothing. Brand yourself with the key words and examples that show off your uniqueness. These steps make it easier for an employer to find you and get a full picture of you as a person and as a professional (Adams, 2012). Finally, use your rhetorical skills to send a message of interest but not desperation, which implies a lacking skill set or lack of social skills. "Seek recommendations from your contacts but avoid anything that screams 'I'm looking for a new job.' You'll tip off your employer, and you'll look desperate to other recruiters" (Volmar, 2010, p. 7).

Just as you are using technology to find a job, employers are using technology to build a full understanding of you. Most large organizations (and some small ones) are allowing tracking software to evaluate all the communication that you send out as part of your application.

ATS

Applicant Tracking Software (ATS) is one of the most basic software programs used by recruiters (Hauser, 2001). In general, ATS searches for key words linked to credentials and experience and then ranks candidates by how well they match the job opening (Vaas, 2012). In this day and age, you can almost assume that organizations will want to take advantage of anything that eases their search process. So, you can expect that your online résumé, along with every  other electronic communication that you send (e.g., email inquiries about the job, cover letters, thank you notes, etc.), will be screened by ATS.

The good news for our sudden embrace of this software is that ATS can make the application process easier for you, save money for companies, and broaden the candidate pool (Wessel, 2012). On the other hand, ATS makes it hard for applicants to stand out (Amare & Manning, 2009; Knowledge@Wharton, 2012b) and survive the initial screening step. Why is this? Basically, ATS typically screens out 50% of total applicants (Weber & Silverman, 2012)! The wonderful aspect of this is that the software eliminates candidates with typos, no connection to the open position, and those with poor communication skills (error-prone job seekers beware!). Unfortunately, ATS cannot read *potential* and can just as easily screen out qualified candidates for not using the correct key terms or not using them in context (Weber and Silverman, 2012).

There is no single, fail-proof plan of attack for navigating ATS; however, these guidelines from Vaas (2010) can increase your chances of not getting cut before a real, live human has a chance to evaluate you:

+ do not apply to the same job multiple times

+ although ATS does look for key words, simply using the words are not enough—they must be highly descriptive and used in context

+ do not abbreviate or use acronyms; the ATS will not understand

+ avoid misspellings in any communication medium that you submit and never leave parts of the application blank

7

You are in! You have made it past the software and someone is actually looking at your materials. Congratulations. Now comes the part where you want to make sure that you have ethically posted materials so that the person reading your portfolio feels confident to bring you in for an interview.

The Legality of Posting Online Information

By now, most job seekers know the dangers of posting embarrassing or career limiting information and pictures. However, sometimes, posting examples of work samples in an electronic portfolio can cause credibility (and legal) problems for the job seeker—especially if the work sample is the intellectual property of the company (Condon, 2009). For example, if you have created a PowerPoint slideshow while working with one company and it contains that company's logo or private information then you cannot legally post that slideshow online as an example of your work. That work is owned by your former employer. Furthermore, honesty, while important in traditional job searches, is vital in digital résumés and portfolios because information is so easily and readily checked. Those who enhance their résumé with better grades or stretch their description of work responsibilities will be easily and quickly discovered and probably will not have their credibility restored (Casserly, 2012).

Creating an Online Presence—Get Yourself Out There!

While a poorly presented Facebook profile can diminish chances of receiving a call back, no online presence at all can be worse. Imagine attempting to find the best place to go for dinner in a new town. You would look online to see what recommendations you could find. If you find absolutely nothing on a restaurant but an address online with no further details, it is a risk to make that your selection. Employers tend to not want to risk the resources of an interview on a candidate whose merit cannot be verified (Smith, 2011). Ways to develop a positive online presence include joining online professional association directories (McGregor, 2010) and creating an online portfolio of work samples that match the desired job (Condon, 2009).

You will want to use all of your online resources to make sure that your introductory materials (your résumé and cover letter) are viewed! If they are viewed then you will want to make sure that they are crafted in the absolute best way possible. All résumés have the same purpose but, whether it be online or the traditional print version, you must choose the format and the content that is best suited to your situation.

RÉSUMÉ FORMATS

Take a look at as many résumés as you can. Look online. Look at your friends' résumés. Look at every résumé that the company for which you want to work has posted. Notice anything? Résumés can look very different and, disappointingly, similar, too. Job applicants who are trying to stand out might choose formatting that is confusing or cluttered. Those new to the process have a tendency to

go online and just copy (in format only, we hope) the layout of another. Selecting the appropriate format for your résumé is the same as selecting the appropriate channel for your message (Berlo, 1960). You must choose wisely to achieve the feedback that you desire.

The Layout and Style of Your Résumé

If you do not want to look like everyone else, who do you want to look like? You, of course. But, who are you on this page? Now is the time to consider the stylistic look that best demonstrates you while still staying appropriate to the industry and the job. For instance, if you are working in a creative industry such as advertising or graphic design then you have the leeway to have a more stylized résumé look (Schultze, Kim, & Bolles, 2012, p. 9). If you are an applicant to a very traditional law firm then keep away from the bold colors, lines and graphics, and maintain a more basic overall visual feel for your résumé.

Choose your look by first seeing what others have done and then making alterations toward a look that best suits your situation. Résumé experts suggest that you keep things simple, uncluttered, and that the document guides the eye from the primary information to the support (see Schultze, Kim, & Bolles, 2012). You can follow those guidelines through any number of layouts. For several examples, consider looking at the résumé images supplied by Workbloom (2012) or any other online resource. (We will spend time later in this chapter on the use of bold, italics, and other *content specific* style.)

7

Templates and Trends

As you look at others' résumés, you will start to see trends. For example, résumé writers often use the same categories on their résumés. Also, time and time again, you will see the same layout and the same font. You will begin to notice that if you are not focused on the content but step back to examine the *look* then many résumés appear to be the same document with a different name. They probably are. These résumés most likely have been created through the use of a template.

A **template** is a styling tool in a word processing program that provides a pattern in which users can fill in details to produce a document. While using a standard format can help to get you started with the creation of a résumé (what goes on it and a sense of looks or layouts), you will soon realize the drawbacks with such a form (Washington & Kanter, 2009). First, you will look like everyone else. Your résumé will not stand out. Second, you will not be able to include new categories that are not on the template and often you may not be able to add or delete the offered categories. Third, you will be forced to stick to a given layout that has been seen time and time again.

Avoid template downfalls by starting with a blank page and making your own decisions about what should go on that page. You should start by considering what look best suits your style (lines, fonts, bullet style) followed by considering what format—chronological or functional—is more appropriate.

Organizational Formats

Putting together your résumé includes more than just designing a pretty page— it is about organizing your information to grab and inspire a potential employer. Organizational formats should suit your purpose and reveal your background in the most appealing way. You have a few choices of format but, just as you will go back and later alter the content of your résumé to suit a specific job, know that you may also want to go back and alter the *format* on some versions of your résumé to suit a specific employer's needs as well.

General Formatting

To start, try to organize your résumé in a **sandwich approach** (meaning that the most important information should come first then the second most important information will go last and the least important, but still highly relevant, information goes in the middle). This will likely be the order in which employers will read your résumé, so you do not want to bury the most important information when there is no guarantee the employer will get to it. At the initial stage of screening résumés, employers spend an average of less than 30 seconds scanning each résumé (Markey & Campell, 1996), so make sure that you do not hide the good stuff!

The two most common formats for résumé writing are *chronological* and *functional*. These two résumé formats are means of arranging the categorized content sections of your résumé. Which one you select should be determined by how much experience you have and what you want to communicate.

Chronological Formats

The **chronological résumé format** organizes your experiences by time. While the true definition of any chronological organization is from the first to the last, most résumés using this format are actually in **reverse chronological order**, which directs you to arrange your experience from the most recent positions and work (no pun intended) down to least recent.

❖ **Manager**, *Cliffhanger Garage Band*, Austin, TX	May 2006–Present
❖ **Wait Staff**, *Brunches R Us*, Grover Beach, CA	June 2004–April 2006
❖ **Hostess**, *Johnny Brenda's*, Philadelphia, PA	January 2002–April 2004

(See how the most recent jobs come first and then go backwards to the least recent experience?)

A reverse chronological organizational format helps an employer to see what you are currently *able* to do and how your experience *led* to those abilities. You will adopt this format to show a clear *history* of your experiences and/or to highlight progressive career *growth* and advancement. When done well, the chronological format allows employers to quickly get a snapshot of how you have built your skill set over time. For this reason, it is the most accepted—if not expected—format among hiring authorities (Thoms, McMasters, Roberts, & Dombkowski, 1999).

A word of caution to those who now assume that you will use this format. Just because something is expected, does not mean that you should automatically do it. There are some problems associated with the use of this format that might highlight issues in your experience (Weinstein, 2012). For instance, chronological formats:

- highlight gaps in your employment

- negatively show frequent changes in jobs or careers, making you look scattered in your focus

- work against those with little to no work experience because time progression will highlight inexperience rather than allow you to draw attention to volunteer work, special projects, or coursework

Functional Format

For those career-minded folks who see more problems than gains in presenting their experience with a chronological résumé format, consider instead the functional format. The **functional résumé format** organizes the experience section of your résumé by *specific skill sets*. To clarify the method of this format, think back to your last business talk. A speech on fashion could certainly be given chronologically (e.g., moving from one decade to the next) but it could also be given by *function* or by category (e.g., classic, couture, grunge, ready-to-wear). Functional résumés are means of grouping your background by skills and accomplishments. If you have had one job for a very long period of time but within that job you have had important groups of experience then a functional résumé helps to highlight your skill sets. The look of a functional résumé is something like this:

Professional Summary
(brief paragraph here about qualifications)

Selected Accomplishments
bulleted list
details
details

Professional Expertise
Management
details here
more details

Horticultural Supervision
details here
more details

Business Analysis
details here
more details

Employment History
Job Title
Company
limited details here

Job Title
Company
limited details here

Education
Degree
School information

You can see in this example that, rather than organizing information on the résumé by time, the skills and accomplishments become the organizational headers.

Just because you show skill *categories* does not mean that you do not list job experience. You will de-emphasize your job timeline by placing it after your skill groups—perhaps even toward the bottom of your résumé (see example) and some applicants, especially executives, might even select not to put dates of any kind next to those employment details. This is just a list of past employers but the details of the individual jobs have already been laid out in the functional expertise categories!

Consider using a functional résumé format if you have very little or a very significant amount of job experience, have made career changes (for example, those people who started out nursing but want to become an advertising executive!), or if you have had gaps in employment. It is also a great way to re-order your experience so that you are highlighting applicable sets of job-related skills.

Suppose you are applying to a position as a web designer and you worked at a web design agency up until last year. However, your previous jobs as well as your current job are as an administrative assistant. While this new job will certainly have some applicable skills, you know the web design experience is more likely to impress the employer. You can include a section called "Relevant Web Design Experience" (where you include your most relevant experiences in reverse chronological order) and then a section *after* called "Administrative Experience" (where you include your remaining experiences in reverse chronological order).

While the functional résumé format may make flaunting your transferrable skills easier, it too should be used with caution. Since it is not the most widely used format and not as straightforward as a chronological format, employers may not fully understand your functional communication. If you are not careful, a functional format can lead to confusion, skepticism, or even annoyance if the amount of experience is unclear. Some employers may even think that use of this format means that you are trying to hide something (Olsen, 2006). Be specific and clear to show that person that you are simply using the rhetorical tool suited best to both of you!

7

You know about the formats that are available to you for organizing your information, however, you still might be unsure which organization will best serve your needs. To make this decision easier, consider what you want *on* your résumé (the content) and then decide how to organize that content to add to or polish off your masterpiece.

CONTENT: WHAT TO INCLUDE AND WHAT NOT TO INCLUDE

The goal of every line of your résumé is to keep the employer reading. That person should want to know what comes next and be excited for the story that will unfold. By the time the employer reaches the end of your résumé story, you will have shown that you are worthy of an interview. The content of your résumé is the meat (or tofu) of your story!

If you have ever read a story that seems to meander and not get to its point then you know the pain of many hiring managers. Résumés have very little time to get to the point—sometimes mere moments (Thoms, McMasters, Roberts, & Dombkowski, 1999). It is crucial that you do not include unnecessary information or fluff on your résumé. Every word, phrase, and line on your résumé is valuable real estate; therefore, you must be thoughtful of what to include and what to *not* include.

Length: How Long Should Your Résumé Be?

The first question that most folks ask when preparing a résumé is, "How long should it be?" What they are really asking is, "How much information should I include on my résumé?" Good question. Once again, there is no formula. Some people who have been in their industry a very long time or have made significant accomplishments will have résumés beyond ten pages. Many industries will expect résumés of this length. Those starting out will likely not have a lengthy résumé and might be stretching to fill a single sheet. The reality is that almost everyone needs a one-page version of their résumé (Schultze, Kim, & Bolles, 2012).

Even people with multiple-page résumés are expected to have a one-page version of their longer documents to offer as career summaries. Although you may have limited experience, you will want to fill an entire page (the rest of this chapter will help you know how to do that) in order to show that even your limited experience represents a wide skill set. If you are newly out of school but have a good deal of experience to highlight then going to a second page *may* be appropriate depending on your industry. Be sure that if you do decide to extend that standard page length that you are not so brief as to imply that an edit could have done the job. If you have spilled over to the next page—use it! Be sure to fill at least three quarters of your final page.

Crucial Contact

Once you start to fill your page, start with the crucial information—who and where you are. Having your name and contact information is necessary for all résumés. It does not matter what industry you hope to join, all employers that are hiring will want to know who you are and how to reach you. You will want to make this visible and easy to read.

The layout of your document will dictate where to put these crucial details but this résumé information has its own distinct style and guidelines. First, unlike other sections of your résumé, your contact information will not have a special heading such as "Contact Information" (no worries—the employer gets that). Instead, simply place the information at the top of the page under or near your name. You will also want to guide the reader's eye to the information by increasing the size of your name (perhaps to a 16-point font) but leaving your contact details a smaller size.

Your contact information speaks volumes about what kind of job you will do. First, you will not want to give the employer more work than necessary by listing more than one address or telephone number. Why would this person want to spend time tracking you down when someone else is so easy to reach? You will also want this information to show that you are detail-oriented and professional.

> **Contact Information Formatting Guidelines**
> - List your full nine-digit zip code; this shows you off as detail-oriented
>
> - Double-check any abbreviations of your state and address; for example, the commonly accepted abbreviation is "PA" not "Pa"
>
> - Avoid "cool" voicemail messages, email addresses, or hold music—what is fun and funny for you can often leave a bad impression with an employer (Southam, 2006)

You now have a résumé look and have let people know how to find you. You have not yet let people know who you are. This will happen with the selection of the categories on your résumé and what you list within each of them.

Potential Categories

Categories are the groups of information that label (with headers) your applicable experience. These elements serve to organize your information and they speak volumes about the kind of job or industry that you are seeking out. Think of your categories and category headers as the preview highlights for the 6 o'clock news. These will say the relevant sound bites and the details will come later. Select the categories that best sell your skills for the particular job that you want. Remember, there is no single formula to résumé creation. Make your decisions about categories based on what will link you to the job and never based upon what a template told you to do.

Objective Category

An objective is an *optional* element of the résumé. Your **objective** should quickly and concisely let the reader know your professional career goals at that very moment. This is a hotly debated component of résumé writing, where some experts insist you need one (Hoheb, 2002; Smith, 2002) and others insist that it is highly problematic to have one (Ross & Young, 2005; Washington & Kanter, 2009). Why?

Objectives are slivers of who you are in a moment, which can either be highly relevant or drastically off-base. Think of it this way: if you are applying to a specific job based upon a listed advertisement then the employer already knows your objective...*to get that job!* This means that including it is a waste of valuable space—that real estate mentioned previously. Your cover letter gives you the opportunity to expand on your goals, so again, your objective becomes rather redundant.

There are, however, some instances where an objective can be useful. One useful time may be if you are *not* applying to a specific position but instead you are sending your résumé to your dream company in hopes that they will have an opening in your area in the near future. In other words, you are targeting a company with whom you would like to be employed and need to let them know the capacity in which you would like to do this. If this is the case then it is important for the company to know what you are looking for and an objective can serve this purpose.

Another situation where an objective may be useful is if you are looking for employment by networking. For example, you talked to your aunt, uncle, friend, professor—whomever—and they told you they would be happy to pass along your résumé. Of course, in this instance, there is not a posted position to which you are applying, so again, it becomes important to make clear what *you* are looking for in a work setting. If you are indeed including an objective statement, here are some guidelines to follow:

- Be short and concise (one sentence, two at the most)

- Do not be so specific that you eliminate opportunities in which you might be interested (such as including specific job titles rather than focusing on a range of jobs you would be willing to consider)

- Try to incorporate your most marketable skills in the objective

Consider some examples of objectives that help and some that can clearly work against the applicant.

> **Objective Issues Resolved**
>
> <u>Not specific enough—BAD</u>: "To obtain an internship allowing me to utilize my knowledge and expertise in different areas."
>
> <u>More specific—GOOD</u>: "To obtain an internship in Human Resources, with a specific interest in training and development."
>
> <u>Wordy yet vague—BAD</u>: "Looking to obtain a successful career with a progressive company that will utilize my education, skills and experience in an executive capacity, where I can effectively contribute to the overall growth of the company in a way that best utilizes my diverse skill set."
>
> <u>Descriptive yet concise—GOOD</u>: "To secure an entry-level paralegal position at Smith Law Associates, exploring the field of tax law and collection."

Summary of Qualifications/Summary of Skills Category

The summary section is another *optional* element that you can include in place of or in addition to an objective statement. **Summary of qualifications** is a category that serves as a brief abstract of your professional life. They are most likely found on résumés of those who work within a precise field of experience or executives in the field, but can sometimes work for those who are attempting to highlight an element of one's vast experience (NACE, 2011).

Consider your summary to be a teaser or preview for what is to come. Your goal is to convince the reader to read on. It should help the employer answer the question, "What can this person do for me?" To answer that question, include three to six high impact statements that showcase your strongest selling points for that particular position. Prioritize these statements so that the most important, impressive, and relevant come first. You can see how these summaries might be used for both a mid-level position and for someone looking to obtain a far more executive job.

7

Editorial Assistant

Key Qualifications:

- Published author and conference speaker
- Three years experience as an English tutor
- Facilitated SAT prep training to diverse student population
- Skilled web page designer

PROFESSIONAL SUMMARY

Attorney with significant international experience and a focus on high stakes litigation, saving client resources through corporate management; Areas of focus include: international manufacturing, commercial agreements, employment law, and corporate governance.

As with all résumé information, you will need to tailor your summary to meet the needs of a particular job. Again, this is not about lying—it is about finding elements of your skill set to sell and others to leave out because they do not fit into the message that you are sending in this situation.

Education Category

The education section is likely to be the only non-optional category on any résumé. Most individuals have some kind of education or training and this is your chance to brag about that status. If you are in college or a recent graduate then bravo! You have current specialized training that is not to be ignored. You may have taken fabulous classes (e.g., Business Communication) or even achieved recognition on a Dean's list. This could be the highlight of your résumé that serves to lead off the document or it could be the culmination of your superb explanation of your skills.

Allow your education information to sell you. It might be brief (most executives leave this as a *mention* near the end of résumés) or lengthy (many almost-graduates lead with their upcoming degree and even add relevant coursework to this section). When you are applying to internships or first entering the professional workforce, your education information will be limited and listed just below your contact information. On the other hand, if your experience sections are stronger, then you will want to move your education section to the end of your résumé. You will need to determine what works best for your situation but, in general, there are some practical guidelines:

- list your university or college training in reverse chronological order (put in the name of the school and the city or state to be clear)

- list all places of education (you do not want to be accused of lying when you list only one school but have taken coursework or even spent years at another institution)

- include the full name of your degree, not the abbreviation (e.g., Bachelor of Arts rather than BA) or let the audience know that you are still, "Major: Undeclared."

- clarify the date of your graduation or expected graduation

- only list your GPA if it *sells* you, which means in most cases not listing anything below a 3.5 (do not worry if your GPA is a bit lower—Bill Gates did not have a stellar GPA and he still did just fine for himself!)

- avoid listing your high school degree; for those who are pursuing a college degree, it is implied that you have earned a high school diploma, therefore, no need to include your high school information here

Education

West Chester University of PA
Expected Graduation: May 2011
Bachelor of Science; Department of Biology
GPA: 3.9

You may do more than just list the basic information. You may wish to add additional details or subpoints/categories that will help show what you have learned during your education. If so, keep the formatting clear and the information relevant. This may include elements such as a double major, a minor or concentration, programs of study abroad, relevant coursework, or academic honors.

There are many designs or layouts to use for this section but here are few good ideas to help you consider what works best for you.

7

Education

West Chester University of PA
Bachelor of Arts: Department of Communication Studies
Anticipated Graduation: June 2014
Summa Cum Laude

Course Highlights:

- Principles of Public Relations
- Web Page Design
- Principles of Marketing

- Advanced Public Speaking
- Persuasion
- Computers & Applications

EDUCATION

❑ University of California San Diego
❑ **Bachelor of Science, Department of Finance/Minor in Information Technology**
❑ AACSB Accredited University
❑ *3.8 GPA*
❑ Expected Graduation: December 2013

Education

Avery Institute for Creative Minds – San Francisco, CA
Anticipated Graduation: May 2010
Bachelor of Science in Science Technology
Secondary Education Certification

Delaware County Community College – Media, PA
Graduation Date: May 2007
Associate of Science in Biology

Experience Category

Before beginning a discussion on experience, it is important for you to know that no matter where you are in your career, if you are drafting a résumé, *you have experience*. One of the most common concerns of those who are early in their career paths, including students, is that they have "no experience." That is simply not true. If you are in college, if you have been in a club, if you have helped just about anybody to do just about anything—then you have experience! Your concern should be how to best show off that experience and link it to the job for which you are applying.

An experience section emphasizes your past and present employment or your participation in relevant activities. It is likely the lengthiest portion of your résumé because this is the place where you demonstrate your capabilities to potential employers. As with all of your materials and any business talk, you will want to link your terminology to the audience (in this case, to the job description). For this reason, you should rarely, if ever, use the header "Experience."

The title "Experience" actually means nothing because it is too vague. You must customize your headings to describe your experience as they relate to the job, often by mirroring the exact language from the job advertisement. That's right—if it says, "need experienced sales consultant" and your résumé lists a "Retail Sales Experience" category, make the quick edit in language to "Sales Consultant Experience." This new description is still accurate but is also now showing the employer the buzz words that will catch the eye of the hiring manager or ATS. You may discover you need more than one category to represent your relevant experiences.

Some possible headings for your experience may be:

- Work History (for a brief list of jobs in a functional résumé)

- Field Work

- Volunteer Work

- Internships

- Research Assistantships

- Editorial Work

- Management Experience

- (Or any title linked to the position: Public Relations Experience; Teaching Experience; Broadcasting Experience; Nursing Experience; etc.)

As with your résumé itself, you will want to consider the layout of this content element before launching into the details. Note in the following example how the position title pops. The name of the company should be included along with the month and year that you started and finished the work (current jobs are listed as "current" or "present"). Next, the layout guides the eye toward the descriptions. (*Remember that this is just an example of organization; you may be using a different look, which is great—as long as you include all the relevant parts!*)

> **Position Title**
> *Name of Company,* City, State   Month/Year–Month/Year
> * Job tasks, skills acquired, and accomplishments—starting with action word
> * Do your best to keep each item to one line
> * Be concise and avoid full sentences
> * Use variety in language choice

Activities and Honors Category

In some instances, what makes you the most marketable may not be your work experience but something altogether unique, such as out-of-the-classroom activities and special awards. Including an "Honors" section is optional (and should not be included if you do not have these) but can be crucial if you lack work experience or training/background in the field. If you have a good deal of activities and/or relevant awards, you can make a fantastic impression. An awards and/or activities section (which can be combined or listed as completely different categories) might include the following:

* Academic awards and scholarships

* Membership in campus, national, or international organizations

* Leadership positions held in campus, national, or international organizations

* University and community service/volunteer positions

You will choose the categories that are relevant to you. Be sure not to combine too many. If an employer sees the category, "Volunteer Experience, Activities, Honors, Memberships," then you look a bit scattered rather than exceptionally accomplished!

The relevance of the activities and the importance of the activity will help you decide how to format this section. You might list a single club experience like a job because you did so much for it—or you might find that a simple and to-the-point list serves you much better. For example:

President, English Club

West Chester University, West Chester, PA   August 2007–Current

- Organize and plan student networking events

- Collaborate with university faculty to plan campus-wide activities

- Recruit students, resulting in 55% membership increase in one year

- Plan and oversee essay writing contest

- Tutor and mentor underprivileged youth in inner city

- Manage all organization fundraising efforts (raising over $5000 in two years)

ASU Campus Activities
- Member   Student Government   August 2007–Present
- President   Investment Club   January 2008–Present
- Treasurer   Accounting Association   August 2008–May 2009

Computers and the "Other" Skills Category

Let us take a moment to address the infamous "Other Skills" category. What does it mean? If you have to ask—or worse, if a potential employer does—then these skills are not likely to sell you very well. Just like any other section, your skills sections should absolutely link to the job that you want. First, the section is optional. Second, the skills that you list should also appear *in the descriptions* of past/current jobs (e.g., if you list that you are skilled in PowerPoint usage, make sure that you have this as part of your college training from your SPK 230 course, or if you state that you have mastered website design, be sure to describe how you put together the website for your summer job at *Claudia's Organic Farm*). ATS systems will select you out if you list skills that are not part of your described work and if you list inapplicable skills.

Many students believe that they are well-suited to label their "Other" skills as "Computer Skills" instead (Schultze, Kim, & Bolles, 2012). Computer skills are perhaps the most useful and generally applicable skills, but most everyone has the basics so listing the three Microsoft Office programs (Word®, PowerPoint, Excel) does nothing to show that you actually have skills with any of these. If you only have a few computer skills then drop the section and simply insert the language into the descriptions of actual jobs. List only the computer languages and programs in which you have *strong skills* and always be honest about your abilities. If you cannot apply a formula in an Excel spreadsheet and easily run a macro, do not list this software as one of your "skills."

7

COMPUTER SKILLS
- Proficient with operating systems using all recent versions of Windows
- Skilled in using all Microsoft Office programs
- Visual Basic, SQL, and web page design expertise
- Certificate in computer security

If you do decide to list skills, consider offering categories that best link to both you and the job—whether it be computer skills or something else. Having a skills section that is linked quite specifically to you and the job does a great deal to help you to stand out from other applicants. These skills might include:

- Foreign languages

- Research skills

- Specialized training

- Budget creation

- Writing skills

- Certifications (although, depending on relevance, these might instead be a sub-category of "Education")

- Etc. (do not use this term but know that other skills besides these do exist)

As a final note, be sure that the skills that you include are not just relevant to the position but are also professional. Walking on your hands is undoubtedly a pretty impressive skill, but there are few jobs for which it would be useful.

High School Information—A Non-Category

If you are a college freshman, it is fine to incorporate high school experiences. However, as your college career progresses, you should be acquiring new skills and experiences and should phase out the high school information (completely phase these out by your junior year). Are there exceptions? Certainly. When you have truly exceptional experiences from your high school days (such as you were the school valedictorian or you started and ran the school television station, etc.), then do include them on your college résumé. Be sure that even these are in some way relevant to the position for which you are applying. If you have nothing else to put on your résumé, then, of course, you will need to include high school experience. When you, however, have reached your junior year and have nothing new to add to your résumé, take notice of this issue and develop a plan for activities and planned experiences that will be beneficial when applying to post-graduation jobs.

RÉSUMÉ LANGUAGE AND STYLE

Regardless of the organizational format and the categories that you list, it is important to use your skills as a business communicator to help showcase yourself through the language and style of this résumé medium. **Résumé content style** is the visual design of your descriptions to include such elements as bold, italics, capitalization, bullets, text positioning, and fonts. **Résumé language** is your use of terminology in the descriptions of your experience. Both your résumé language and résumé style should captivate but not distract.

Résumé Content Style

The visual style of your résumé should allow your résumé to look professional and be easy for the employer to quickly read. Some experts will suggest that you adopt a full-sentence format for your descriptions while most others will suggest using a brief, bulleted format over sentences. There is no specific formula for what your particular résumé should look like but there are several good indications of what it should *not* look like.

To keep your style useful and not distracting, be sure to give attention to those elements that pull the eye away from the content rather than into it.

+ **Ink Color:** Color copies are harder to read and see than crisp black ink. If you use an element of color then color print, use the highest quality print. If you are using an electronic medium, know that your résumé will get printed and, if that employer does not have your high quality printer, the version that actually gets passed around might not have the most professional look.

+ **Font Size and Type:** As a general rule, you will want to simplify what you do in terms of font size and type. You will want to choose a font style suited to your personality. Just like with visual aids, font will say something about you. As a reminder from our discussion of visual aids, fonts generate their own emotional meaning and have their own personalities (Li & Suen, 2010). For example:

    ■ **Garamond** = classic, old fashioned, sophisticated, favorably judged

    ■ **Times New Roman** = stable, mature, formal, efficient, not easily read, serious

- **Arial**: stable, formal, serious/less serious than serif, direct, friendly

- **Comic Sans**: fun, unreliable

- **Helvetica**: stable, generic, bold

- **Courier**: conformist, dull, unimaginative

Fonts are reflective of your individual style. Try not to have too much style going on. This means that you should use no more than two kinds of fonts in the body of your résumé, use a 10–12 point font size (depending on font type) for content, but a larger size for your name and a bit smaller for contact information.

+ **Bullet Format:** If your résumé is supposed to guide the eye but the reader has a hard time doing more than simply trying to track the bullets, you are in trouble. Always be sure to line up your bullets/tabbed content throughout the *entire* résumé. Use bullets like an outline with one type representing a major idea and different styles for supporting levels. If you do choose to use bullets, only do so if you have three or more items to list. Bullets are used to cut down on text. If you have nothing more than a single line to bullet, it draws attention to your lack of editing (and your lack of experience!).

+ **Formatting for Emphasis:** If you have ever "heard" a PowerPoint presentation that used every available sound then you know the feeling that an employer gets when picking up a résumé that overuses formatting for emphasis. CAPS and **bold** and *italics* and underlining…enough already! Limit the use of formatting. Be consistent across categories of your résumé when you do use it. Remove the hyperlink from your email or website listing (this both makes it hard to read and clutters the visual style). As always, create a line for the eye.

You can arrange and format your résumé in a variety of ways; just make sure it is appealing to the eye and professional. Do not get crazy with use of color or font style. The contradiction is this: you want your résumé to look different than others so it stands out (which is why you avoid using templates) but don't want the style to be so different that it becomes more of the focus than your information. The examples provided in this book are just that, examples. They are not the only way of formatting your overall résumé or individual sections. If you format well, you increase the chances that an employer will get as far as reading the *content* of your résumé.

Résumé Language and Descriptions of Content

A résumé is a written document deserving of all of the same attention to detail as your most important college paper. Whether you have had one job or twenty, the descriptions of what you have done should convey to a potential employer that you are a unique and worthwhile asset. Furthermore, regardless of whether you are posting your résumé online or printing it out, it will absolutely be reviewed for writing clarity and accuracy! We have already discussed in detail the use of ATS for evaluating your writing style; now we need to help you craft a writing style that will pass any evaluation.

Think of it this way: your résumé is the best work of non-fiction that you could ever produce. It should be interesting, captivating, honest, and understandable. It should guide the reader from one section to the next and the ultimate result should be a sense of satisfaction and even enthusiasm from the reader! This is one of the few times that you will get to talk completely about you—but as all good communicators do, you must make it a message that the audience wants or that you can convince them that they want.

Just Plain Ole Good Writing

When you began your journey into understanding business talk, our first discussion was about how communication is sent and received (see the Communication Models from Aristotle, Lasswell, Schramm, etc.). In the realm of résumés, an effective communication is one where the message fits the medium. Since our "business talk" medium here is a written one (not to worry—you will be *talking* about this written work soon enough in your interview!) then you must adhere to the basics of good writing.

Good writing has become more difficult in the modern world. When is the last time that you checked your text message for proper grammar and punctuation? How often do you evaluate your quick emails to see if there is subject–verb accuracy? Unfortunately, we almost never do these things and are in the habit of "bad" writing. This is your chance to pay attention to those details and get it right for the audience, which means no all-caps text, abbreviations, poor grammar, or inaccurate punctuation (e.g., there are no periods at the end of phrases but all sentences should have them!).

Treat your résumé document like a speech. Each job is like a topic sentence/claim that now must be explained with specific data and precise support. You used both quantitative and qualitative evidence in your speech; use it again in your résumé! *Provide numbers whenever possible.* Give the names and appropriate labels for all listed elements. Organize your bulleted information so that it has **logos** or "makes sense" to the reader. This means that your résumé will never include a claim that cannot be supported. (Imagine that your résumé lists "excelled at conflict negotiation" on it and when you are asked about this in an interview you have *nothing* to say. Eek! If there is not a good example of support then, as with spoken presentations, do not include it.)

Our proclivity to text rather than write or call also has us using odd tenses. Actually, not so much odd as just *wrong*. For example, if a job is in the past, then use a past tense for descriptions. If the job is one that you hold currently, put it in present tense. If you see an example that uses "-ing" on the end of most descriptions, know that it is almost always misleading. "-ing" (a present participle, if you were wondering) means that you are doing that certain action *right then and there* so this is neither accurate nor easy to read. (You are "managing customer accounts"—or so it says on your page. Are you doing this as I am reading your résumé? If not, or if you do not know, then swap the ending. For example, on your résumé exchange "write" for "writing" or "manage" for "managing," etc. This will help you to be more clear.)

Good writing is about descriptive clarity without repetition. It is great to say that you "created all public relations materials," but when you add to that that you "created formal correspondences" and "created new memberships," enough! OK. We get it—you are creative. That being said, we have lost the meaning of your descriptions and only have assigned one word to all that you have done. By being descriptive but without repetition (and without slipping in synonyms that do not make sense), you better become a whole person to the reader.

Content to Include

It is good to know, as you are attempting to link your (potentially imperfect) background to your (potentially ideal) job, that there are certain skills that will transfer from any job to any other job. (For instance, communication, writing, computer skills, problem solving, team work, leadership, organization, decision making, and time management are all transferrable skills.) Think about what the job to which you are applying to entails and requires, and then work on including the language that frames your previous experience so that it meets those requirements. (This does not mean make up skills so that some skills are not relevant to one position but are highly relevant to another; include information only when it is relevant but do not forget to include it when it is!)

If that employer wants "strong communication skills" then do not have your résumé simply list a public speaking class. No; instead be sure to have phrases such as "learned effective communication skills" or "applied communication strategies" to help describe your work at past jobs or in various clubs or volunteer work. As part of connecting you to the job, be sure to frame as much of your past experiences as you can in a way that makes their relevance to the job that you want extraordinarily clear. For example, it certainly does not make sense to spend a great deal of time discussing your skill and aptitude for mopping a floor, as you learned in your janitorial job, when you are applying for an accounting job. While you do want to mention that your janitorial position helped you with being more thorough, there is no need to dwell on too many details.

Student Teacher: 10th Grade English

ABC High School, Philadelphia, PA   August 2008–December 2008
- Prepared and implemented lessons, regularly assessing student progress
- Integrated technology into lessons, assignments, and classroom activities
- Served as mentor to writing club, increasing membership by 20 percent
- Established and maintained positive relationships with students and parents
- Collaborated with co-teachers to ensure student-centered instruction

Journalism Intern

Philadelphia Daily Times, Philadelphia, PA   Summer 2008
- Conducted interviews and wrote articles on a weekly basis
- Generated and researched ideas for feature stories
- Edited and revised stories created by other reporters
- Observed and interacted in all business aspects of a major publication
- Utilized Quark Express, Adobe Photoshop, and Microsoft Office Suite

Content to Exclude

As you go about drafting your message, there are a few items that you should avoid including on your résumé or as part of your document. Obviously, do not include the irrelevant stuff—but what else? Eliminate any element that will hurt the appeal of your résumé and perhaps communicate the wrong message about you.

- **Unprofessional Elements:** If you have an email that is more fun than office appropriate (e.g., "hotmama@gmail.com") then this is the time to change it or have two accounts and use your more professional one here. Additionally, you will want to eliminate things that are about you personally rather than your skill set. Unless you are applying for an acting gig, take off the picture, reference to your height, weight, eye color, or hobbies. It does not matter what worked in the movies...*never scent your résumé* or print it on paper that is hard to read such as bright colors or strong watermarks.

- **The Killer Typo:** Of all of the recommendations given in this chapter thus far, most importantly, *make sure your résumé is error-free!* You must proofread over and over. Have friends, classmates, teachers, and co-workers review and critique your materials for you. The reality is that you may be able to earn an A on a paper with a typo or even two; however, this is not the case with a résumé. Your résumé is a representation of the work that you will do as an employee. It is the one and only piece of evidence that the employer has to determine if you are worthy of an interview. One teeny, tiny typo can be the difference between getting an interview and not.

+ **Avoid "References Upon Request":** A blurb of "references available upon request" was the standard long ago. It said that you were able to provide contact information for people who could attest to your high qualities. Nowadays, however, no one will hire you if there are *not* folks to attest to your employment character. Thus, there is no need for this line on your page and it is, in fact, a waste of precious space. You will, however, want to attach a second page with those professional and personal references (typically about three of each), or have it ready to go the minute someone asks for it.

+ **Just Too Darn Much:** As you are writing, remember to edit. Most examples (even some in this text) are verbose, meaning that they are simply overwhelming with words and text. Too much on a page can be daunting to a reader so use word economy and edit down.

Buzz Words and Linking Terms

You already know to use the buzz words from the job advertisement in your résumé, but what about those buzz words that make you sound energetic, interesting, and motivated? You will want to use these *cautiously*. You will want to include in each descriptive bullet some type of terminology that makes your individual approach to the task memorable such as, "use leadership skills to ensure that the executive board approaches tasks enthusiastically." This speaks well of you and your style. You never want to use the phrase "responsibilities included" or any version of the term "responsible" given that this will imply that you were required to do something and did so with a bad attitude.

What you will want to do is use positive action words sparingly. Avoid overused words and phrases or you will come off as cliché and unimaginative (see Zupek, 2010). This means avoiding phrases like: people person, go-getter, team player, hard working, multi-tasker, self-starter, results, goal oriented.

Just as we advise in traditional writing, digital résumés as well as social media profiles should avoid the buzz words that signal you are just like everyone else. The most overused business buzzwords of 2011 according to LinkedIn are creative, organizational, effective, extensive experience, track record, motivated, innovative, problem solving, communication skills, dynamic (Casserly, 2011).

Elaboration

It might sound like a contradiction to be told to use word economy but also to elaborate. Unfortunately, both are necessary. What elaboration means in this context is that you want your descriptions to come to life. If the job advertisement says, "Need account executive with good communication skills" and your description simply mimics this back with no elaboration then you will neither pass the ATS or the hiring manager's scrutiny. Remember, do not sound like a job ad! (Do not just list responsibilities but let people know who you are.)

In an ideal world, your résumé would serve as the only introductory document that employers would need. It is not. Most employers will want you to craft a cover letter. The cover letter serves many functions but one is certainly to balance out the bad résumés that are so often sent. If your résumé clearly links

you to the job, what else could they need? Most people do not link their résumés to the job but instead produce one résumé for all applications. The cover letter is the place that they show specific links. You will already have an amazing résumé but your cover letter can be crafted to be one more piece of evidence that puts you a cut above the rest!

COVER LETTER CREATION

Dear Sir or Madam:
You have an opening for XY position. I am a great person to fill XY position. I have done great things. Please call me.

Does this sound all too familiar? Is it perhaps rather close to the ideas you have expressed in a cover letter of your own to a potential employer? Or, have you looked at a template online and been told that your letter should look something like that example? This makes sense. The basic elements are there but what is missing is the constructs of good communication and knowing the rhetorical situation. If you want to do better, *know* and *be about* your audience!

A **cover letter** is used to make an introduction to an employer, introduce your résumé, and get you an interview (Donlin, 2008). They can be sent to find out about jobs, to reply to an advertisement, to begin communication with an employer, or to take action on a job referral. Consider this your first in-depth interaction with the person who will eventually be your boss. As such, you want to both be yourself and be impressive.

Cover Letters per Industry

Just like your résumé, cover letters have no set number of pages but a single-page cover letter is *typical*. The idea of the cover letter is to get a potential employer to read your résumé and a lengthy novel may hinder his or her enthusiasm for picking up the next document. Some industries will expect a lengthier introduction (for instance, academics tend to have two- or three-page cover letters along with over ten-page résumés!) while others will not want much from you at all. To understand what is best for your industry, talk to your mentor, past graduates, those in the industry, and use the wonderful worldwide web to do a bit of reading.

The information you are required to include or hope to include to best connect to the employer will help to determine the length of your cover letter. You certainly may include all of the elements described below and still be inside that single page criteria. This means that again, word economy will be your friend!

Cover Letter Content

Unlike the basic elements shown previously ("Dear Sir or Madam"), we know that messages are far more likely to be accepted when they are for our particular audience in that particular moment. Think of your cover letter like this:

+ What do *they* want?

+ What will make *them* feel good?

+ What will be respectful?

Aristotle, if he were alive today, would absolutely tell us that the same appeals that are needed in any communication are needed here: **pathos** (an emotional connection to the audience), **logos** (clear organization), and **ethos** (credibility of the speaker). Your cover letter can make all of these appeals. The way that you connect to potential employers is through the strategic use of your cover letter content, which is each of your cover letter paragraphs.

Most cover letters are produced to contain three components. These components may come across in anything from three individual paragraphs on a single page to numerous paragraphs, bulleted lists, and data on several pages. For the purposes of clarity here, we will call them your *three paragraphs*.

Paragraph One

As with your résumé, your cover letter is about highlighting the links between you, the job, the industry, and even the employer. This first paragraph is about those links. Most cover letters simply use this first section to introduce the applicant and state the desired position. "To Whom It May Concern: I am a senior at ASU and am looking for a job in Marketing. I see you have a position open and hope you will consider me." (Gracious! Can you imagine being an employer and reading hundreds of those?)

Standard openings to cover letters blend together and are not very interesting to read. Now imagine that you pick up a page and the first thing you read is about you! It might be a compliment about a recent award. It may be recognition of the impressive goals that your company has set. You may even see that this letter is from the person who called you last week—and you know this because the first paragraph specifically mentions the call and something that the two of you discussed. These are the memorable letters.

To be memorable, make this paragraph about connecting you to the employer. Give examples of what you know about the person or company from your research. Do not include negative information about the company or try to critique the company so you can be their problem solver (yikes!). Keep the information focused and have it lead to the reason why you are applying for this job with this company. Consider the last (not the first) sentence listing the actual position that you desire.

Dear Mr. Cannizzaro,

I so enjoyed our conversation in February. It was a good opportunity to catch up and I was excited to hear that All-Tri is looking for new talent. As you know, I have had a long interest in and experience with Public Relations. My time as a Public Relations intern on the McDonald's Team this past summer at All-Tri showed me that your reputation as one of the most prestigious organizations in the Austin area is well deserved. I hope to join your organization on a more permanent basis as an entry level PR associate.

Paragraph Two

Your second cover letter paragraph is about becoming a more real and substantial person in the eyes of your potential employer. Résumés are for listing your experience. Cover letters are for creating images through narratives. Once you have told the employer what job you want, you must get them to see you in the position. This means detailing a very brief story (with a beginning, middle, and end) that applies a skill needed in the desired job. If the job needs you to work in groups, tell a story of how you led your team in a class-based project for your Introduction to Management course. If the position requires you to manage a budget, talk about the time that you worked on the University Fall concert and both allocated as well as managed thousands of dollars.

The best means of telling your story is to organize it just like you will later in an interview—by first explaining the problem or situation, then your action, and finally the result. Give a specific instance/narrative rather than several vague examples. The story should relate to something on your résumé (i.e., if you tell a story about your summer job at Home Depot, make sure you have listed that job on your résumé). Even though this is a story, you'll need to make it short and to the point, being vivid and specific with great word economy. Finally, apply that skill to the current company or position.

> Working in the communication industry has allowed me to refine my skills working with the public. I wanted to relay to you an instance that occurred while I was working at *Candy for all Occasions*. A woman had placed an order two days before it was expected, and due to a miscommunication between her and another employee, her order was filled incorrectly. These circumstances put me in the difficult situation of mediating between the owner, who was on the phone, and the customer to rectify the situation by conforming to the language of each party, negotiating a resolution that would satisfy the customer's need while keeping the cost of reproduction at a minimum and saving face for the company. As a result, the situation left the customer satisfied and the order filled to her liking and me with an enlightened idea of what I would want for a career. With a background in both customer service and business, I believe that my qualifications would be applicable in an agency setting—such as All-Tri.

As you put together your story, you will want to use word economy but you may need to include some additional details that could break this into two paragraphs, a bulleted list within the paragraph, or even a quote that gets included. Choose the format that best works for your situation.

Paragraph Three

The last cover letter paragraph must leave a good impression with the potential employer. This is where you should be **proactive**. As you finish your letter, let the reader know that you will be in touch. This must not mean that you are rude, pushy, or presumptive. Do not be obnoxious and state that this conversation *will* lead to an interview or state any other type of expectation. (For instance, avoid the specificity of stating that you will be in touch "to set up an interview" or "call at 9 a.m. on Monday the 21st to speak to you about the position.") If you get too presumptuous then your cover letter and all of your other materials will not make it further than the circular file bin next to the hiring manager's desk or be handed around the office—not to showcase your skills, but as an example of how the next generation never learned manners. Instead, let the person know that you will follow up or check in *to see what he or she needs*, then, most important, do so.

> I look forward to providing you with further details about my qualifications (in person, or via phone, or email). Please contact me at your earliest convenience. I will follow up with you to see what other information you may need from me during the week of June 28, 2010. Thank you for your time and consideration.

If appropriate, mention your enclosed résumé (if you have enclosed or attached one) or any other materials. The great result of this paragraph is that you put the ball in your court. In this section, you can also thank the employer for reading your letter and considering you for the job. Finally, be sure to sign off appropriately. Swap out statements such as "Holla Back" or "Kisses" for more professional formal endings such as "Yours truly/Sincerely/Sincerely yours" (or another formal ending).

Cover Letter Language

Like your résumé, a cover letter is a chance to prove your communication skills, and it is part of the first impression that you will relay. As such, you want to spend extra time on what and how you will say it. Most of these details are consistent with the résumé language criteria, but this is a letter (in full sentences) so you will want to give it the attention of a paper or report that you would be writing.

> **Cover Letter Writing Reminders**
> + Remember to avoid rambling.
>
> + Focus on what you can contribute to the employer—for that job, not just in general (think in terms of specific experience, skills, or knowledge).
>
> + Reduce your use of the word "I" (although using this word is acceptable in moderation); this document is about you but too much "I" use can imply self-centeredness.
>
> + Make sure your letter is neat; avoid spelling errors, grammatical errors, typographical errors, smudged or unclear ink.
>
> + Have someone else proofread and critique your letter.

7

The Look of Your Cover Letter

As you can see from the examples given here and the full example shown on the following page, your cover letter should follow the "look" of your résumé. This means that you should use the header and style of your résumé for the cover letter. Consider this to be your own personal letterhead that will help an employer see how all of your documents go together (e.g., your résumé, cover letter, reference page). You will want this to be professional down to the pen that you use to sign your letter.

Signature

Your personal touch to your cover letter is your signature. After writing your closing line (e.g., Sincerely, Kind Regards, etc.), hit the enter key three or four times to give room for your signature. Keep that signature the appropriate size—John Hancock scrawls are best left for the Declaration of Independence—and legible!

While it is doubtful that any potential employer is using handwriting analysis to understand your personality from this turn of your pen, it *is* likely that your signature will leave an impression. Thus, always sign your letter. Use a good pen (no Sharpies, pencils, felt tip, or basic ballpoints, but you do not need a $300 Montblanc either). Gel pens and roller-ball fine point pens have clean dark lines  with strong professional appeal. Because you are giving each document a personalized look, you do not want to look like this job is just another something at which you are throwing an application, which can be the case when you do not even bother to sign your letter. This can also happen when you have electronic submissions. Simply type your name but then change the font to a cursive style and increase the size ever so slightly. This shows a personal touch.

JENNIFER SMITH

12 South Drive
West Temple, PA 19460-9345
484.555.6987
js123smith@kanan.edu

All-Tri Communications
c/o Mr. Tom Cannizzaro
200 South Broad Street
Austin, TX 19102-3899

June 5, 2011

Dear Mr. Cannizzaro,

I so enjoyed our conversation in February. It was a good opportunity to catch up and I was excited to hear that All-Tri is looking for new talent. As you know, I have had a long interest in and experience with Public Relations. My time as a Public Relations intern on the McDonald's Team this past summer at All-Tri showed me that your reputation as one of the most prestigious organizations in the Austin area was well deserved. I hope to join your organization on a more permanent basis as an entry level PR associate.

Working in the Communication industry has allowed me to refine my skills working with the public. I wanted to relay to you an instance that occurred while I was working at *Candy for all Occasions*. A woman had placed an order two days before it was expected, and due to a miscommunication between her and another employee, her order was filled incorrectly. These circumstances put me in the difficult situation of mediating between the owner, who was on the phone, and the customer to rectify the situation by conforming to the language of each party, negotiating a resolution that would satisfy the customer's need while keeping the cost of reproduction at a minimum and saving face for the company. As a result, the situation left the customer satisfied and the order filled to her liking and me with an enlightened idea of what I would want for a career. With a background in both customer service and business, I believe that my qualifications would be applicable in an agency setting—such as All-Tri.

From my experience, I refined organizational skills, participated in planning meetings, and enhanced networking skills. These learning experiences are why I am so interested in gaining further experience through your company; I consider myself a hard-working, goal-oriented, personable, and resourceful worker who would like to work for a company with the same ethic. I look forward to providing you with further details about my qualifications (in person, or via phone or email). Please contact me at your earliest convenience. I will follow up with you to see what other information you may need from me during the week of June 28, 2010. Thank you for your time and consideration.

Sincerely,

Jennifer Smith

Jennifer Smith

7

WHEN AND HOW TO SEND YOUR MATERIALS

With all of the efforts that you have gone through to make sure that your materials look good, it would defeat the entire purpose of your efforts to have them show up looking ill-formatted and full of errors. Anyone who has ever opened a document that was crafted on a different computer using a different version of software knows how this impacts the appeal of what you are reading. Remember that this is all about message effectiveness, so an employer opening something like this will immediately have less of an emotional connection to your work than to another. If you are posting your documents online, sending them via email, or even uploading them to a blog or website, be sure to convert all of your materials into a stable format. Saving your documents in a PDF will save you from any conversion nightmares.

A portable document format (PDF) is a picture of your document that is held stable when sent to other machines. You have likely viewed documents in this format for school, when doing research, or at work. If you have Word 2007 or above (or a Mac) then you already have the ability to "save as" and select the option of a PDF. Earlier versions of the software can create PDF files by going to the print window and "printing" the document as a PDF or you can use any number of free online converters.

Note: If these directions are confusing, search the internet for "create PDF free" to find a plethora of sites that are happy to do this for you! Also, remove personal contact information before posting your PDF online.

YOUR APPROACH TO THE RÉSUMÉ AND COVER LETTER PROCESS

Crafting your introductory materials (your résumé and cover letter) should be approached with all the enthusiasm that you have for obtaining the job and sitting down for an interview. Even if you have never produced either of these documents before, approach each of these with confidence! Your first résumé may need quite a bit of work. Your first cover letter might not send the message that you hope it will. This is your first time, or perhaps the first time that you have crafted them as explained here. Just like with the research for your business talk, you will craft, recreate, revise, update, and continue to work on each as you move through your career. Each time that you update, you will find that you are more skilled at sending this type of message. Each time that you send your message, you have a better chance of landing the interview for your ideal job!

8

INTERVIEWS AS BUSINESS TALK

"So many people out there have no idea what they want to do for a living, but they think that by going on job interviews they'll magically figure it out. If you're not sure, that message comes out loud and clear in the interview."

—*Todd Bermont, Dean of the Careers College*

"Never wear a backward baseball cap to an interview unless applying for the job of umpire."

—*Dan Zevin, NPR correspondent, author*

TWO-WAY COMMUNICATION

If you have watched almost any reality show or even if you have ever been trolling around YouTube, you have likely seen examples of some truly horrible interviews. These might be due to lack of preparation on either party's part or simply bad behavior. On the other hand, examples of interviewees who shine and connect or interviewers who ask ideal strategic questions are harder to find. The good thing is that media examples of bad interviews tend to be staged or simply the most extreme cases. It is not likely that you will ever actually experience an interview that is truly outrageous; however, you may experience one where the meaning between you and the other person is anything but shared. Effective communicators understand that successful job interviews are an exchange of information that requires significant preparation from *both* parties.

Interviews are *two-way, relational communication exchanges, which serve as a specialized form of oral task-related communication.* The task? Both the employer and the job candidate must determine if they are the strongest match for one another (Friedman, 2012). *Interviewers* evaluate an applicant's suitability relative to all the other people (even an image of the ideal candidate) that have applied for a given position. *Interviewees* must respond and even ask questions in a way that demonstrates attributes of that ideal candidate. Both parties must work diligently to evaluate each other. When either person is not performing at his or her best, then we have a bad interview (that just might make it onto YouTube).

This chapter intertwines discussions of the two roles of interviewing: the task of being interviewed and the task of interviewing someone else. By understanding how employers are organizing and sending their messages to interviewees, those being interviewed are better able to interpret and reply to those messages.

THE CANDIDATE SEARCH

During your very first interview, look across the room: the person interviewing you was once sitting in your shoes. One of the reasons that he or she may excel as an interviewer is because that person knows what it is like to be interviewed! One of the reasons that he or she may not excel is because that person has not created an effective means of obtaining needed information. Like all forms of communication, successful *interview communication* depends on an understanding of the audience and an appreciation of the process. That process begins with knowing what each person wants to get out of the interview exchange.

What Employers Want

Interviewers want to fill positions with someone who will do the best job possible. If the job calls for computer programming then the employer wants the best computer programmer—but the employer may also want the best programmer with the best attitude who also has limited external training so as to not have to worry about losing bad habits. Employers will always have a set of criteria that serves as the basis for their evaluation.

Criteria are *standards for judgment*. Employers will look to see if you have particular foundational requirements and the strength or merit of that criteria. These criteria may include any or all of the following:

+ **Skills**: education, testable computer skills, languages

+ **Experience**: past work in the field, types of work/training, management

+ **Ability to learn**: accomplishments in past jobs, awards, honors

+ **Personality**: demeanor, humor, approachability, respect, long-term goals that fit with company or position goals

+ **Emotional intelligence** (discussed in depth in the Meeting and Leading chapter): adaptability, interpersonal ability, stress management, and mood (Chia, 2005)

If an employer knows exactly what to look for then the task of finding a person to fill a position is much easier. However, not all interviewers will have thoroughly thought through what they want before they start the interview process or have prepared to look for criteria.

The more an interviewer prepares for an interview, the better he or she will be able to evaluate a candidate's ability to do the best job. And, yet, we must be honest. Not everyone who interviews you will be prepared. Some may glance at a résumé five minutes before the interview, while others will carefully compare the job description with the information you have provided days before the scheduled meeting. Remillard (2012) tells us that less than 10% of hiring managers even share details of the job descriptions with co-workers who are interviewing candidates! Whether by choice or by default, the range of interviewer preparation will vary. What applicants must never do is assume that interviewers will not be prepared or have not thoroughly gone through the process of finding out everything possible to evaluate them.

8

How Employers Find Applicants

Do you have a LinkedIn profile? Have you submitted your résumé to CareerBuilder or given copies to family and friends? As an interviewee, we can think of all sorts of ways to put ourselves out there—but the process is just as important on the other side. Those trying to fill a vacant position must conduct an effective search. Consider the following timeline for bringing a new person into a company.

Steps to Hiring New Employees

1. See a need.

2. Create an advertisement or job description.

3. Consider applicants (interns, out of house, job fairs, social media, etc.).

4. Select candidates for interviews.

5. Organize and conduct interviews.

6. Make a selection.

Whether you know it or not, you are likely already part of a job search simply by existing in the modern world. According to Schawbel (2011), we are on trend to have our online presence simply replace our résumés in the not-too-distant future. This means that any information about us that is already online or retrievable through public access will one day become part of how employers find us for jobs, deny us jobs or even interviews, and part of how they will craft interview questions. Thus, your task now as either a potential interviewer or a potential interviewee must be to immediately understand online presence.

Searching for an Online Presence—and the Law

Dan Schawbel (2010) asks in *Manage Your Online Reputation—Before Someone Else Does*, "Did you know you're being Googled right now? You are" (para. 1). He tells us that almost 80% of recruiters are using search engines to look at you, and nearly 65% are using social networks to check you out! Why would they do such a thing? There are actually several reasons that an employer will want to search the online presence of a potential employee, and just as many reasons that he or she should not.

First, certain jobs require specific types of checks. For example, if the job requires working with children, the employer will most likely do a criminal background check to make sure the applicant does not have a child abuse history. Clean driving records may be required for jobs where you will be doing a lot of driving. If you know you have not done anything, do not be scared. This is not a personal reflection on their first impression of you—it is just the law. If a company does decide to do a background check on you, *it is their responsibility to provide you with written notice that it will be conducted and obtain your permission to begin the check* ("Using Consumer Reports," 2012), but understand that they may not always choose to do so. Second, companies will want to verify your information. Typically, these checks happen before you would be allowed to start your first day of work but, as Scott Thompson who lied on his résumé and was fired after four months on the job at Yahoo will tell you, they may happen at any point of your employment (Pepitone, 2012).

Third, at some point before an offer is presented, companies more often than not will conduct reference checks. You may have submitted a few names along with your résumé but companies will need to verify if those people indeed hold the roles that you say that they do and if the relationship that you list is honest (after all, if the only person that you can get to say nice things about you is your sister who gave you a part-time job last summer, there is reason for concern).

Finally, interviewing is expensive but searching someone's online presence is essentially free. If you can find out about someone's job history, relationships, political positions, social life, and even criminal background (yes, this is online, too!) without leaving your office then this is a good means of determining if you want someone to have a particular position in your company.

Many people wonder if all this rooting around in our personal lives is legal, let alone moral. We cannot answer the latter but there are guidelines about how employers may use online information (which is not to say that some will not ignore these guidelines):

+ employers cannot use irrelevant criteria (such as age or gender) found on social media sites to make hiring decisions

+ social media recruiting should use the same searches at the same point in the process for every applicant

+ some information, such as medical records, is confidential and may not legally be used in employee searches regardless of being able to find it online

+ companies that perform credit checks must adhere to the requirements of the Fair Credit Reporting Act

+ employers are not required to give applicants notification of searches (but most recommend a heads up for ethical reasons and to be able to preemptively address any potential concerns)

8

Contact your state's fair employment agency to familiarize yourself with your rights on these issues.

Online research provides a quick and easy way to get an impression of an interviewee. If you do use these methods in your search, be sure to print or save screen shots (for later reference rather than needing to search again) if you see something that causes you to question the candidate's candor, professionalism, or judgment so that you may address the issue in a professional manner. If you are interviewing, consider managing how you will be viewed online *long* before beginning the job search.

Managing How You Will Be Viewed Online

In a 2010 report commissioned by Microsoft, only 15% of respondents thought online information about themselves had an effect on job prospects. However, 75% of employers reported they conducted online research about applicants (Privacy Rights Clearinghouse, 2010). In other words, you should regularly check your online identity and be careful what you post! Before even thinking about applying for a job is the time to clean up your Facebook, LinkedIn, Twitter, Pinterest, or other social networking pages. Delete all of those unnecessary photos *and* comments that you have posted or that your friends have posted about you. Another way to find website content related to you is to conduct a Google search on YOU. You may be surprised to see what will surface. In order to be sure that you have the potential to get an interview invitation and that you are not confronted with painful information when you get there, *manage your online presence*.

Dan Schawbel (2010) recommends some unique online management ideas that go beyond simply changing your settings to private (which are easy to override) and taking down pictures before closing accounts to remove them from archives. He suggests:

1. Purchase your own domain name.

2. Develop a blog and connect it with your name.

3. Claim your name on social networks before someone else does.

4. Contribute content to other sites so you can offer your own background/bio before others create one for you.

You may not want to go this far to assert your online presence, but given that someone will, it seems best that you get there first. If you do not manage potential issues then you may never even be called in for an interview. If you do, you are more likely to have the chance to go through the exciting interview process!

INTERVIEW COORDINATION

From our discussion, thus far, and from our focus on business communication, there seems to be just one type of interview—the one to get you the job. In truth, there are many types of interviews and knowing all of them can actually help you to do well with the others. Here are a few interview purposes you need to know:

+ **Informational** (applicant-initiated, typically pre-interview)

+ **Performance** (employer-initiated, regular interval work assessment)

+ **Counseling** (applicant or employer-initiated, therapeutic focus)

+ **Interrogation** (employer-initiated, investigatory)

+ **Grievance** (applicant-initiated, conflict resolution)

+ **Exit** (employer-initiated, offer employer feedback)

+ **Employment** (employer-initiated, evaluating applicant suitability)

You may use the informational interview to gain information about a job or company. You may use the performance interview to let others know how well or not well they are doing at their current jobs. You might want to schedule a counseling interview after a potential employer finds that picture of you from New Year's Eve. We encourage you to move forward with each of those interviews but this text will discuss only the **employment interview**. These interviews will be your entrance into the business world and preparation begins with knowing how many people will be involved in the process.

Interview Types: Alone or Together?

In some interview settings, it will be you speaking to a panel of people from the company (i.e., one to many). In other settings, you may be in front of one company representative surrounded by other interviewees (i.e., many to one). And, without making the math too complicated, the situation can include a group or panel in both interviewer and interviewee positions (i.e., many to many).

The **group vs. individual interview ratio** refers to the number of people on each side of the interview table. You are probably most familiar with the one-on-one

8

setting where you sit by yourself across from one company representative and have a discussion. Changes in our modern economy have created a surge in the number of applicants applying for individual positions (Chan, 2010). When this is the case, companies tend to bring in groups for initial screenings before having only the top candidates come back for secondary (or several) interviews.

Have you ever seen *The Apprentice* or *Celebrity Apprentice*? Donald Trump provides an excellent example of the infamous group interview. Why infamous? Trump does not appear to be at all interested in shared meaning! He turns these information-gathering sessions into dramatic finger-pointing communication breakdowns. This might make good TV but, in truth, group interviews are no different than individual interviews in terms of their purpose. Applicants are being compared to the person that the company wants to hire (actual or imagined). Group interviews may be less familiar to us but they simply give us an opportunity to interact with the competition!

Interview Mediums

Not only will the number of people in the room vary, but the room itself is a variable. Interviews are not always conducted in the traditional fashion of a company calling you into their offices, sitting you in a room, and asking you questions. Today, interviews will happen in a variety of modes and settings.

Telephone Interviews

> It happens all the time: we get a résumé that everyone thinks is really exciting. Terrific grades. All kinds of powerful-sounding jobs…And then I call them up, and I can't stand talking to them…Before moving on to a full-fledged in-person interview, we usually use a phone screen to make sure that we're not wasting time and money on someone who is just seriously not smart. (Spolsky, 2006, para. 1)

Telephone interviews are time and money savers. Typically, phone interviews are conducted by secondary employees (i.e., not the big boss) or by a Human Resources department representative. The time of the interview can vary from a few minutes to well over an hour. A strong benefit of phone interviews is that this process cannot be visually focused  (such as on what you are wearing or look like) but instead must focus on qualifications (Hilpern, 2003). However, nonverbal communication does come through in phone interviews. Slouching over a desk, playing with pens or items around you, or a focus on something other than the discussion can all be heard right through the phone lines. Treat this interview as seriously as you would any other because even though interviews conducted using this medium are evaluated more positively than face-to-face encounters (Straus, Miles, & Levesque, 2001), they are still your first and only chance to make a first impression!

Face-to-Face Interviews

The employer's impressions about you in your interview carry more weight than your résumé or cover letter, so both employers and applicants should *want* to meet you face-to-face. In fact, Muir (2005) states that how applicants promote themselves before meeting an employer is nowhere near as critical as the behavior shown in person to either confirm or counter the desires that the employer has for the ideal candidate. That might just be fancy talk for "seeing is believing!"

Meeting face-to-face allows others to see how you project yourself and if what they have come to believe from your application materials is indeed the truth. **Traditional face-to-face interviews** are exactly what you would expect in terms of having a live and in-person chat with a person about a job. The unspoken focus of these interviews will be on nonverbal messages. If you, for instance, list on your résumé that you have held executive positions where you have led others but come in to the interview seeming unsure, insecure, and confused about the details of how to direct a team then that is a telling sign for an interviewer. If you have a fantastic bulk of experience but come in with a bad attitude and unprepared, you take away any hope that the employer had about hiring a rock star! (And, likely, any hope that you will get the job regardless of how good you look on paper!)

In this day and age, your interview may take a technological path. You may be asked to have a *mediated* **face-to-face interview** using videoconferencing technology. According to Barbara Kiviat's (2009) article in *Time*, "How Skype Is Changing the Job Interview," such practices are becoming a trend to save travel time for applicants and company resources given to on-site interviews. As with any new business communication tool, this technology still has its bugs. Internet connections fail, screensavers of you on vacation come up, both parties use different video technology and cannot sync up. There are lots of potential issues. With time and comfort, these issues are lessening every day. What has not changed is how to get ready for the mediated face-to-face interview.

Prepare and practice ahead for mediated interviews whether you are the interviewer or interviewee. No matter how many miles separate you, this is still an interview! Dress as you would if you were meeting the interviewers in person (you can still be seen to a large degree and may have to stand, so no sweat pants!), be sure to have good lighting, ensure that your backdrop is professional, and above all make the necessary preparations to ensure there are no interruptions (Bibey,

8

2010). If you have made it this far and the company wants to see just a bit more of how you are prepared to take the job, be ready to give a case presentation.

The **case presentation** interview is often employed by management-consulting firms, as well as investment-banking companies, and is increasingly being used by other types of corporations as at least part of the job-interviewing process. These interviews ask that applicants conduct research (even during a brief break in the face-to-face interview) and come back to present findings, suggestions, or technical trainings (Bhattacharyya, Patil, & Sargunan, 2010).

The digital marketing company Acquity Group's representative, during an interview with the *Los Angeles Times*, explained how their job candidates must come up with a pitch on the spot to promote the virtues of Acquity.

> Jim Newman, Acquity's executive vice president of operations, recalled a promising job seeker who seemed confident and articulate through his presentation. That is, until he inserted some X-rated imagery into the pitch. "It was awkward," Newman said. "Otherwise, he was pretty good. But then all of a sudden it was like, 'What is this guy going to say when he's in front of a client?' He didn't get the job." (Hsu, 2012, p. 2)

Case presentation interviews are designed to scrutinize the skills that are especially important to the individual job as well as to see how you manage stress and interact with others. Experts (see Hansen, 2006) agree on many of the fine points for approaching case presentation interviews:

+   listen carefully to the question/problem posed

+   do not be afraid to ask questions

+   prioritize issues and objectives

+   remember that rarely is there one "right" answer

+   construct a logical framework (logos!) with which to explore the critical issues of the case

+   practice extensively when possible

+   do not be afraid to think outside the box (creativity and brainstorming are likely just what the interviewer is looking for!)

Case study presentations examine your ability to manage a situation as much as they examine your particular skill set. If the job requires that you have even more specific skills, do not be surprised if you get tested on them!

Skill Testing Interviews

If the position that you seek requires specific skills or knowledge, companies may require applicants to take a test to show that they have these required skills. If you are interviewing an applicant and need skills, know that a well-designed test can get you valuable evaluative data! Interview tests may be scheduled before face-to-face interviews, during them, or even after. Some examples of **reasoning tests** examine one's verbal, numeric, abstract, spatial, or mechanical abilities. Some examples of **performance tests** include tests of typing skills, software skills, statistical knowledge, or computer programming languages (Psychometric-success.com, 2009). Tests may be multiple choice, timed, etc. (indeed, just like school!).

If your potential employer asks that you take a test, consider going online to take several versions of a practice test before logging in to take the actual test. Previsor.com (formerly Brainbench.com) has an array of skill assessment tests and resources that are particularly helpful for this need. Be sure to ask what version of the software the test will be in and using what operating system because differences between versions may mask your actual aptitude. Once you have mastered the type of interview, you will want to know about the structure of the interaction itself.

Interview Organization

Although interviews vary in purpose along with the number of people and the medium of communication, all interviews follow a natural structure. That structure, or *organization*, is much like a speech: interviews include an opening, a middle, and a closing—each with its own goal. Knowing these will help you as an interviewer to put together the best interaction assessing candidates' abilities. Knowing these as an interviewee will help you to feel more in control and understand what to expect and when to interject! (And, let's face it, we know that not all interviewers will be as prepared as we would hope.)

The Opening

When you open a speech, you must connect to your audience and introduce communication that will best lead to *shared meaning*, regardless of sender and receiver *shared experience*. We learned earlier, when discussing communication models, that effective communication requires strategic selection of content and mediums as well as the encouragement of feedback. Interviews are just the same! You must set up and open with a structure that helps to encourage revealing information on both sides. To do so in an interview, the interviewer should offer the following elements to verbally guide the remainder of the communication exchange and as part of making initial assessments.

8

Interviewer Opening Steps

1. **Start with a brief statement.** The opening is your time to develop rapport. Greet the applicant and help him or her to know your role as well as, if appropriate, the time that the interview will take (Rutgers, 2010).

2. **Define the interaction.** Given that there are many types of interviews, it is both useful and ethical (see the Ethics chapter) to let the interviewee know exactly what type of interview (e.g., informational, grievance, employment, etc.) will take place.

3. **Direct the time.** Much like your speech preview, you will give the applicant an overview of the order of the interaction. You do not need to reveal information that will skew the process (such as letting the person know that he or she will be taking a computer skills test if this is supposed to gauge unstudied aptitude). You can simply state that this process will include, for example, time to meet with all of the department heads, a tour of the facility, and then lunch with the marketing department. Now, expectations are set and you can move on.

After you have opened your interview, you will want to move on to the meat of the interaction. Before you do so, take a moment to do a status check. If you are interviewing, did you clarify the three elements? If not, why? If you are being interviewed and the elements were not made clear to you, this is the time to (politely) ask questions about the process so that everyone is on the same page. Schramm (1954) will be proud if you give feedback to make sure that full communication is occurring! Now, you can launch into the time for finding out about the person or people across from you.

The Middle

Take a moment to review the purpose of an interview laid out at the beginning of this chapter. This is a time for employers *and* potential employees to evaluate one another. If you know what information you hope to get out of the process (i.e., such as what kind of manager the applicant will be or how the candidate uses logic to evaluate problems), then you are better able to choose an interview structure that will reveal that information.

Interviews can be either structured or unstructured. **Structured** interviews have a clear plan of action and lend themselves to particular types of questions to gather specific information (Wiesnerf & Cronshaw, 1988), whereas **unstructured** interviews are often unplanned and left to the interviewer's whim and, thus, have less than half the success of gathering useful data (Wiesnerf & Cronshaw). Employers are moving away from purely unstructured interviews because structured interviews offer greater comparability among candidates and validity (Oliphant, Hansen, & Oliphant, 2008). If an interview is structured, this means that it will adopt a particular sequence.

Interview sequencing refers to the types and orders of questions asked as a means of drawing out particular information (Hayes, 1994). The most common (but certainly not all of the) sequences are:

+ Tunnel

+ Funnel

+ Inverted funnel

Tunnel sequences ask a series of closed-ended questions (i.e., those questions that have a set number or specific replies such as "yes" or "no" along with "male" or "female") (Hayes, 1994). Tunnel sequences are often used as pre-screening tactics because the closed-ended questions provide information that can quickly filter out unqualified candidates. If you are being interviewed and are only hearing closed-ended questions—or get interrupted when you try to elaborate—most likely the interviewer is not angry at you but is instead simply the person pre-screening you; so, keep your answers short and to the point! If you find that you are getting open-ended questions then you will have a chance to provide answers, which we will discuss more in depth below.

Funnel sequences mix both closed- and open-ended questions that begin with general questions and then narrow the focus (like a funnel) into more specific questions.

> For example, you might ask a respondent to describe his or her opinion about retail licensing policies in general before asking for opinions of specific policy options. This approach is useful if the specific questions will give the respondent information that could change his or her initial assessment. (UC Davis, n.d.)

Inverted funnel sequences also mix both closed- and open-ended questions but flip the funnel upside down so that the most targeted questions come up front and the general ones conclude.

> For example, you might ask about the individual activities of a coalition before asking for the coalition's effectiveness overall. The respondent may give a more detailed response to the question about overall effectiveness because the earlier question will have made him or her think about the specific activities. (UC Davis, n.d.)

Obviously, the middle of the interview is the most crucial information-gathering part of the process. Interviewers probe the person (or people) to determine the viability of the candidates. Interviewees attempt to make the best impression while

8

also evaluating the person interviewing them. The following sections will guide you through the process of that crucial information exchange and evaluation. It is the purpose here only to outline the overall structure of the interview—the big picture! Once you have gained all of that telling and detailed information generated from this exchange, the final step will be to close the interview.

The Closing

The end of the questioning portion of the interview does not mean the end of the evaluation or communication. In fact, if you think of any interview where at the end there was a long pause while you thought, "How do I wrap this up?" then you know the importance of the last few moments of interaction.

After the last question, the interviewer should conclude by removing any ambiguity from the application process (such as what comes next). If this is not done, the interviewee should feel comfortable asking about a potential timeline and addressing any final questions (Rennar, 2010; Rutgers, 2010) about the company and the process. Be sure to have covered the following:

Interviewer Closing Steps

1. **Provide a timeline:** Thank the applicant for his or her time and explain what will happen next. Tell the applicant when the hiring decision will be made and how it will be communicated.

2. **Answer questions and allow the applicant to add information.** The applicant's objectives are to gather information about the position and sell him or herself. Provide the opportunity for the applicant to accomplish these objectives.

An effective wrap-up will help to ease the candidate's mind (which results in less of those premature calls for updates) whether you have decided to move forward with that candidate or not. Now you are in a position to reflect on the information that you have obtained as an interviewer and as an interviewee to determine if a working relationship will be established. The information on which you are most likely to reflect is from the middle of the interview—the exchange of questions.

AN EXCHANGE OF QUESTIONS

Have you worked on an Excel spreadsheet? What type of projects have you managed using Excel? Can you tell me about other database management systems that you have used?

Do you catch a trend here? Clearly, someone asking these questions has a specific need to hire an employee with experience using the software program Excel or a similar database management program. This same interviewer may also ask about one's greatest strengths and weaknesses or other general questions, but this cluster shows a specific interest by using purposeful questions. Questions may be employed (no pun intended) to gather a vast array of information but each will have a purpose.

Interviewer Question Purposes

Interview questions will be developed in one of two ways with which you are already quite familiar: **closed-ended** or **open-ended questions**. You will be on the lookout for these questions as an indication as to which of the interview sequences that your interviewer has (hopefully) adopted, but should also know more about how each is used to gather information. Either closed- or open-ended questions can be used to gather particular information: general, situational, or behavioral.

Interviewees can expect **general purpose questions** in most traditional interviews. This type of questioning is focused on the applicant as a general employee and perhaps as a fit with the company or team but less so on one's abilities, skills, or potential growth. In this type of interview, how well a candidate manages the interview process will be highlighted. See if these general purpose questions with limited probative ability look familiar:

- What are your greatest strengths?

- Tell me about a weakness and how you manage it.

- If you were a tree, what kind of tree would you be?

- What do you admire in a boss?

- How many basketballs can you fit into a school bus?

Situational purpose interview questions pose specific job-related situations. Situational questions are designed to elicit analytical or problem-solving responses but are on the spot and, therefore, give candidates limited preparation (note: case presentations, discussed previously, are more elaborate versions of the situational question interview). See if these situational purpose questions look familiar:

- Have you worked on an Excel spreadsheet?

- What type of projects have you managed using Excel?

- Can you explain how you have used other database management systems in the past?

8

+ What three problems did you have working on the database system at your last job and how did you manage those issues?

Behavioral purpose interview questions may not focus on how well a person interviews as much as what specific traits, actual experience, or ability to perform in a potential job-related circumstance that the applicant can offer (Oliphant, Hansen, & Oliphant, 2008). Questions may include:

+ "What kind of leader are you?"

+ "Would you rather work in a team or individually? Why and explain this."

+ "How often did you consult team members during your training at GenEx corporation?"

+ "Have you ever used your listening abilities to achieve goals?"

Behavioral interviews can be broken down into even more specific types based on question development, such as target selection questions. **Target selection** works like a focus group system of asking questions with questions organized around specific key job criteria (Lazarus, 2008). This would include asking numerous questions centered on leadership ability or asking for a series of examples of ways to manage co-worker conflict.

Interviewees should expect to have both open and closed types of questions that evaluate them on a general, situational, or behavioral level (Oliphant, Hansen, & Oliphant, 2008). Responses to these questions during interviews will give an employer clues about a candidate's personality and ability to succeed in the organization, so knowing how to answer them well is crucial!

Answering Interview Questions

You can often guess what interview structure you will encounter (funnel, tunnel, inverted funnel, no structure at all) based on the type of the interview being conducted—employment, informational, exit, etc.—and how far along in the process that you are. You can also *guess* on the questions that you will receive. Both of these, however, are guesses. You are far better off in knowing how to formulate answers if you are prepared for any situation and all types of interview questions. These questions will likely fall into three categories: **expected**, **dreaded**, and **illegal**.

Types of Questions

Expected questions are those that are based on you, the industry, and the job position. For example, if you are applying to a job that insists on PowerPoint skills then you should *expect* to get asked about your particular skill level with that software. Answering an expected question is accomplished by considering why the question has been asked and for what type of answer the employer is looking. (Caution: Providing employers with answers that they want does not mean lying; you can strategically offer some information and not other details but all of your examples should be true!) Consider the following general purpose, potentially expected questions and why they might have been asked. These questions and the indications of why they might be asked were drawn from a variety of sources (Lazarus, 2008; Messmer, 2004; Navarro, 2006; Pearce, 2006; Thornbury & White, 2006; Williams, 2006; Woloshin, 2008).

+ **Tell me about yourself.** Employers do not want extensive history of your life. Pick the jobs that apply to the position and say one concrete achievement about each one or present yourself as an overall *brand*.

+ **What is your current salary/benefits expectation?** Employers love to have you start this discussion (hopefully your offer is low and they can give it to you without you ever knowing your higher value). Avoid discussing salary and refocus on the job's responsibilities, and that you trust the employer will give a fair wage when he or she offers the job. If pushed, offer your mid-range dependent on benefits or a salary range based on research.

+ **Why do you want to work for us?** Employers want to know what you know about them and what qualifications make you a good fit to their existing needs.

+ **Tell me about your biggest weakness.** "None" is not an acceptable answer or even true (sorry!)—neither is "being too gosh darn perfect." Yuck. Employers want to evaluate your honesty and work ethic to fix issues. For example, "Being so detail-oriented means I take a lot of time on projects. However, I make sure I allot enough time so I can meet deadlines." (Be sure to offer a specific answer, as discussed below.)

+ **Tell me about your biggest strength/most successful project.** Employers are looking for specifics to gauge your idea of success. Frame this in terms of your past employers' goals and be sure to link this strength with the prospective company's goals. (Never take sole credit for any success that was not truly an individual effort.)

8

A **dreaded question** will be unique to you. You might get asked what type of tree you would be (a typical question to determine how you see yourself and if you can think metaphorically). Some candidates may dislike such abstract questions (i.e., they "dread" them) while others see these questions as a challenge and, therefore, look forward to responding. A dreaded question is one that you have your own personal reasons for hoping that an interviewer will not ask you but you must be prepared in case they do. For instance (drawn again from the same above sources), these might be questions that some people will dread getting:

- **Can you explain this gap in employment?** Employers want to be sure that you are not lazy and are attempting to see if you were fired. If you were laid off because of an economic downturn or quit because of a change in family situation, feel free to say so. Then talk about what you have to done to stay current in your field, such as volunteering in professional organizations.

- **Tell me about your worst employer.** *Never* badmouth a past employer. Employers want to test your tactfulness. In fact, negative talk about a current or past boss was one of the top mistakes listed by hiring managers, according to a 2012 CareerBuilder Survey ("Hiring Managers Share," 2012). If your last boss was horrible, then find something to say about how the environment was challenging.

- **Describe how you successfully persuaded a group to adopt your point of view. How did you achieve this?** Employers hope to see what type of leader you will be (see the Leadership chapter). Frame your response to your then-employer's goals, and focus on the importance of conflict resolution and interpersonal cooperation skills.

Finally, you should be prepared to answer illegal questions, which means you should find examples and practice responses. In general, any question that allows an employer to evaluate you based upon criteria that does not pertain to the job is an **illegal question**. Neuson (2007), author of *Avoid Discrimination Claims When Interviewing Job Candidates*, classifies illegal discriminatory categories into the following:

- **Age:** including questions that ask how many years you have been out of school; it is, however, acceptable to ask if you meet age requirements to work for the state or business

- **Marital status:** whether you have children, plan to have children, or your spouse's occupation

- **Gender:** including whether you are comfortable working with the opposite gender

- **Race/national origin:** where your parents are from, where you were born, origin of last name, if English is a second language, language spoken at home, how long you have lived in the United States, if you are a citizen; it is, however, acceptable to ask for proof of eligibility to work if you are offered the job

- **Religion:** church you attend, if you attend church, religious holidays, if you can work on Sunday

- **Disability:** physical or mental limitations outside the purview of the job; it is, however, acceptable to ask if you can do the essential functions of the job without accommodation and ask for physical checks on this if you are offered the job

- **Sexual orientation:** questions about relationships and partners or living arrangements

Here is the tricky part…a question from most of these areas is not going to be illegal in *all* circumstances. If you are asked about your age when being over a particular age is required for the job then this question is not illegal. If you are asked about your gender when entering the Olympics to compete in a particular gender category then, while rude and lacking tact, this question is *not* illegal. Answering these questions is, again, all about you understanding what the person hopes to gain by asking the question.

- **Is that a religious tattoo I see? Are you engaged? Do you have kids? Are you seeing anyone? What kind of last name is Grimsely? How old are you, anyway? Do you own a car?** To be fair, some illegal questions may be asked because the employer hopes to better understand your ability to do the job based on factors outside of work conditions (like getting to and from work). When this is the case, put the employers at ease by addressing what appears to be the true concern. For example, to address employer questions about children, consider offering a statement like, "Some may be concerned that employees with kids can often be late or miss work. I can assure you that I am aware of the job's requirements and always prioritize my day to avoid any unnecessary conflicts with meeting those requirements." This type of answer is known as **strategic ambiguity**, where you give the impression of having provided information even without offering a direct response (see Paul & Strbiak, 1997). Finally, remember that your job as the interviewee requires you to uncover information about whether or not *you* will be truly happy in the job. Too many uncomfortable questions could indicate an unpleasant office environment.

If you are still feeling unsure about what you should or should not ask when interviewing someone (or when being interviewed), you should know that there are actually specific laws about what is legal in employment settings. Knowing these will help you be an informed and confident interviewee—as well as a lawful and ethical interviewer. According to the U.S. Equal Employment Opportunity Commission (2010), these laws include:

8

- **Title VII of the Civil Rights Act of 1964 (Title VII):** prohibits employment discrimination based on race, color, religion, sex, or national origin

- **The Equal Pay Act of 1963 (EPA):** protects men and women who perform substantially equal work in the same establishment from sex-based wage discrimination

- **The Age Discrimination in Employment Act of 1967 (ADEA):** protects individuals who are 40 years of age or older

- **Title I and Title V of the Americans with Disabilities Act of 1990, as amended (ADA):** prohibit employment discrimination against qualified individuals with disabilities in the private sector, and in state and local governments

- **Sections 501 and 505 of the Rehabilitation Act of 1973:** prohibit discrimination against qualified individuals with disabilities who work in the federal government

- **Title II of the Genetic Information Nondiscrimination Act of 2008 (GINA):** prohibits employment discrimination based on genetic information about an applicant, employee, or former employee

- **The Civil Rights Act of 1991:** among other things, provides monetary damages in cases of intentional employment discrimination

Now that you know the type of questions that you will encounter in an interview setting, you should turn your attention to how to organize, answer, and behave in this communication setting.

Organizing Answers

If you are asked a closed-ended, general purpose question (e.g., "Do you have a CPR certification?") then there is not much of an answer to organize. You respond "yes" or "no." If, however, you are asked open-ended situational or behavioral purpose questions then one-word answers will not ingratiate you with your interviewer! Now you must have developed and *organized* responses.

Interview answers, as with speeches, that have no organization are difficult to follow and remember. For this reason, most job search sites have acronyms for how you should organize your answers to interview questions (STAR, PAR, SAR, S-PAR, etc.) (Hansen, 2012). Each of these means just about the same thing. For our purposes, **PAR (Problem-Action-Results)** is the easiest response organization to use. Put simply, you should organize your answers to open-ended questions by first, **P)** setting out a problem or situation that you faced then **A)** note what action that you took, and **R)** give detailed results of your action. The following example shows you how all of this can happen in just a few sentences!

1. *What major challenges and problems did you face in your Business Management degree? How did you handle them?*

   P: "The workload was especially difficult because expectations in this major are so high and realistic for post-graduation. The most challenging course that I took was Interviewing (COM 300) with Dr. Cypher.

   A: While this course was demanding with a Corporate Research Project, three speeches including an Elevator Speech about ourselves, and two interviews, I found that working efficiently with a calendar and organizing small tasks helped me to feel proficient with my progress.

   R: This tactic must have worked because I received a high grade in the course (a B+) along with a glowing letter of recommendation, which was included in my application packet given to you. It is that efficiency that I now can apply in this position given that the job description asks for applicants who can handle heavy workloads!"

Specifics are the key to being memorable in your interview. Anyone can talk about their aptitude for leadership when asked about a good quality, but someone who can explain how he or she took on a leadership role and then turned a problem into a fantastic result...well, now *that* is impressive!

The above example is a great means of crafting a memorable and easy-to-follow answer. That is just the type of thing that will keep the interviewer thinking about you after you have left the room. However, while the above may be what you actually *say* in the interview, consider using an abbreviated form in your prep work to lessen the preparation work and so that you can easily draw to mind all of your prepared examples (this process is similar to creating an extemporaneous public speaking outline with just key words to remind you of your arguments).

1. *What major challenges and problems did you face in your Business Management degree? How did you handle them?*

   P: Workload (Cypher class)

   A: Work efficiently

   R: High grade & letter of rec.

As you are preparing your PAR notes, keep in mind that this is an organized conversation and the natural you will be the best seller of you! Be sure not to memorize your answers; the key to interviewing success is simply being prepared for the questions and having a mental outline to follow when responding to each question.

To be natural, avoid clichés. "People-person" is overused and "I'm looking for a new challenge" gives the impression that you are about to be fired from your current job (Cejka & Taylor, 2007). Keep your responses succinct—do not rattle on and on. Being conversational and engaged is great but being *too* chatty will backfire on you. As with a natural conversation, watch for signs that show that the interviewer is getting bored, such as looking at the clock or watch, or if they stop taking notes ("A word of caution for chatty job candidates," 2008). Be familiar with the technical language of the job and be sure to tailor all of your answers to include the company or job, showing that you have done your homework (Lipovsky, 2006).

As part of your homework, practice your *emotional* confidence. There is no crying in interviewing! If you do something embarrassing (like reaching over and spilling your interviewer's coffee…oops), do not panic. First, apologize. Second, you could try to lighten the mood by saying something like, "I got so excited by what we were talking about that I spilled your coffee. I'm so sorry." Third, *clean up the mess.* Fourth, offer to pay for a replacement or to take care of any cleaning. And finally, apologize very succinctly again in your thank you letter after the interview.

Overly emotional responses put the interviewer in the position of being your psychologist (Hoffman, 2008), which is awkward for both parties. Avoid showing too much negative emotion. That includes keeping quiet about the traffic jam on the way to the interview or the rainy weather in your area. And finally, remember to always be polite. Being defensive or argumentative with the interviewer will get you nowhere.

Tactics for When You Cannot Answer a Question

As you prepare to be interviewed, be sure not to just get ready for the intelligent and seemingly appropriate questions. You will not believe what some people will ask you! Clive Muir (2008) put together a list of ludicrous but actual interview questions:

+ Would you like a cup of tea or coffee before we start? Don't worry, that isn't a trick question…or is it?

+ Imagine you are a frog. Which beer do you prefer and why?

+ If you won $20 million in the lottery, what would you do with the money?

+ I know we're not allowed to ask this (ha ha), but what is your religion?

+ Why the hell would you want to work here?

Depending on the question, you have several options. You could say, "I am not clear how that would relate to the job. Would you mind explaining this to me?" (Be sure to do this with a pleasant demeanor—a snarky tone will turn things around badly.) Another potential response is "If I understand the question correctly, you would like to know…(followed by a quick and relevant revision of the statement to something job pertinent)." This demonstrates your ability to listen and communicate effectively (Thornbury & White, 2006). As you respond to your own revision of the question, make sure that you spin your response in a solution-oriented way (Crawford, 2007).

All questions, even illegal questions, need a response. Silence is not an option. Neither is taking on a confrontational manner. Your response does not always need to give a direct answer to the question but you cannot stare mutely at a person who just asked you something. Consider using **strategic ambiguity**, where you give the impression of having provided information even without offering a direct response (see Paul & Strbiak, 1997). Conversely, if the question is about information that you do not currently have, offer to get back to the interviewer with the answer—and then don't forget do so.

The bottom line is that your answers should, whenever possible, draw the discussion back to the employer's needs. The employer has already reviewed your credentials (we hope!). What they are judging in the interview is your personal character to see if this is a good fit for them.

Asking Questions Back to the Interviewer

Effective interviewers will give you, at some point, an opportunity to ask questions. Remember that the interview is a *conversation*, a two-way interaction, and that you should be prepared to ask questions throughout the process or at least during the closing interaction. In fact, this is your chance to show your interest in the company and see how well you will fit in their organization. Rennar (2010) suggests the following question categories (specific questions taken from: Conklin, 2007, Lazarus, 2008):

- **About the position:** Is position newly created? If not, how long has the position been vacant? If hired, what resources would I have to accomplish the job's goals in first 6 months?

- **About the company:** How is job performance evaluated? What are the company's strategies to remain competitive and what is my role in that?

- **About environment:** Was the predecessor promoted or did s/he leave? What is the typical day or week like?

- **About expectations:** What qualities would the ideal candidate have, and what skills and abilities would go above and beyond expectations?

8

Be careful. You do not yet have the job so questions about what the company can do to adjust to your specific desires and needs (or the salary that you want) should be held until you have an offer. Do not initiate any discussion of salary or benefits during initial interviews. In a survey of 150 senior executives by Accountemps ("When is money worth mentioning," 2009), respondents mentioned that the salary question was posed by 12% of employers in the initial phone call, followed by 30% in the first interview after that. Only 12% said that the issue was raised when an offer had been made. Why is this the case? If your salary expectations are too high, the employer does not want to waste time having you do lengthier interviews with hiring decision-makers. Williams (2006) smartly argues that you do your best to postpone this discussion until an offer has been made. Remember, it is not about *you*, but your *fit* with them. Understanding that fit is as much their job as it is yours. So, ask questions…and do it with confidence!

EVALUATING EACH OTHER—A TWO-WAY STREET

As you are both asking questions of one another, you will be engaging in mutual evaluation. Remember that the interview is a two-way street. Sure, the employer evaluates you, but you should also be evaluating them. Approach all interviews with the mindset that you are entering into a negotiation (Mavunga & Kombe, 2008).

As the job-seeker, you are coming from a weaker position than the employer. The more knowledge you have about the company, the better able you will be to ask questions, offer informed answers, and evaluate opportunities. Interviewees should prepare by researching the company and finding practice questions.

Evaluating Them

Have you ever gone into a test *knowing* that you were not prepared? How did that feel? Not good, right? Going into an interview not prepared feels about the same. Oddly enough, according to Drs. Hansen and Hansen (2006), people go into interviews unprepared all the time.

> Most career experts agree that few interviewees prepare adequately for interviews (and) that, while college students spend in excess of 4,000 hours studying and attending class to prepare for their career, the average interviewee spends less than an hour preparing for a job interview. (para. 4)

More recently, the *Los Angeles Times* (Hsu, 2012) reported that 18% of those seeking employment spend under an hour preparing for an upcoming interview, while 53% of survey respondents said they spend less than two hours doing so.

Even worse, when asked if they would go socializing the night before a job interview, 27% of interviewees said that they would on the condition that they return home at a reasonable time, while another 2% would have no problem in going out for the night (Huffington Post, 2010).

Perhaps this lack of preparation is because people are not sure *how* to prepare for an interview. It is easier than you may think. Candidates should take steps to know the company, find practice questions, and show up to make a good impression.

Know the Person—Know the Company

It is simply good practice to do your research on a company before you interview with them. Not only does being familiar with a company's mission and its history help you to answer questions, but it will also help you decide whether that company provides an environment where you want to work. It is also a good means of finding out how skills from your past experience might transfer to a variety of industries (Bowers, 2009).

This information is relatively easy to find given the availability of information on the internet. First, look up some basics about the company, including the company's history, mission, goals, and performance (Pearce, 2010; Rennar, 2005). Next, go a bit further to find out the stability of the company by searching news articles, trade publications, and a variety of resources (Bowers, 2009):

- Business Wire
- WetFeet.com
- Hoover's Online
- Annual Reports Library
- Forbes Lists of Best Companies

- Thomas Register
- Wright Research Center
- EarningsWhispers.com
- What kinds of things do you want to know?

Try to answer these questions (from Bowers, 2009):

- How old is the company?
- How large is the company?
- What are its products or services?
- Who are its customers?
- Who are its major competitors?
- What is its reputation/industry standing?

- How many women and minorities are in key roles?
- What are its short- and long-term goals?
- Have there been recent employee layoffs?
- What training programs are offered?

8

Finally, conduct a few **informational interviews** with experts in the industry, or even with someone from the company itself. These search techniques are ultimately in your best interest. You might uncover dirt that makes you think carefully about whether you want to work with the company (Crawford, 2007). The last thing you want to do is to accept a position in a company that is about to close, has shady practices, or does not make good on promises made to candidates.

Preparing to Be Evaluated

When you go to a company website and find pages not working, grammatical errors, or blurry images, these visual elements give you pause about the professionalism of the company. Online research can be a quick method to find information on companies and people as well as a fantastic resource for finding resources to prepare *you* to be interviewed.

Finding Practice Questions

Finding interview questions will help you to start the necessary rehearsal element of your interview. How so? Go into any search engine. Search for "interview questions" and you will find *thousands* of interview questions. Many of these questions are rather **expected** (e.g., "Tell me about yourself"), some of them for you might be **dreaded** (i.e., "If you were a color, what color would you be and why?"), and some of them could be **illegal** (e.g., "Are you planning on putting on any weight in the near future?"). You can easily find infinite general questions. Now, go through and alter the questions to be specific to you, the industry, the company, or the job. Supplement these questions by asking people in the industry or those who have been at their careers long enough to have conducted several interviews for questions that they believe you might get. Your next element of practice should be to prep and ready yourself for a visual evaluation.

Managing Visual Evaluations

Have you ever gone to a party and realized you were over or underdressed? Remember how awkwardly, painfully uncomfortable you felt? Imagine how you would feel if you walked into your interview and saw every employee in shorts and t-shirts while you were strutting around in a three-piece wool suit? Worse—what if the employer said, "We like you…but don't you have anything more appropriate to wear?" This *actual example* of a question asked to an interviewee is a good indication of how the wrong look can throw off the whole interview experience even when you look "professional."

The person interviewing you is looking for *visual similarity and attractiveness* in interviewees. Some things are beyond our control. For instance, communication scholars Neuliep and McCroskey (2001) found that people tend to view others of the same ethnicity as more attractive than those of other ethnicities. Some things, however, such as what we wear *are* within our control. "It's the ultimate sartorial irony: Less restrictive dress codes were supposed to make life more comfortable for everyone. Instead, with the old rules gone, many people are in a state of dress-down confusion" (Field, 2000, para. 2). When it comes to interviewing or delivering a business talk, consider that physical appearance, such as business-casual or highly professional attire, plays a role in connection. For instance:

+ **More formal attire is more respected:** young professionals prefer a more casual atmosphere but still link levels of professional attire with levels of authority (Cardon & Okoro, 2009)

+ **Backlash from too casual attire is increasing:** companies who have seen too casually dressed employees are reacting by creating and enforcing specific formal attire policies (Field, 2000; Kiddie, 2009; Reddick, 2007)

+ **Formality is specific to industries:** what is considered appropriately business-casual in one industry will be considered too casual in another industry (Haefner, 2008)

+ **Less makeup signals confidence:** moderate cosmetics helped women be perceived as healthier and more confident than those without (Nash, et al., 2006; also see Cox and Glick's, 1986, *Résumé evaluations and cosmetics use: When more is not better*)

Managing Behavioral Evaluations

By now, you should begin to feel confident in your ability to look professional and to answer common interview questions. The last step in negotiating an interview is to be sure that you behave in a way that communicates the message that you hope to send. Again, this is a two-way street so appropriate behavior should be adopted by both the interviewee and the interviewer.

On the side of the interviewee, you will want to consider all of your non-verbal communication as well as your pre-interview preparation behavior. In short:

+ **Be early and stay late:** If you show up early then you are on time. If you show up on time then you are five minutes late. This old adage works well for the interview setting. If you are late for an interview, your chance of getting the job is almost nil. Why? First of all, it implies a low value of the position. It also reflects poorly on your future behavior if you do get hired. And, finally, it is

8

disrespectful to the people who have set aside their time to get to know you. Arrive ten minutes early (Thornbury & White, 2006). Any earlier than that and your nerves will start to fray.

To make it on time, incorporate your travel into your preparation. Travel to the location, when possible, a week or a few days before the interview, during the same time of day. Locate where to park, any funds you will need for parking or travel, and possible complications with your route or time. Allot yourself enough time on both ends—never have to run out of an interview that is going well just because it is going long (Lazarus, 2004).

- **Be "on" early on:** Be "on" during the last turn in the directions. This means that as you turn into the parking lot, be aware that anyone could be seeing and evaluating you. Do NOT brush your teeth in the car, change out of fuzzy slippers, or squeeze into your pantyhose.

- **Silence anything that makes a sound:** Cell phones, watches, iPads—any gadget whose sound cannot be turned off should be left at home. This includes a huge pile of change in your pockets, loud keys, or jewelry. All of these serve as small distractions to any focus on you.

- **Bring copies of your résumé, a pad of paper, and a pen.** Take notes. It shows your interest in what the other person is saying. On the pad (or iPad), write down your questions for them so you do not forget to ask, answers to questions, or names to remember. This conveys serious interest.

- **Practice rapport-building behavior.** Appearing disinterested during the interview is one of the top mistakes that job seekers make, according to a 2011 nationwide survey of hiring managers ("Hiring Managers Share," 2012). Instead, practice all the cues of showing interest. Smile. Krunhuber and his colleagues (2009) studied different types of smiles and concluded that those with authentic smiles received higher personal, job, and expression ratings compared to those with fake smiles or neutral expressions. Sit up straight, do not fidget, lean forward when listening, adopt a firm handshake—all of these slight gestures will project confidence and comfort (Giles, 2010).

- **Adjust to group interview settings.** The number of the people in the room when you interview ought to simply be a matter of where to give your eye contact. When someone speaks, it is important that you look at that person. If it is someone interviewing you or someone sitting next to you being interviewed, look at him or her. Make sure that you give the speaker the attention that you would want. It shows an interviewer that you respect him or her and an interviewee that you are not intimidated.

On the side of the interviewer, non-verbal communication is a matter of conveying demeanor that invites open responses...and playing it cool! If your behavior alienates the best candidate, you have done yourself a huge disservice. A survey conducted by the consulting firm Development Dimensions International (DDI), along with Monster.com (2007) that included nearly 628 staffing directors, 1,250 hiring managers, and 3,725 job seekers, identified *interviewer behaviors* that adversely affect candidate willingness to work at the company, such as:

+ Acting like she/he has no time to talk to me (70 percent)

+ Withholding information about position (57 percent)

+ Turning the interview into cross-examination (51 percent)

+ Showing up late (48 percent)

+ Appearing unprepared for interview (47 percent)

+ Asking questions unrelated to job skills (43 percent)

Similar studies (RGL, 2011) found that companies lose qualified candidates when the interviewer is unfriendly or silent, takes a phone call or checks a cell phone or computer, appears disorganized, is rude or arrogant, limits eye contact, or primarily asks closed-ended questions. Instead, get the applicant excited about the job by showing your own enthusiasm. Set the tone for the position by holding high expectations of yourself as an interviewer.

When the big day comes, you may be nervous but you will not be unprepared. You might be worried about making the right impression but you will have the tools for effective communication regardless of which side of the table that you are on. You will move through the interview skillfully and be ready to take the next step. Now is the time for post-interview communication.

POST-INTERVIEW INTERACTION

You are still being interviewed even after you leave the interview. *Huh?* That must sound like a strange statement but it is true. Once you leave the meeting that you have had with the company or boss or even the initial screening with HR, interviewee behavior is still being evaluated and you are still in the midst of needing to make an impression. Most folks forget this step but those who do not make the right impression and are more likely to land a job!

8

Write a Thank You Letter

Say thank you. Your mom has probably been telling you this for years and now is when it will really pay off—literally. The most crucial element of your follow-up is a **thank you letter**.

> "Thank you letters are important in this market, now more than ever," said Lisa Verde, director of recruiting for Matrix Resources, Inc., an international IT recruiting firm. They are important, Verde explained, because hardly anyone sends them, yet companies expect them, and a thank you or follow-up letter can make the difference between getting a job and getting overlooked. (Joss, 2003)

As a rule of thumb, if the employer uses email to contact you, it is acceptable to use the same medium to communicate back during the process, but a hard copy thank you should be used to conclude the process. Old-fashioned, handwritten letters are still preferable to email (Powers, 2000) even if the latter is also becoming more acceptable.

Keep the letter short and spelled correctly. (This is a letter to a potential boss—not a Facebook posting.) Mention something specific and interesting that was discussed during your interview and then reiterate your interest in the position. Most importantly, mail this letter immediately, preferably on the same day.

How to Inquire about Your Status

You felt good about that interview. Now you sit back and wait. You wait a week, and no one calls. What do you do now? First, reflect back on the timeline that you (should have) established in the closing of the interview. If the interviewer said that it would be at least two weeks before you would hear anything, relax! If the interviewer said that you would hear within 48 hours, then you need to follow up once that time has passed. Second, wait one or two more days before calling or emailing the main interviewer. Even if they have made a decision, it can take time on their part to finalize how to move forward. Certainly, make sure you do not hassle the person *before the specified date* that he or she gave you at the end of the interview (Thornbury & White, 2006).

When you do follow up, be sure that you are polite and not insistent. If you need to continue to follow up, keep the tone the same. A busy employer will like nothing less than multiple desperate phone calls from a person that he or she is still debating on hiring. Check in. Ask for another timeline. If you have more to offer, such as an updated résumé with new experience or a change in contact information, this is a good reason to touch base!

What to Do with an Offer and Negotiating a Salary

You will most likely receive a job offer through a phone call from the employer. If you are made an offer, you must be prepared to negotiate it from a position of knowledge. Wait to accept until you know the terms of the offer—starting date, salary, and benefits. Feel free to say you are excited about the opportunity and get the details before rushing into a "YIPPEE! Of course, I will work for you!" declaration. Instead, know and calmly list your needs and evaluate the offer to see if it meets most, if not all, of them. Do your research on the standard salary for that job, at that time, and in that location as well as benefits for similar positions in your area of residence. Use search engines such as Salary.com to find comparable wages.

Resist the urge to give a potential employer any type of specific salary number because any offer will definitely be targeted to your initial suggestion—even if it is unreasonably low. Throw the ball into their court by saying something like, "Let's talk about job requirements and expectations, then determine a fair salary for the job." As noted above, if you can get by with not giving a number first, you gain the upper hand; however, if you feel that the employer will not move on to the next level of interviewing unless you give an answer, be prepared to state the going industry rate in your area (this is where your research comes in useful) and be flexible in negotiating. For example, the company may not be able to increase the compensation, but might be willing to throw in more vacation days, or allow you to telecommute once in a while. Begin negotiating by thanking the employer for the offer. And always, always ask graciously and respectfully.

GO FORTH AND INTERVIEW!

Interviews are planned conversations. To be fair, they are not always planned but they *should* be. These are times for companies to evaluate your suitability for a job relative to others. Who are these others? They can be the other people that have also applied for the job or even an ideal person that the employer has in mind. Who you are might be that ideal person or even someone looking for the ideal person. The key here is that now you are equipped with the communication skills to interview, be interviewed, and evaluate job decisions. Next, imagine yourself in the career you have been working toward. Let's go even further and say you have done so well in your career that you have been promoted to a position of leadership. Do not be nervous. We know you can do it, and the next chapter will show you how.

8

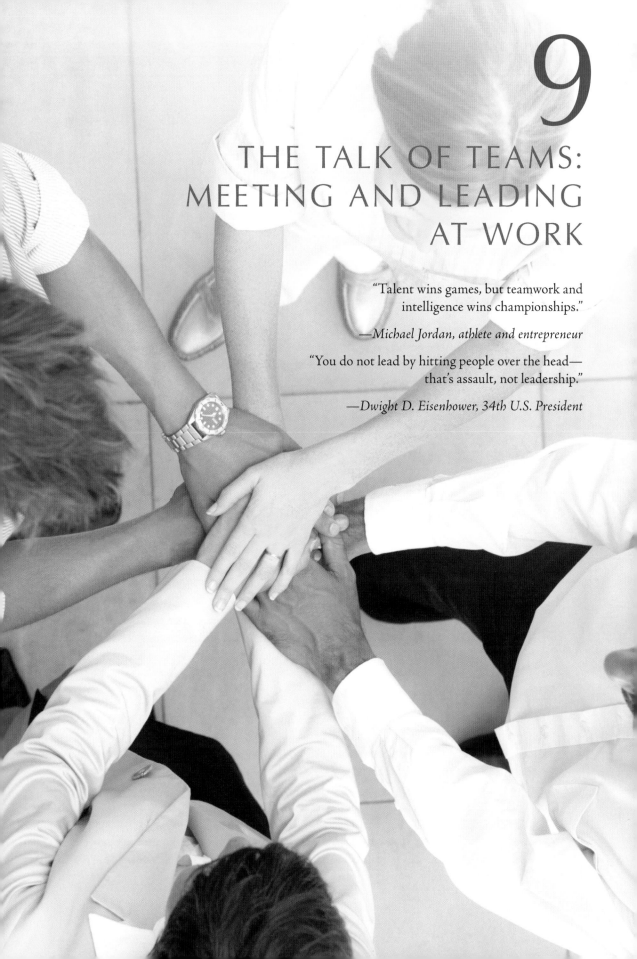

9

THE TALK OF TEAMS: MEETING AND LEADING AT WORK

"Talent wins games, but teamwork and intelligence wins championships."

—*Michael Jordan, athlete and entrepreneur*

"You do not lead by hitting people over the head— that's assault, not leadership."

—*Dwight D. Eisenhower, 34th U.S. President*

BUSINESS TALK...IN THE SETTING OF A TEAM

If you have made it this far—both through this text and through your career—then it is likely that you will now have the chance to work with others. It may be the case that your boss assigns you to work in a group or even that she asks you to lead a work group! This is fantastic. This means that your business talk, thus far, has placed you in the eyes of your organization as an expert with skills to follow. Congratulations! Now, before you end your readings on business talk either thinking (positively) that if you are a good talker then you are a good leader or thinking (negatively) that working with a group is something to dread, consider some truths about team-based communication in professional settings.

Teamwork has been credited with producing inspirational success stories, such as the survival and rescue of the thirty-three miners trapped in a Chilean copper-gold mine in 2010 (Buschschluter, 2010; Knowledge@Wharton, 2012c). Alternatively, teamwork has been blamed for tragedies such as the explosions of the U.S. space shuttles *Challenger* and *Columbia* (Dimitroff, Schmidt, & Bond, 2005). While your own workplace experience may never reach these extremes, chances are that you have already experienced a rewarding team situation, as well as one that made you swear that you would never work in a group setting ever, ever again. Whether you live for working with others or avoid it, it is rare that you will find a professional setting where you do not need to work in a group or meet with others.

Meetings and teamwork dominate how we work in professional settings. Sometimes you may be on long-term projects with others, other times you may have only one meeting a week or even a month to provide status reports on individual projects. In any case, working with others is so dominant in professional settings that it is no surprise that the ability to work in teams is the *number one* characteristic employers seek in new graduates (NACE, 2011)! Those who excel at this skill can find the rewards of leading a group in a professional setting. You may find that you are asked, expected, hope, or find no other option than leading those with whom you are working, so you will want to have the skill to step into this role as well. Leadership is not just something listed on your résumé—it is a skill that comes with understanding and practice.

If you want to demonstrate the type of leadership, or even team participation, that results in professional creativity, cohesion, productivity, and results—as well as kudos from the boss—then you will need to understand the elements of effective meeting and leading. You will need to leave our discussion of business talk knowing how a group forms and progresses over time, the roles that are adopted when co-workers meet, as well as how they manage (and occasionally even hope for) conflict. You will need to know the traits of leadership that will help you reach your team goals and how to navigate the practice of directing a meeting through a goal-oriented agenda. This is your moment. You have mastered all the aspects of individual business talk—and now you must master that talk with others!

MEETING (AND WORKING) WITH A TEAM

"Who are you?"
"What do you do?"
"Wow—you can do that?"
"Look what we can do together."

Does this sound familiar? We experience group work and meeting with others in very similar patterns each time that we come together. Think of the patterns of your last team or professional meeting. You got together for the first time. There was a bit of tension and then there were some breakthroughs. You started to figure each other out (who would step up, who would drop the ball, and who would keep you laughing). Finally, you determined how to move toward your goal using the resources of your group. This is a common pattern of group experience. If your last group experience did not work exactly like this, you likely can look back and still find similarities to this pattern. Groups emerge and develop. Understanding this process can get you to your goal more quickly than just sitting in a meeting and wondering what to do next!

How Groups "Emerge" and Develop

What does it mean to emerge? Basically, **emerging** means that some element (in this case, the elements of working in a team) will become apparent, important, and prominent over time. From the pattern listed above, you can understand how the roles that you adopt when meeting with others, such as who should be selected as the leader of the group will emerge over time. Your group will not magically appear completely formed and ready to get down to business. Give yourself (and those in your meeting) a little leeway to figure out how you will all work together. Scholars for years have been attempting to figure out the ways that groups meet and communicate in an attempt to help them to be as effective as possible.

To give you a leg up on the competition, who might take twice the time trying to figure out what will come next, consider some of what we know about meeting in a group. Group communication theories attempt to explain the team experiences by suggesting trends and providing a general understanding of the patterns that most groups will experience.

The goal here is *not* to cover every single aspect of team work theories but to showcase the ones that best describe the trends in group research which are applicable to how you will function in your professional life! Let's look at groups first in the broadest sense and overall picture—the element of emerging through stress.

9

Bormann's Recurring Pattern Model

All groups encounter stress. We know this is true from our own experiences. We also know that stress can be both a good and a bad thing. "I am being transferred to a division under a manager that I don't like"—bad stress. "I just got promoted to team leader!"—good stress! All individuals encounter stress as part of life and all groups encounter stress as part of functioning. Bormann (1990), in his **Recurring Pattern Model**, called those stresses "tensions" and explained that every group goes through two types of interacting tensions: primary and secondary.

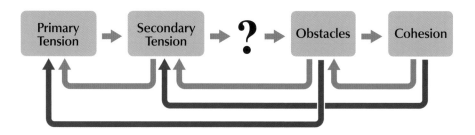

Bormann's Model

Primary tension refers to the stress that those in a first meeting or initial team interaction feel both about being in a group setting and the uncertainty surrounding the roles that they might play. When we first gather in a meeting or group work setting, we normally wonder about who the people are in our group as well as what our interactions will be like. This is normal. Even groups that have a long history of meeting can have primary tensions at the beginning of a new project. Some signs of these tensions are feelings of caution or hesitancy in offering information or even failing to engage in typical communication patterns. If you have ever had a long awkward period of silence in an initial group meeting, then you know what this means. Other signs include group members being overly polite or doing everything possible to avoid conflict. In short, primary tension is the tension of not having yet established group norms.

The means of getting past primary tension occur during the time that it takes to establish norms for that team or group. This might happen when people tell appropriate jokes and lighten the stress of initial interactions (inappropriate jokes increase tension and may establish group norms but not such that the group can move past this initial phase). Some people will share personal stories and experiences to help establish their identity with others (Bormann & Bormann, 1988).

Secondary tensions occur as groups move toward a decision-making phase. During this stage, conflict may arise as group members debate what to do and how to reach their goals. As those in the meeting or on the team attempt to influence one another (Bormann, 1990), there will be power struggles, differences of opinion, personality differences, and the development of norms. Secondary tension will see the rise of group conflict. Before you start thinking of how to avoid this phase, Beebe and Masterson (2003) suggested that even the most cohesive groups will go through some form of conflict—and that conflict can be useful! The absence of tension can indicate that group members are bored or unmotivated. Rather than avoid tension at all costs, group leaders should: remember that conflict is inevitable, set limits within which this conflict may occur, and remember that creativity causes positive tensions.

The final elements of Bormann's Recurring Pattern Model suggest that movement through primary and secondary tensions *can* lead to group cohesion (yea!). You might now assume that when you can get through those initial phases then you will always come out better on the other end. Sadly, Bormann (1990) and—reality television—tell us that not all groups leave the tension phases. Some meetings are short and cannot get to this point; hopefully, you will meet again (and again, and again). Some groups have many meetings but simply never move past one of the tension phases, or even slip back into a tension phase with the addition of a new member or new idea. Bormann (1990) explained that groups who remain caught in the tension phase—and many groups do—can never directly address obstacles or overcome opposing forces. This is why Bormann's model (the previous diagram) is not listed in "phases" but as a continuum that can keep cycling back. What we learn from him is that it is important to address tension if your group ever hopes to move forward!

Bormann's Recurring Pattern Model provides a wonderful overview of what you will face walking into almost any initial meeting in a professional setting. His phases, however, do not give us a full picture of what might happen as we are attempting to be productive in our meetings. You may be better able to figure out the kind of business talk which will help your meetings be most productive by looking at a few other views on group communication.

Tuckman's Group Development Model

Tuckman's (1965) **Group Development Model** is equally useful for understanding our experiences in business meetings, teams, and group settings. Unlike Bormann's (1990) cyclical model, Tuckman described five linear stages of team development: forming, storming, norming, and performing. Adjourning was later added to make a fifth stage.

9

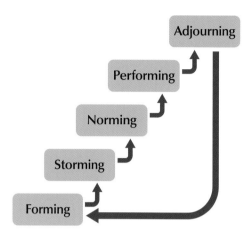

Tuckman's Model

During the **forming stage** of Tuckman's Model, team members take time to share information about themselves and learn about their tasks through explicit discussions or implicitly through nonverbal cues, such as status symbols or physical traits. Ideally, team members also establish trust, clarify group goals, and develop shared expectations in this stage. When forming, some group members may be confused, uncommitted, or become unwilling to listen or participate in efforts to resolve issues.

In the **storming stage**, conflicts emerge as team members work to identify appropriate roles and tasks. This can be an uncomfortable stage where it may seem like the group may never reach cohesion. However, avoiding this stage can result in poor decisions that do not take the group into the next phase—norming. Groups able to resolve conflicts move to the **norming stage**. In this stage, your team would come to an agreement on how to work together, strengthen relationships, and come to a strong and unified understanding of member obligations. In reaching this single-mindedness, the team members increase their trust in one another and have a clearly coordinated process. During the **performing** stage, team members, now confident about what needs to be done and actively helping each other, will work on completing all of the assignments necessary to achieve the team's overall goal. Later, a fifth stage was added to this model, the **adjourning stage** (Tuckman & Jenson, 1977), which described the end of the meeting and disbanding of the team after completion of the project.

If these stages do not resonate with your own team experiences then perhaps Fisher's Decision Emergence Theory will better describe your last group project or best direct the *decisions* for your upcoming team meeting.

Fisher's Decision Emergence Theory

Fisher's (1970) **Decision Emergence Theory (DET)** explains how it is that, when we meet at work, we go from "eek—we have a problem" to "yea—we have a decision!" The DET is an explanation of the complex communicative process that problem-solving groups go through in reaching consensus about a decision (Fisher). He offered four linear phases that groups experience as they try to reach decisions: orientation, conflict, emergence, and reinforcement.

Fisher's Model

In the **orientation phase** of teams making decisions, team members will try to make others feel comfortable by putting a high emphasis on clarification and agreement, being vague to avoid conflict, acting politely, developing roles while reducing social tension, and getting acquainted. The goal of orientation (just like when you went through it as a freshman in college!) is to reduce uncertainty.

Tensions occur as the group moves into the **conflict phase**. During this time, team members must begin to discuss decision alternatives; argumentativeness becomes the norm. As with any discussion where more than one option exists, the team members will offer ideas and begin to criticize each other's ideas. This will be a time when the dislike of ideas and people will be expressed as the social inhibitions of orientation diminish! Be ready for this phase. It is a time of potential. During conflict, attempts to persuade must be used and leaders will emerge. Fisher (1970) reminded us that without a conflict (a positive notion), teams will reach decisions that are limited and less creative. When groups do not experience conflict—or avoid it—then bad behavior has been enforced leading team members to emerge as an unhealthy group.

Emergence is the longest and most gradual phase in Fisher's (1970) description. Perhaps this is the case because emergence is when we all tend to get a bit more ambiguous and less critical—at least less vocally critical! Being in this phase allows team members to save face when their ideas are clearly not going to be adopted as

9

part of the final decisions. Members will begin to compromise in order to achieve consensus and the group does less to make decisions. The decisions instead naturally *emerge* from the group interaction.

What all teams hope to reach is the **reinforcement phase**, or the time when groups reach decision consensus! At this time, you will want to see that all of the members of your team (or those in your meeting) are committed to the decision. Decisions should reflect *real agreement* rather than conflict avoidance. Your group will want to feel good about their decision. So, when favorable views of the decision proposal are expressed, these views should receive agreement and *reinforcement*. This is a time, according to Fisher (n.d.), for "a strong spirit of unity and verbal backslapping by the members" (p. 260).

If you are feeling empowered about walking into your next team meeting or you have come to a sudden realization of why folks backed off of a bad idea in your last group effort then you are well on your way to using business talk with others. This, however, is just the beginning of understanding how to communicate in such a dynamic setting. Crafting effective teams means understanding the individual roles that each team member will adopt and how their communication is impacted by those roles. Management-based research by Chong (2007) suggests that performance of a team is based upon the *roles* that the team members play. The distribution of those roles in the group depends on the: 1) purpose of the group and 2) the stage of group development.

Team Member Roles through Tasks and Relationships

We know that groups or teams get together for a purpose. Some teams are solving a problem (and might use Fisher's DET to do so) while other groups get together for social reasons (and can be tracked through Bormann's tension types). In any case, within these teams are team members, and team members must play specific roles in order for the group to move forward in its functional process. A team is made up of all sorts of people. How these people interact and relate to one another is a key factor in determining how successful the team will be at achieving its mission.

Most research on role behaviors is based on the work of two influential organizational theorists: Kenneth Benne and Paul Sheats (1948). Their work defined twenty-six different group roles that can be played by one or more people within a group. While this might seem like ancient work to reference for your modern-day meeting experience, it is this work that is the foundation of our group role research today. Benne and Sheats' "group roles" research remains a useful (and interesting) way of looking at team behavior. They defined three categories of group roles: *task-related roles, relationship maintenance roles, and dysfunctional/individualistic roles.*

Teamwork Task-Related Roles

Roles that support the task dimension of teamwork are those that help the group directly achieve its goals. The team needs these roles to be present for all the parts of the job to get finished! While you may see this as a very long list for a team that might have just four or five people, Benne and Sheats (1948) found that a single person might play numerous roles. Try to look at the following list and identify who on a past team might have held each, which ones you have held, and which ones might have been held by your team leader. These teamwork task-related roles include (see Benne & Sheats, p. 43):

+ **Initiator/Contributor:** suggests or proposes new ideas, solutions, goals, or even ways of organizing the task ahead

+ **Information Seeker:** asks for factual adequacy, authoritative information, and facts pertinent to the problem being discussed

+ **Opinion Seeker:** asks for a clarification of the values pertinent to what the team is undertaking or of values involved in suggestions

+ **Information Giver:** offers facts or generalizations which are "authoritative" to him or her and relates his or her own relevant experience to the problem

+ **Opinion Giver:** states beliefs or opinions about suggestions made with the emphasis on his or her own proposal of what should be the team's values (not views of facts or information)

+ **Elaborator:** spells out suggestions through examples or definitions, offers a rationale for previously made suggestions, and tries to see how an idea or suggestion would work out if adopted by the team

+ **Coordinator:** shows (or clarifies) how various ideas and suggestions can relate to one another, tries to pull ideas and suggestions together, or tries to coordinate the activities of various members

+ **Orienter:** defines the position of the team with respect to its goals by summarizing what has occurred, points out any departures from agreed-upon directions or goals, and raises questions about the direction that the team discussion is taking

+ **Evaluator/Critic:** evaluates the team's work on a set standard (such as the logic of the ideas or how practical they are in context)

+ **Energizer:** motivates the team to action or to increase the quality of team actions

+ **Procedural Technician:** performs routine tasks such as keeping minutes, monitoring the budget, or making sure meetings start and end on time

+ **Recorder:** writes down ideas and is the "group/team memory"

9

Teamwork Relationship Maintenance Roles

Task-related roles are about getting the work done. Teams, however, cannot get the work done if the group is struggling to get along. Benne and Sheats (1948) understood that all groups adopt roles that work to support individual relationships and make people feel comfortable. This might be understood as the 'pathos' of the team. Those adopting these roles do not directly help the group to achieve goals but, without them, the group *will* ultimately fail. Relationship maintenance roles (see Benne & Sheats, p. 44) include:

- **Encourager:** praises, agrees with, and accepts others' ideas with warmth and solidarity toward other group members

- **Harmonizer:** mediates the differences between other members, attempts to reconcile disagreements, relieves tension in conflict situations through jokes and tension-relieving activities

- **Compromiser:** jumps in to manage any conflict in which his idea or position is involved. He may offer compromise by yielding status, admitting his error, by disciplining himself to maintain group harmony, or by "coming halfway" in moving along with the group

- **Gatekeeper/Expediter:** facilitates "talk-time" by calling on some members or discouraging the participation of others so that specific individuals do not take over or some do not participate

- **Standard Setter:** sets the bar high for group success through his or her own behavior and what is deemed acceptable for other's work

- **Follower:** all groups need a person who will passively go along with what is suggested and serve as an audience in group discussion and decision making

Helpful team roles can be easy to recognize and welcomed by the group. However, anyone who has ever been in a group situation can tell you about dysfunctional roles. A great deal of research has catalogued **self-oriented** roles that distract a group from its goals.

Teamwork Dysfunctional/Individualistic Roles

No doubt you have been in a group with some team members whose behavior has hindered the overall process. You may even have been one of those people, knowingly or unknowingly. "Attempts by 'members' of a group to satisfy individual needs which are irrelevant to the group task and which are non-oriented or negatively oriented to group building and maintenance (create) problems (with) group and member training" (Benne & Sheats, 1948, p. 45). This might sound like you just want to get rid of any of these dysfunctional folks right away. Wait! What we learn from group communication research is that these roles exist for a reason. If you simply suppress or exclude them then a group cannot determine what it needs to change in order to move ahead successfully. Look for these roles—and then read on about how to manage them when they surface.

- **Aggressor:** works in a variety of ways to deflate the status of others, disapproves of others' ideas and values, attacks ideas or group work, jokes aggressively, takes credit for another's work

- **Blocker:** tends to be negative and resistant, disagreeing with others without having a reason, and goes back to old ideas after the team has decided to move on

- **Recognition Seeker:** works in various ways to call attention to him or herself, whether through boasting, reporting on personal achievements, avoiding "follower" roles, and acting out

- **Self-Confessor:** uses team time to express personal ideologies, non-group-oriented "feelings" or insights

- **"Playboy"/Social Loafer:** (in a term coined by the authors to reflect the time) makes a show of lack of involvement in the process and disinterest in the group with cynicism and nonchalance

- **Dominator:** manipulates the team through flattery, aggressive directing, or interruptions in order to assert superiority

- **Help-Seeker:** tries to gain sympathy from team members through expressions of inferiority, cries for help, and expressions of confusion, whether valid or not

- **Special Interest Pleader:** asserts a personal agenda to promote a particular bias

You certainly may have more than one task dimension role while simultaneously having a few relationship maintenance roles. In addition, the roles that you personally will play may change with each group, or you may combine roles. For example, you may generate ideas, ask questions, and harmonize the group. Other members may have roles that overlap with yours. What is critical is that you pay attention to what roles are being adopted. If you see a role that has not been adopted and, therefore, whose work is not being accomplished, then you should help the group by playing that role. For example, one role that is not always popular is the harmonizer role because this group member addresses some of the dysfunctional roles that, sadly, occur in many groups.

9

ADDRESSING CONFLICT IN A MEETING

Too often, team members happily report to their supervisors, bosses, or co-workers (and even professors) that there is no conflict in their groups. Unfortunately, instead of good news, that statement should be perceived as a red flag warning of danger ahead. Although you may not like it, *conflict is good for groups*. Without conflict, groups tend to make poor choices, have members who are less committed, and generally lose their opportunity for great achievements (Janis, 1972, 1982). The good news is that you do not have to *like* conflict to *manage* it!

Types of Conflict in Groups

Before conflict can be managed, types of conflict must be defined. **Conflict**, by definition, occurs when two or more interdependent parties perceive incompatible goals. We engage in conflict and disagree when we are dependent on that other person to meet our goals and perceive that he or she is blocking us from those goals (for example, our competition for a job or promotion, a person who took credit for our work, or a colleague who attempted to have our work not be published or presented). There are three types of conflict.

When you think about conflict, you may imagine two people arguing. They are loud and using words designed to hurt. That attempt to hurt is an example of emotional or **affective conflict** (Parayitam & Dooley, 2009). Affective conflict is what most people think about when they think about the concept of conflict. **Behavioral conflict**, or physical aggression (Parayitam & Dooley), is destructive to relationships as well as property and, while it is hopefully rare in a professional setting, it still must be considered when you are addressing conflict at work! Finally, **cognitive conflict** is an intellectual disagreement that considers competing perspectives and can be resolved rationally by careful consideration (Parayitam & Dooley). Cognitive conflict is good! Cognitive conflict leads to open-minded debate, which fosters new and better ideas as well as to the avoidance of the unquestioning conformity (Blanco, 2007).

When people argue *ideas* then they have the chance to merge suggestions into better plans. However, because people tend to think of conflict negatively (as the affective and behavioral conflict that destroys relationships and hurts groups), they become conflict avoidant. This means that while they try not to have conflict, they are also more likely to engage in groupthink!

Groupthink—Bad Conflict Avoidance

Irving Janis, a psychology researcher at Yale University, coined the term **groupthink** (Janis, 1972, 1982), which refers to the tendency for groups to agree simply for the sake of agreeing and avoid what they perceive as negative conflict. Groupthink occurs when groups do not engage in *productive* conflict during decision-making meetings. The result? A poor decision! There are numerous instances of cataloged groupthink leading to disastrous decisions. Janis' own work points to Nazi Germany's decision to invade the Soviet Union in 1941, the United States' Bay of Pigs Invasion, and the Watergate Scandal. Additional studies point out the bad decisions created by groupthink in cases such as the collapse of SwissAir (Hermann & Rammal, 2010) and the space shuttle *Challenger* catastrophe (Dimitroff, Schmidt & Bond, 2005; Moorhead, Ference, & Neck, 1991).

According to Janis (1972, 1982), there are particular conditions that foster the development of the groupthink mentality—and symptoms that let us know that we have gone down this path. In brief, you should be cautious of the following **conditions of groupthink**, which are: 1) a high level of cohesiveness and attachment to solidarity, 2) group isolation, and 3) time sensitivity.

If you believe that all of these conditions exist during your meeting or with your team, do not fret—you still have time to cautiously avoid this bad decision-making path. If, however, you begin to see some of the following symptoms, then you may have already stumbled down this path and need to stop, rewind, and try again. According to Janis and Mann (1977), the **symptoms of groupthink** are:

+ **An illusion of invulnerability**: members of the group ignore obvious dangers and risk

+ **Collective rationalization**: members of the group discredit contrary thinking

+ **Illusions of morality**: members of the group ignore ethical consequences

+ **Excessive stereotyping**: members of the group produce stereotypes of rivals

+ **Pressure of conformity**: members of the group pressure other members to believe asserted stereotypes

+ **Self-censorship**: members of the group withhold dissenting views

9

+ **"Mindguards"**: members of the group will withhold information that is adverse to the group's complacency

Groupthink is far too common, and it is easy for newly formed teams or groups in initial meetings to fall victim during their early phases of interaction. You may have been disappointed when groupthink prevented your team in class from receiving the A you wanted, but think of the real-world cases presented previously. From the invasion of another country to the loss of life in a scientific endeavor, looking inward and not considering external influence is not just a poor evaluation of the rhetorical situation, it is a dangerous choice.

In short—*groupthink is bad*. Instead of avoiding conflict, learn to manage it. There are practices that allow members of a team and its leader to engage in that inevitable conflict in a way that does not lead to groupthink, shut down decision-making processes, or leave groups floundering in secondary tensions. The only way to solve affective or behavioral conflict is to turn it into cognitive conflict.

Creating Conflict on Purpose

We know that affective or behavioral conflict must be addressed in meetings or teamwork to avoid the negative norms and goal blocking that they create. We also know that cognitive conflict can help to avoid groupthink and improve ideas. So—start to fight?! Absolutely not. Creating cognitive conflict is a skilled procedure best outlined in the reflective thinking approach to problem-solving.

The Reflective Thinking Approach

While several models to problem-solving and conflict creation exist, the **Reflective Thinking Approach** to problem solving (developed by John Dewey of the Dewey-Decimal System) is the basis for most modern problem-solving methods for groups (Dewey, 1910; see Dewey 1933 for an updated version). Dewey's method is a structured, organized series of logical, rational steps (often in the form of questions) that he bases on the scientific method of *defining, analyzing,* and *solving* a problem. The version of this approach (shown on the following page) has been updated by Gouran and Hirokawa (1996) who studied decision making in small groups and found that the order of Dewey's steps was less important than making sure that each and every one of the critical functions were completed in a group's decision-making process—including those that create conflict! So, in order to make sure that you create cognitive and resolvable conflict, adhere to the following steps:

1. **Identify the problem:** Teams must make sure that they are focused on the correct problem. Dewey suggested putting the problem in the form of a question, such as, "Why are we losing accounts to our competitors?"

2. **Research the problem:** Ensure that the team investigates the problem from all angles and gathers all available data so that members may understand the *whole* problem. Again, form this like a question, such as, "What procedures do our competitors offer that we do not?" or "What do we not know about available resources for our clients?"

3. **Identify criteria for an ideal solution:** Teams need to explicitly state the lens through which they will evaluate all possible solutions before they begin to come up with solutions. Your question in this area might be, "Do we want the *cheapest* solution or the one that is *fastest* to implement?"

4. **Generate possible solutions:** This is the brainstorming phase and more *is* better! Assume that it takes at least ten adequate solutions to produce one brilliant one. This is not the time to criticize ideas even when they do not have merit in your eyes. This is the time when you will begin to feel that cognitive conflict and must hold back turning it into behavioral or emotional conflict. You will want people to disagree, come up with outside-of-the-box ideas, avoid self-censoring, and generate their own suggestions. Consider asking your team, "Have we thought of every possible method of fixing this regardless of our ability or desire?"

   A proven technique for brainstorming, developed by advertising executive Alex Osborn (1953), calls for:
   + No criticism of ideas during brainstorming
   + Aiming for large quantities of ideas
   + Building on each other's ideas
   + Encouraging wild and exaggerated ideas

5. **Evaluate pros and cons of the top solutions:** Team members will have to engage in debate. You will want everyone in your meeting to consider both the positive and negative aspects of each solution (not just what you like or don't like). You will want to value the merit of ideas over the notion of cohesiveness, look to outside evaluations of all ideas, and give yourself enough time to reach the best solution. Ask of every idea, "Does this idea fit within our criteria (such as is it cheap or is it fast)?" and "How can we make this happen, if at all?"

6. **Select the best solution:** One meeting may not be enough time to go through these steps and then vote or build consensus on the best one. You will want to make sure at this point that you are emerging from conflict and reinforcing the backing of the best solution. Go back to your pre-determined criteria (Step 3) to determine how you want to select the best solution. Your final question will be, "Are we all willing to agree that this is the best possible decision for this particular problem?"

9

Obviously, using the reflective thinking approach is useful when a group or team has a decision to make or a problem to solve. It can best manage existing conflict from the members by putting the interaction into a structured process. And, ironically, if you start out solving a problem without any cognitive conflict then the decision-making process will naturally create it—and that's a good thing!

Choosing to adopt a reflective approach and choosing to ensure that all the needed roles of the task and relationship maintenance have been adopted are not typically the choices of a follower. You might be wondering how it is that you can direct your next meeting to engage in good conflict and move toward its goals. If you are thinking this, then you are already thinking like a leader! Leadership is the last area of concern for you in your path to effective business talks.

BECOMING THE LEADER OF YOUR GROUP

You might have read the previous list of team roles and thought, "OK—but who is actually *in charge?*" The person in charge may adopt any of the roles listed but is, indeed, the one that we will call the leader. For many people, including most of the early scholars of team dynamics, the most important role in a group is that of the "leader." **Leadership**, for our purposes, is influencing and guiding a group to go beyond its current status to achieve collective goals. This is something in which *all* group members can share (Pearce, Manz, & Sims Jr., 2009). Entire classes, undergraduate and graduate degrees, business seminars, numerous

books and presentations have been devoted to the study of team leadership. Of course, leadership *theory* is complex and evolving. There are countless studies and theories of leadership to help guide an adoption of this role, some of which have transformed how we understand leaders and others that have been discounted over time.

Initial Views on Leadership

Perhaps the most well-known theory about leadership is the **Great Man Theory** (yes, original theories about leadership were about men but much has changed with time!). The basic idea behind this theory was that great leaders are born that way. Those who followed this ideal would say that Martin Luther King, Steve Jobs, Margaret Thatcher—all of these people were born with the skills to lead and, thus, they naturally took up the role.

But, if you have ever stepped into a leadership role during one meeting but happily let someone else do that work on a different team, then you might question the validity of this theory. You would not be alone. After reviewing 287 studies conducted between 1904 and 1970, Stogdill (1948, 1974) concluded that leadership success was *not* based on personality traits (the natural characteristics of the person). Instead, he found that a person's natural characteristics would make them successful leaders in some situations but not others and that two leaders with different personalities could be successful in the same situation.

Today we know that being a successful leader is a fairly complex concept. We know that leaders are not born but are groomed by situations and training. We know that *the Great Man Theory is invalid* and that leadership is often shared across team members. After all, there is no leader in the world today who does not have a fleet of staff sharing the weight of the work. Your team should be no different. The more people in your group who pull their weight—who adopt the leadership role when the task is within their expertise—the better your group will be. How you will know when to jump in as a leader may very well be decided by how well you read the needs of the situation. People with high levels of emotional intelligence adopt a leadership role when that is what is needed and then step into other roles when a leader is not needed.

Emotional Intelligence

One of the major parts in the leadership success equation is emotional intelligence (also known as "EI") and was first proposed by Peter Salovey and John Mayer (1990), then made popular by Daniel Goleman (1998, 2006). **Emotional intelligence** "refers to the abilities to recognize and regulate emotions in ourselves and in others" (Goleman, 2006, p. 2). What does this mean for business? Well, if your boss walks into the room where you and your officemate just finished yelling at each other (which you should never do) and he or she cannot even tell that something is wrong, then either you two are fantastic actors or your boss has low emotional intelligence. Imagine the problems that arise or the issues that cannot be solved when our leaders do not have high emotional intelligence.

Because emotional intelligence describes traits that would seem quite important for leaders to possess (e.g., abstract reasoning, social competence, etc.), Mandell and Pherwani (2003) conducted an experiment to determine whether or not there was correlation between emotional intelligence and successful leadership. Not only did they find a direct relationship between emotional intelligence and transformational (visionary) leadership skills (for a review of this type of management style see Chapter One), but they also found that women scored higher on emotional intelligence tests than did men! (Sorry guys…you do some things better than women, too!)

9

Using emotional intelligence, thus, should not only help you to determine whether or not to adopt a leadership position, but help you to do well in that position. By choosing to bring in all information both emotional and intellectual, you can become a leader who *influences* your team to effectively move toward its goals.

Leadership Styles of Influence

Yes. Leadership is about influence. As a leader, you will move your team in a particular direction, apply metatalk to manage conflict, and see that your team completes its tasks. Yet, how you lead will depend on the style of leadership that comes naturally to you as well as your style of conflict management. Paul Hersey and Ken Blanchard (1969; Hersey, Blanchard, & Johnson, 2007) articulated four styles of **situational leadership** that explained how leaders can influence their teams in particular circumstances, and their popular theory continues to be the basis for leadership training courses. For your purposes, the following leadership styles of influence can help guide you to pilot the direction of any meeting or team project during your time of leadership. These styles are:

+ **Telling (Authoritarian):** This style uses only one-way communication, which does not ask for feedback; put simply, "tell" people what to do and provide close supervision. A telling style works well when group participants are unmotivated and the leader has information needed by the group. (In a group of peers, giving orders can be uncomfortable, but sometimes group members are willing to let someone else be in charge.)

+ **Selling (Coaching):** Like the telling style, selling leadership still has the leader in charge of directing the group but now embraces two-way communication/feedback and provides emotional support so that those in the meeting or on the team "buy-in" to the decisions; the selling style works well when group members are motivated but may need more direction because of a lack of experience or knowledge.

+ **Participating (Collaborative):** As with the Benne and Sheats (1948) division of group roles discussed earlier, this leadership style of influence is dictated by the task and relationship elements of teamwork; participative leaders will focus less on task management and more on relationship maintenance because team members are already motivated and have useful information or experience to share. Situations calling for this leadership are about shared-decision making with a leader who is a co-member of the group, rather than the "boss."

+ **Delegating:** Delegating style is when the leader is part of the decision-making process and will stay involved to monitor the group work but primary responsibility for making final decisions has been passed to the team members who are both knowledgeable and motivated!

As you can see, different situations will call you to use different types of leadership styles. What you choose is based on who is on your team (and the rhetorical situation) as well as accounting for who shows up for each individual meeting.

Imagine that you have a motivated and knowledgeable team where, as the primary expert, you have taken on a leadership role. Suddenly, your boss comes in and changes the task of the group. Same team, same you—different project. Now you have a group that is unmotivated and far less informed. You likely will have to switch from a delegating style to a telling style in order to accomplish your new goals. As with topic selection for any presentation or business talk, you must take into consideration the audience in crafting your message (are they hostile, wavering, or supportive?). As a leader, you are crafting a message to motivate your team. Take into consideration the needs, motivation, and expertise of your team to select the best style.

As with leadership, all of the interaction between team members will be situational. You might have a group that is happily moving along one day and then angry and dysfunctional the next. Before you judge your co-workers, take a step back to think of yourself. Have you ever had a bad day? Have you ever snapped at a friend, co-worker, or even a boss or professor? You know that this is not because of them but because your needs and concerns have changed on that day or with that project. Everyone does it. However, now in a leadership role, the responsibility of managing those situational needs will fall onto you.

To do that, team leaders can engage in a stylized conversational pattern called metatalk or engage in leader-based conflict management styles.

Talking about Conflict

When one of your team members adopts a negative role or is determined to engage in negative conflict, the best way to address this is to talk about it. One useful form of business talk is the strategy of metatalk. In its simplest terms, **metatalk** means talking cooperatively about how the team is communicating (Swain, 1998).

9

Instead of having arguments or getting caught up in the details of a disagreement or hidden meanings behind comments, metatalk allows team members to focus on the communication strategies that should be used when disagreement occurs. From reading the initial chapters of this text on communication models and effective listening, you already have the skills to do much of this!

For instance, consider the "criticism sandwich." Before a person in a meeting can even make a negative comment, you can talk about *how* criticism should be offered. Instead of just laying out the negative ideas, team leaders can ask that all criticism is "sandwiched" between constructive and positive comments. This is a strategic way of deciding *how* to engage in communication but not directing team members on *what* to say. It also is a reliable reference when people get off track and offer affective conflict comments. If an aggressor team member says to you or another in the meeting, "Why did you do that? You're stupid," then you could get defensive and say, "No I'm not!"—or you could step outside of the attack all together and engage in metatalk through a comment about the attack itself and how the criticism was communicated. Remember that conversation in meetings can sometimes turn combative. Knowing how to respond when you are in the middle of a verbal battle is important to your confidence as a team leader and establishing goal-oriented norms.

Leaders Managing Conflict

According to business consultants and management professors Kenneth Thomas and Ralph Kilmann, conflict management is not a one-size-fits-all process (Thomas & Kilmann, 2004). If you use the same conflict management style in every situation, then you are not reading the rhetorical situation and responding appropriately. Thomas and Kilmann created a conflict styles grid that helps guide leaders in assessing how best to adopt conflict management strategies. Again, like Benne and Sheats (1948), they remind us that all leadership in conflict situations must consider **concern for the task** and **concern for the relationship**.

According to Thomas and Kilmann's (2004) theory, your level of concern for each of these team-based elements should determine your conflict resolution approach.

	Low Concern for the Relationship	Moderate Concern for the Relationship	High Concern for the Relationship
Low Concern for Winning	Avoid conflict		Accommodate to their goals
Moderate Concern		Compromise	
High Concern for Winning	Compete to win		Collaborate to find a win-win solution

Thomas and Kilmann's Conflict Styles Grid

Seeing the grid can help us to find where our particular situation fits into how we should approach the conflict, but to truly understand the actions of each style, consider how you would manage conflict in a meeting with each.

+ **Avoidance Approach to Conflict:** In avoidance, the conflict is simply not addressed. Team leaders have a *low concern for the task and the relationship*, and sometimes, this is appropriate. For example, imagine you want to buy a unique but unimportant item on eBay. While the seller really wants to make the transaction with you, he is only willing to sell it at a price that you cannot afford. The best solution is to walk away. Neither party reaches their goal, and the relationship dissolves. No harm—no foul.

+ **Accommodation Approach to Conflict:** Avoidance of conflict *prioritizes the relationship* over the task. Some team leaders know that the task at hand is not terribly important (such as the color to paint the break room or selecting doughnuts or yogurt for the snack at your next meeting) but the relationship will determine how the team functions in the future. When another person cares very much about the task but the group or the leader does not, to best meet long-term goals, leaders will accommodate the relationship needs and sacrifice the task.

+ **Compromise Approach to Conflict:** Compromise (often misunderstood because our kindergarten teachers drilled it into us that compromise is *always* best) is another *situationally* appropriate conflict management technique where both sides give up some part of their task needs and/or relationship needs. In a true compromise, each party agrees to give up something so that they can get something in return. Since both parties lose something with this

9

approach, it should be used *only when the goal is not critical.* Case in point, if you are arguing over whether or not to order pink or yellow Post-It® notes it might be best to compromise. Go with the color that does not thrill you this time and choose your color the next time. Here, compromise is good. However, if your conflict is about who will be promoted first, you or a co-worker—and you know that you deserve (and need) the pay bump—consider a competing approach!

+ **Competing Approach to Conflict:** Sometimes you want to win at all costs and you are not worried if you make an enemy in the process. If you do not care—or do not need to care—about the relationship, then competing is a great strategy for getting something you really want. Competition sacrifices the relationship for the task or goal. This works well with trying to get that promotion over another or in cases of not putting up with sexual harassment!

+ **Collaborating Approach to Conflict:** Obviously, a win-win (*where the task and the relationship are valued*) is the ideal solution. Many people advocate using this strategy all of the time but you know that it is only situationally appropriate. First, collaborating takes significant time, energy, and creativity to produce a true win-win solution. Second, it takes the investment of both sides (perhaps your leaders and followers or even leaders from two different teams). Therefore, remember that collaborating will not be feasible or even worth the investment in every situation.

While each of the above strategies is talked about through the lens of leadership, note how they are also appropriate when you are not the leader of your group. You may face a conflict situation between yourself and another team member. You might be the leader on one task but the follower on another (the important concept of *shared leadership*). Regardless of your role, these strategies for managing conflict scenarios should be a useful guide to you whenever you are faced with goal-oriented disagreements.

By having some strategies to manage conflict at your fingertips, you are one step closer to having a functioning team or meeting. If your group can say that they regularly disagree with one another, but do not experience the negative effects of conflict, then you have a cohesive and effective group! This is the goal that any team member or leader should work toward. As part of pursuing this goal, it will be the job of everyone on the team to spend time *preparing* for meetings and it will be your job as the leader to help everyone in this important task.

PREPARING FOR PRODUCTIVE MEETINGS

Research indicates that team productivity and even organizational success is linked to the strength of team meetings (Kauffeld & Lehmann-Willenbrock, 2012). However, say the words, "We should have a meeting!" and you can almost hear the groans if not see the eyes roll. Unfortunately, too many poorly run meetings organized by ill-prepared hosts have given these important team interactions a bad reputation. Just like speeches and interviews, successful meetings do not happen by accident. Maximizing group input and participation requires the meeting organizer (if you are the leader then this is you!) to prepare by identifying meeting goals as well as writing and distributing an agenda.

"Do We Need to Meet?"—The Art of Determining Meeting Goals

If you run a search for "business meeting" on the internet you will find innumerable suggestions for how to run effective meetings along with a fair number of rants about ineffective meetings. Technology architect Craig Borysowich (2005) remarked that, "[b]oth the private and public sectors are a complete wasteland of time-wasting, soul-sucking, bad meetings. It needs to stop!" (para. 1). This is why, before meeting agendas are drafted and conference rooms secured, the meeting organizer must ask herself, "Do we even need to meet?" The answer to this question comes from identifying the goal of each meeting. Meetings have a goal so that participants can arrive prepared to offer meaningful participation (Willets, 2011).

Meetings are rich channels of communication. If you reflect back on our first chapter discussion of communication models or even the coverage of research such as interviews versus surveys, you will remember that there are times that you will want to use a rich channel and times that you will not. Meeting participants have the advantage of being able to transmit a significant amount of verbal and nonverbal information—thus, it is a rich channel. The downside is that the richness of this channel requires a significant time investment, which is something in short supply for today's professionals (Krattenmaker, 2007).

Meetings should be reserved for situations that *require* face-to-face (whether mediated or in-person) group interaction. Situations that might call for a meeting include problem solving, anticipating problems, identifying opportunities, or coaching (Lloyd, 2012). If the goal of the meeting is to deliver brief progress reports or the distribution of materials for an upcoming project then a less rich channel such as email, which accomplishes the goal without zapping the time and energy of meeting participants, is likely a better choice. If you have decided that your

9

meeting is warranted (by identifying the goal of your team's interaction), you are now ready to give your attention to how you will, as a leader, direct the communicative expectations of your team members to support—instead of impede—the flow of communication. This begins with the setting of a meeting agenda.

Writing an Agenda

One of the most important ingredients for effective meeting communication is a well-written agenda. An **agenda** is a list of tasks that the group will undertake during the meeting. You have likely seen these throughout your life in a variety of settings and given them very little attention. You may have done this, in part, because the agenda itself was not created and distributed in a way that grabbed your attention or facilitated communication. As your team's leader or the person charged with drafting such an important document (this might also be the role of the coordinator, orienter, or even procedural technician—all of which are roles that can also be held while you lead), you will want to do just a bit better than the average agenda maker!

Good agendas:

+ Remind people to attend (through clarifications of meeting times and locations)

+ Articulate the meeting goal and what must be accomplished (which will help to keep the leader and team members on track!)

+ Let people know what resources to bring along

+ Provide details of who will cover what issue (to remind task leaders to prepare and allow those who miss meetings or details to follow up)

Every organization and industry has a different way of writing agendas, so there is no set standard or style that you can apply to all situations. In fact, some groups have the agenda format written into their by-laws or are legally bound to follow the agenda once it has been published. Some agendas are short and sweet and delivered by email while others arrive via FedEx® with a binder of supporting material attached. Despite the variation in agenda styles and requirements, typical agendas will contain the following common elements.

Agenda Common Elements

+ **Clear headers:** Anyone scanning the document should immediately be able to see the details such as the who, what, where, and when (time and date).

+ **Identified objectives:** An objective is the outcome or goal of the meeting (not the process of how to get there). Good objectives are clear, positively worded and achievable.

- **Assigned topics and times:** Effective agendas assign someone to each particular meeting task and note how long this discussion should take in the meeting as well as give a general description. For example, a discussion item on a proposed media relations campaign might read: "Media Outreach (10:00 to 10:20 a.m.): *Communications Director Patricia Ornst will lead a discussion on the impact of our new media relations campaign.*"

Agenda Example

Project:	TechSystem Redesign	
Meeting Purpose:	To identify risks for clients using TechSystem	
Attendees:	R. Johnson (Chair), L. Mannheim, J. Lake, S. Sawville, R. Jackson, T. Smith, J. Schultz, P. Talarico	
Date and Time:	Wednesday 11/17/2010 10:00 a.m.	
Place:	Meeting room 7	

Agenda Item	Person Responsible	Time
1. **Introduction, review agenda, meeting purpose.**	R. Johnson	2 min
2. **Review of risk management process** Identify the basic definition of risk for this technology and consider the approach to risk management previously established for TechSystem.	R. Johnson	10 min
3. **Risk identification brainstorming** Produce an initial, expansive list of risks in all categories through active participation in a non-judgmental think-tank session. (The list will be assessed, prioritized, and maintained in subsequent meetings.)	All (led by P. Talorico)	60 min
4. **Assign tasks, set date for next meeting, review meeting effectiveness**	R. Johnson	15 min

Attachment: Copy of risk management standards and procedures.

9

As you are putting together the agenda for your meeting, craft it so that the focus of your meeting will be to look ahead. Guttman (2009) reminds that while the focus of your meeting might be to "review progress on previously identified cross departmental projects," (p. 18) there should be an emphasis on actions taken and acts to be taken instead of using your time as a reporting session (something that is better left to an email exchange). Pozen (2011) helps us with the practical application of an action agenda by suggesting that all agendas leave a place and time for the "What is next?" element. He states, "At the end of a meeting I will always ask, 'What are the to-dos, who's going to take care of them, and when will they be delivered?' I want the participants to agree on the deliverables and to set their own timetable" (p. 129). Such a smart step on your agenda will make your leadership role easier because team members can actually *see* their responsibilities and the time allotted for completion. If you have crafted an ideal agenda, you will want to make sure that every member of your team reads it in their own preparation for the meeting.

Agenda Distribution

All of your hard work on your agenda will be wasted if participants do not have enough time to review the materials prior to the meeting. Not surprisingly, almost all business scholars agree that meeting agendas should be distributed in advance (see Millard, 2007). Sending an agenda prior to the day of the meeting helps those who arrive to be mentally prepared for discussions, bring critical materials, decide if they need to bring additional team members, and even weigh in on the organization of the meeting itself. So, how much time in advance should it be sent?

The time for agenda distribution depends on the objective of the meeting. For most business meetings, three business days ahead will suffice (so, remember, if your meeting is on a Monday morning, your agenda should be sent by Wednesday afternoon at the latest—not Friday afternoon). For larger meetings, such as a four-hour, twice-a-year board  meeting, the agenda and any supplemental materials ought to be sent at least two weeks to a month ahead of time—depending on the complexity of the proposed discussion items (Baker, 2010). Since you have prepared for your meeting, now it is time to relax…right? Not quite. On the day of your meeting you need to give a bit of attention to meeting room setup to ensure the participants are literally in a space to effectively play their roles in your group.

Using Meeting Space to Help Communication

Savvy meeting organizers use meeting space dimensions to support the goal of the group's discussion. Types of room setup include lecture-style (also known as theater style), classroom, conference, U-shape, E-shape, T-shape, hollow-square and banquet style. While you do not need to become a meeting planner expert overnight, you do need to choose the setup that supports your communication goals. (Hint: If your organization has a meeting planner, make that person your new best friend!) For example, just as the name suggests, the classroom style allows attendees to take notes and provides table space for attendees to look through information, whereas U-shape, E-shape, and T-shape are ideal for smaller meetings and provide opportunities for interaction (for more details, see "Step-by-step," n.d.).

Obviously, you cannot sit 100 people in a circle to watch a presentation, and you cannot have a theater seating style for a small problem-solving discussion. No matter what room setup is chosen, meeting organizers should use strategy if assigning seats for team members. Rowan (1997) recommended that chatty folks are not seated next to each other, vocal opponents are not directly across from each other, and the leader should be seated in a position to make eye contact with all participants. Similar to steps taken before delivering a speech, the meeting organizer should check the physical conditions of the meeting space. (You will want to identify and fix any potential distractions such as the temperature being too hot or too cold, not enough light, a noisy air conditioner, or even bad signage directing your group on how to find you.) If you have a good space and a well-prepared group then the final stage of your business talk will be to use both of these components to help direct the meeting itself.

Establishing Meeting Rules and Expectations

Think back to the first day of class at your college or university. Your professors likely spent the first day going over the expectations of the class. You heard about rules for absences and being late, cell phone policies, and perhaps even how you would be graded on the amount and type of participation that you offered. Your work life will be just the same.

On your first day of orientation, you will be told about the rules of your office. On the first day of your team's meeting, you must set up the rules for your team. Running an effective meeting requires the team leaders to design and communicate a framework for communication. This framework may include letting team members know that they should avoid side conversations, be prepared to discuss particular agenda items, not use cell phones (yes, get used to this policy!), as well as being sure to start and end the meeting on time.

9

Leaders will, also, likely need to initiate conversation to set a standard of participation for team members. Pozen (2011) cautions meeting leaders—especially those who are also the boss—to recognize the difference between providing a meeting focus and *forcing* discussion. Ideally, meeting leaders should promote discussion by opening with a general statement of the situation that reiterates the goals and clarifies the meeting procedures rather than starting with his or her own viewpoint or proposed solution. When meeting leaders force their ideologies this can lead to shutting down needed conversation and debate, especially if participants think the boss has already made decisions (Pozen).

Meeting conversations may or may not be on topic. Some off-topic conversations can be useful! Your team might find that participants are suddenly inspired to solve an issue for tomorrow's meeting (yea, you!); do not ignore this suddenly inspired solution but balance the time given to it so that it does not dominate a meeting whose goal was to focus on another decision. A strategy to balance on- and off-topic conversations is to allow for the ideas to be given but to do what Krattenmaker (2011) calls "parking" these topics (para. 16). This means that you would use the visual aids in the space—perhaps a flip chart or a whiteboard—to document the ideas so that they can be saved and your team can come back to them at a later, more appropriate time.

Your job as team leader will be to facilitate the business talk. You will want to stick to your agenda and work toward your team goals. You will want to follow the rules that you set and lead by example. Displaying the rules in the meeting room and reminding attendees that the guidelines are designed to protect their time can help ensure good-natured compliance from the meeting leader and participants—and you will want your meetings (and your teams) to be a productive professional place!

BUSINESS TALK—THE ROLE OF A LEADER, A FOLLOWER, AND A TEAM

Working in teams can be both rewarding and disappointing. The effectiveness of your team hinges on group communication. An understanding of team roles, conflict resolution strategies, leadership styles, as well as knowing how to properly prepare for meetings can ensure that your team is productive. Though emotions play an unmistakable and important role in team dynamics, remember, though, that effective teams are not concerned with making *all* group members happy *all* of the time. You know that conflict can help to lead to better solutions and that understanding dysfunctional team members can help you to develop a better understanding of how to meet the needs of your group.

It can be intimidating for new employees or even those simply new to a group to figure out how to navigate existing communication patterns. You might find that your talk, which you know is well-researched and effectively organized, is not valued in your workplace. Do not fret. Responding appropriately to your rhetorical situation can take time and certainly a great deal of effort. You know, however, that you were hired because your expertise (and likely your great attitude) are valued. You know that in survey after survey of major employers, communication skills were stated as one of the top qualities that companies desire in applicants (Morreale, 2001;  Morreale & Pearson, 2008; NACE, 2011) and that, through your work on business talk with this text, you have developed those skills and know how desirable you will be to employers.

Remind yourself that communication is what connects one person to another. In a professional setting, communication is how tasks are assigned and clarified as well as how projects are managed. *Communication is how the work actually gets done.* Whether your career goals are in accounting, management, medicine, government service, or any other field, you are now better equipped with the communication strategies necessary to send verbal and nonverbal messages in the settings of speeches, meetings, and interviews. You have a stronger chance of career advancement because you have mastered *business talk*.

9

REFERENCES

Chapter One—Sending Messages

Berlo, D. K. (1960). *The process of communication: An introduction to theory and practice.* New York: Holt, Rinehart and Winston, Inc.

Bisel, R. B., Messersmith, A. S., & Keyton, J. (2009). Understanding organizational culture and communication through a gyroscope metaphor. *Journal of Management Education, 34,* 342–366.

Bitzer, L. (1968). The rhetorical situation. *Philosophy and Rhetoric, 1,* 1–14.

Burns, J. M. (1978). *Leadership.* New York, NY: Harper & Row Publishers.

Daft, R. L., & Lane, P. G. (2008). *The leadership experience* (5th ed.). Mason, OH: South-Western Cengage Learning.

Dunleavy, K. N., Chory, R. M., & Goodboy, A. K. (2010). Responses to deception in the workplace: Perceptions of credibility, power, and trustworthiness. *Communication Studies, 61,* 239–255.

Hall, S. (1980). Encoding/decoding. In Centre for Contemporary Cultural Studies (Ed.), *Culture, media, language: Working papers in cultural studies, 1972–1979* (pp. 128–138). London: Hutchinson.

Han, S., & Shavitt, S. (1994). Persuasion and culture: Advertising appeals in individualistic and collectivistic societies. *Journal of Experimental Social Psychology, 30,* 326–350. Retrieved on July 1, 2012 from http://osil.psy.ua.edu:16080/~Rosanna/Soc_Inf/week13/693_persuasion.pdf.

Hart, R. P. (1994). *Modern rhetorical criticism.* Boston, MA: Allyn and Bacon.

Jakobson, R. (1960). Closing statement: Linguistics and poetics. In T. Sebeok (Ed.), *Style in language* (pp. 350–77). Cambridge, MA: MIT Press.

Johnpress, T. (2003, August 24). Transformational culture can percolate your firm. *Austin Business Journal.* Accessed December 28, 2010 from http://www. bizjournals.com/austin/stories/2003/08/25/smallb2.html.

Johnson, A. M., & Lederer, A. L. (2005, Fall). The effect of communication frequency and channel richness on the convergence between chief executive and chief information officers. *Journal of Management Information Systems, 22*(2), 227–252.

Mayo, E. (1949). Hawthorne and the Western Electric Company: Some further comments on the interview experiment. In E. Mayo (Ed.), *The social problems of an industrial civilization* (pp. 60–76). London: Routledge.

McGregor, D. (1960). *The human side of enterprise.* New York: McGraw Hill.

McQuail, D. (1983). *Mass communication theory: An introduction.* Michigan: Sage Publications.

Morreale, S., & Pearson, J. (2008). Why communication education is important: The centrality of the discipline in the 21st century. *Communication Education, 57*(2), 224–240.

Mortenson, C. D. (1972). Communication models. In C. D. Mortenson (Ed.), *Communication: The study of human communication* (pp. 83–102). NY: McGraw Hill.

NACE. (2011, October 26). National Association of Colleges and Employers. *Job outlook: The candidate skills/qualities that employers want.* Retrieved June 13, 2012 from http://www.naceweb.org/s10262011/candidate_skills_employer_qualities/.

Parra, M. G., Lleó de Nalda, A., & Perles, G. S. M. (2011). Towards a more humanistic understanding of organizational trust. *Journal of Management Development, 30*(6), 605–614.

Russ, G. S., Daft, R. L., & Lengel, R. H. (1990). Media selection and managerial characteristics in organizational communications. *Management Communication Quarterly, 4,* 151–175.

Schramm, W. (1954). How communication works. In W. Schramm (Ed.), *The process and effects of communication* (pp. 3–26). Urbana, IL: University of Illinois Press.

Scott, R. W. (2003). *Organizations: Rational, natural and open systems.* Boston, MA: Prentice Hall.

Shannon, C. E. (1948). A mathematical theory of communication. *Bell System Technical Journal, 27,* 379–423, 623–656.

Shannon, C. E., & Weaver, W. (1949). *The mathematical theory of communication.* Urbana, IL: The University of Illinois Press.

Taylor, F. W. (1911). *The principles of scientific management.* New York: Harper & Brothers.

Watzlawick, P., Beavin, J., & Jackson, D. D. (1967). *Pragmatics of human communication: A study of interactional patterns, pathologies, and paradoxes* (1st ed.). NY: Norton.

Weber, M. (1947). *The theory of social and economic organizations.* Translated by Henderson, A. M., & Parsons, T. New York: Oxford University Press.

Worthy, J. C. (1950). Organizational structure and employee morale. *American Sociological Review, 15,* 169–179.

Chapter Two—Choosing to Receive Messages

Air Force Negotiation Center of Excellence. (2004, March 21). Active listening for mediators. Retrieved on June 15, 2012 from http://www.au.af.mil/au/awc/awcgate/va/mediation/active.htm.

Aristotle [350 B.C.E.]. (1980). *Nicomachean ethics*. Translated by W. D. Ross, 1908, revised by J. O. Urmson. Oxford: Clarendon Press.

Barker, L., Edwards, R., Gaines, C., Gladney, K., & Holley, F. (1980). An investigation of proportional time spent in various communication activities by college students. *Journal of Applied Communications Research, 8*(2), 101. Retrieved from Communication & Mass Media Complete database.

Bierck, R. (2001). How to listen. *Harvard Management Communication Letter, 4*(1), 4. Retrieved from Communication & Mass Media Complete database.

Bitzer, L. (1968). The rhetorical situation. *Philosophy and Rhetoric, 1,* 1–14.

Bordone, R. (2007). Listen up! Your talks may depend on it. *Negotiation, 9*(11). Retrieved from Communication & Mass Media Complete database.

Browne, M., & Keeley, S. (2006). *Asking the right questions: A guide to critical thinking.* Boston, MA: Prentice Hall. Retrieved on June 15, 2012 from http://wps.prenhall.com/hss_browne_askingquest_8/48/12534/3208929.cw/index.html.

Brunner, B. R. (2008). Listening, communication & trust: Practitioners' perspectives of business/organizational relationships. *International Journal of Listening 22*(1), 73–82.

Cashman, Kevin. (2012). *The pause principle.* San Francisco, CA: Berrett–Koehler Publishers Inc.

Chaney, J. (2011). Arnold Schwarzenegger confirms he fathered child with staff member. *Washington Post.* Accessed on June 20, 2012 from http://www.washingtonpost.com/blogs/celebritology/post/arnold-schwarzenegger-confirms-he-fathered-child-with-staff-member/2011/05/17/AFvi7g5G_blog.html.

Dewhurst, S. (2010). Mastering the art of powerful questioning. *Strategic Communication Management, 14*(4), 14.

DiSalvo, V. S. (1980). A summary of current research identifying communication skills in various organizational contexts. *Communication Education, 29,* 283–290.

Encyclopedia of Business and Finance. (2010). Listening skills in business. *Encyclopedia of Business and Finance.* Retrieved on July 30, 2010 from http://www.endnotes.com/business-finance-encyclopedia/listening-skills-busness.

Ferrari, B. T. (2012). *Power listening: Mastering the most critical business skill of all.* New York, NY: Penguin Group.

Festinger, L. (1957). *A theory of cognitive dissonance.* Evanston, IL: Row & Peterson.

Flynn, J., Valikoski, T., & Grau, J. (2008). Listening in the business context: Reviewing the state of research. *International Journal of Listening, 22*(2), 141–151. Retrieved from Communication & Mass Media Complete database.

Fredriksson, L. (1999). Modes of relating in a caring conversation: A research synthesis on presence, touch and listening. *Journal of Advanced Nursing, 30*(5), 1167–1176.

Gergen, C., & Vanourek, G. (2011). *Life entrepreneurs: Ordinary people creating extraordinary lives.* Warren Bennis Series (142). San Francisco, CA: John Wiley & Sons.

Glen, P. (2011). 5 Steps to poor listening: The ordinary professional's guide. *Business Listening.* Accessed on June 8, 2012 from http://www.businesslistening.com/listening_for_IT_pros.php.

Harding, T. S., Finelli, C. J., & Passow, H. J. (2004). Does academic dishonesty relate to unethical behavior in professional practice? An exploratory study. *Science and Engineering Ethics,* 10.

Hart, R. P. (1994). *Seducing America: How television charms the modern voter.* New York, NY: Oxford University Press.

Hartman, J., & McCambridge, J. (2011, March). Optimizing millennials' communication styles. *Business Communication Quarterly, 74*(1), 22–44.

Helmstetter, S. (2005). *The gift.* Park Avenue Press.

Hillyard, S. A., Hink, R. F., Schwent, V. L., & Picton, T. W. (1973). Electrical signs of selective attention in the human brain. *Science, 182,* 177–179.

Kant, I. (1964). *The moral law.* Translated by H. J. Paton. London: Hutchinson & Co. Ltd.

Kant, I. [1785]. (1985). *Foundations of the metaphysics of morals.* (2nd ed). Translated by Lewis White Beck. New York: MacMillan.

Kant, I. (2003). 'On a supposed right to tell lies from benevolent motives.' Translated by T.K. Abbot. Retrieved on June 2, 2011 from http://core.ecu.edu/phil/mccartyr/kant/entry3.htm.

Kidder, R. M. (1995). *How good people make tough choices.* New York: William Morrow.

King, C. (2010). Beyond persuasion: The rhetoric of negotiation in business communication. *Journal of Business Communication, 47*(1), 69–78.

Kunzig, R. (2009). Scraping bottom. *National Geographic.* Accessed on June 20, 2012 from http://ngm.nationalgeographic.com/2009/03/canadian-oil-sands/kunzig-text/1.

Lee, D., & Hatesohl, D. (1993). Listening: Our most used communication skill. *University of Missouri Extension.* Retrieved from http://extension.missouri.edu/publications/DisplayPub.aspx?P=CM150.

Lenzer, R. (2008). Bernie Madoff's $50 billion ponzi scheme. *Forbes.* Accessed on June 20, 2012 from http://www.forbes.com/2008/12/12/madoff-ponzi-hedge-pf-ii-in_rl_1212croesus_inl.html.

Maccoby, M. (2000, January/February). Narcissistic leaders: The incredible pros, the inevitable cons. *Harvard Business Review.* Retrieved on September 15, 2012 from http://hbswk.hbs.edu/archive/1565.html.

Mayer, R. (2005). *How to win any argument: Without raising your voice, losing your cool, or coming to blows.* Pompton Plains, NJ: Career Press.

McCroskey, J. C., Richmond, V. P., & McCroskey, L. L. (2006). *An introduction to communication in the classroom: The role of communication in teaching and training.* Boston: Pearson.

Mill, J. S. (1972). *Later letters. Volume XVI.* Toronto: University of Toronto Press.

Oestreich, D. K. (2009). Asking for feedback. *Oestreich Associates.* Accessed on June 14, 2012 from http://www.unfoldingleadership.com/downloads/AskingforFeedback.pdf.

Posner, M. I., & Petersen, S. E. (1990, March). The attention system of the human brain. *Annual Review of Neuroscience, 13,* 25–42.

Ramsey, R., & Sohi, R. (1997). Listening to your customers: The impact of perceived salesperson listening behavior on relationship outcomes. *Journal of the Academy of Marketing Science, 25*(2), 127. Retrieved from Communication & Mass Media Complete database.

Rifkin, G. (1994, January 23). Profile; the 'iron lady' keeping lotus on track. *The New York Times.* Retrieved on September 16, 2012 from http://www.nytimes.com/1994/01/23/business/profile-the-iron-lady-keeping-lotus-on-track.html?scp=1&sq=Software Development at Lotus June Rokoff&st=nyt.

Ryssdal, K. (2012, March 12). How much productivity will be lost during March Madness. *American Public Media.* Accessed on June 14, 2012 from http://www.marketplace.org/topics/life/final-note/how-much-productivity-will-be-lost-during-march-madness.

Schramm, W. (1954). How communication works. In W. Schramm (Ed.), *The process and effects of communication* (pp. 3–26). Urbana, IL: University of Illinois Press.

Soule, E., Hedahl, M., & Dienhart, J. (2009). Principles of managerial moral responsibility. *Business Ethics Quarterly*, 19(4), 529–552.

Sypher, B. D., Bostrom, R., & Seibert, J. H. (1989). Listening, communication abilities and success at work. *Journal of Business Communication*, 26, 293–303.

Tufte, E. (2005, September). PowerPoint is evil. *Wired News*. Retrieved February 18, 2010 from http://www.wired.com/wired/archive/11.09/ppt2.html.

Vatz, R. E. (1968, Summer). The myth of the rhetorical situation. *Philosophy and Rhetoric*, 6(3), 154–161.

Vatz, R. E. (2007, January). The mythical status of situational rhetoric: Implications for rhetorical critics' relevance in the public arena. *The Review of Communication*, 9(1), 1–5.

Vogt, E., Brown, J., & Isaacs, D. (2003). *The art of powerful questions: Catalyzing insight, innovation, and action.* (1st ed.). Mill Valley, CA: Pegasus Communications, Inc.

Wheeless, L. R. (1975). An investigation of receiver apprehension and social context dimensions of communication apprehension. *The Speech Teacher*, 24, 261–268.

Zofi, Y., & Meltzer, S. (2007, May). Listening takes practice (key component of effective communication). *Legacy of Leadership*. Retrieved from http://www.ltlmagazine.com/print/article/listening-takes-practice?page=2.

Chapter Three—Researching Messages: Having Ethos with Business Audiences

Allen, M., & Preiss, R. (1997). Comparing the persuasiveness of narrative and statistical evidence using meta-analysis. *Communication Research Reports*, 14(2), 125–131.

Bass, A. N. (2010, February). From business dining to public speaking: Tips for acquiring professional presence and its role in the business curricula. *American Journal of Business Education (AJBE)*, 3(2), 57–64.

Bitzer, L. (1954). The rhetorical situation. *Philosophy and Rhetoric*, 1, 1–14.

Bryman, A. (1998). Quantitative and qualitative research strategies in knowing the social world. In T. May and M. Williams (Eds.), *Knowing the social World*. Philadelphia, PA: Open University Press. pp. 138–156.

de Bony, J. (2010, February). Project management and national culture: A Dutch–French case study. *International Journal of Project Management, 28*(2), 173–182.

Fallows, D. (2008). *Search engine use.* Pew Internet & American Life Project.

Firestone, W. A. (1987, October). Meaning in method: The rhetoric of quantitative and qualitative research. *Educational Researcher, 16*(7), 16–21.

Gardner, H. E., & Laskin, E. (2011). *Leading minds: An anatomy of leadership.* New York, NY: Basic Books.

Hall, G. M., & Robinson, N. (2012). *How to present at meetings.* 3rd ed. [online book]. Hoboken, NJ: Wiley Blackwell Publishing.

O'Keefe, D. J. (2002). *Persuasion: Theory & research* (2nd ed.). Thousand Oaks, CA: Sage Publications, Inc.

Pullin, P. (2010). Small talk: Rapport and international communicative competence. *Journal of Business Communication, 47*(4), 455–476.

Purcell, K., Brenner, J., & Rainie, L. (2012). *Search engine use 2012.* Pew Internet & American Life Project.

Talab, R. S. (2001, May/June). Permissions, fair use, and production resources for educators and librarians. *Tech Trends, 45*(3), 7.

Traphagan, T., Traphagan, J., Dickens, L. N., & Resta, P. (2012, February). Changes in college students' perceptions of use of web-based resources for academic tasks with Wikipedia projects: A preliminary exploration. *Interactive Learning Environments.*

Chapter Four—Ideal Business Talk Organization

Halford, G. S., Cowan, N., & Andrews, G. (2007, June). Separating cognitive capacity from knowledge: A new hypothesis. *Trends in Cognitive Sciences, 11*(6), 236–42.

Monroe, A. H. (1935). *Principles and types of speech.* Glenview, IL: Scott Foresman.

O'Keefe, D. J. (2002). *Persuasion: Theory & research* (2nd ed.). Thousand Oaks, CA: Sage Publications, Inc.

Parra, M. G., Lleó de Nalda, A., & Perles, G. S. M. (2011). Towards a more humanistic understanding of organizational trust. *Journal of Management Development, 30*(6), 605–614.

Perloff, R. M. (2003). *The dynamics of persuasion: Communication and attitudes in the 21st century.* Mahwah, NJ: Lawrence Erlbaum Associates, Inc.

Sprague, J., & Stuart, D. (2009). *The speaker's compact handbook.* Boston, MA: Wadsworth, Cengage Learning.

Chapter Five—Aiding Business Talks with Visuals

Ad Age. (2012, June). Database of 100 leading national advertisers. *Marketer Trees 2012.* Retrieved August 28, 2012 from http://adage.com/datacenter/marketertrees2012/.

Akhmadeeva, L., Tukhvatullin, I., & Veytsman, B. (2012, July). Do serifs help in comprehension of printed text? An experiment with Cyrillic readers. *Vision Res, 65*(21), 21–24.

Atkinson, C. (2004). PowerPoint usability: Q&A with Don Norman. *Sociable Media.* Retrieved on July 2, 2007 from http://sociablemedia.com/articles_norman.htm.

Atkinson, M. (2010, September). Objects as visual aids: UK speechwriters' guild conference. *Atkinson Communications.* Retrieved on September 7, 2012 from http://maxatkinson.blogspot.com/2010/09/objects-as-visual-aids-uk-speechwriters.html.

Beaver, D. (2007, April). With visual aids, more is less. *ABA Banking Journal, 99*(4), 61.

Beebe, S. A., & Beebe, S. J. (2009). *Public speaking: An audience centered approach.* Boston, MA: Allyn & Bacon.

Belkin, L. Y. (2009). Emotional contagion in the electronic communication context: Conceptualizing the dynamics and implications of electronic emotional encounters in organizations. *Journal of Organizational Culture, Communication, and Conflict, 13,* 105–122.

Berlo, D. K. (1960). *The process of communication: An introduction to theory and practice.* New York: Holt, Rinehart and Winston, Inc.

Broadbent, D.; Broadbent, M.H. (1980). "Priming and the passive/active model of word recognition" in R. Nickerson (ed.), *Attention and performance, VIII.* New York: Academic Press.

Bumiller, E. (2010, April 27). We have met the enemy and he is PowerPoint. *New York Times,* A1.

Burgoon, M. (1999). Principal investigator, grant 9804. *Arizona Disease Research Control Commission: Adolescent Smoking Prevention.* Retrieved on September 15, 2012 from www.cios.org/EJCPUBLIC/011/3/01136.HTML

Buss, W. C. (2006, March). Stop death by PowerPoint. *Training & Development, 60*(3), 20–22.

Carroll, S. (2007, March). PowerPoint abuse? Oversimplification hinders communication and understanding. *FX One Seven Zero.* Retrieved February 15, 2010 from http://www.fx170.com/?q=article_multimedia.

Chaboyer, W., Wallen, K., Wallis, M., & McMurray, A. M. (2009). Whiteboards: One tool to improve patient flow. *Medical Journal of Australia, 190*(11), 137–144.

Cheesebro, T., O'Connor, L., & Rios, F. (2009). *Communicating in the workplace.* Upper Saddle River, NJ: Prentice Hall.

Cieply, M. (2011, October 30). For home entertainment releases, a rare bright spot. Media and Advertising, *The New York Times online.* Retrieved from http://www.nytimes.com/2011/10/31/business/media/for-home-entertainment-industry-a-bright-spot.html.

Collins, J. (2004, July–August). Education techniques for lifelong learning: Giving a PowerPoint presentation: The art of communicating effectively. *Radiographics, 24*(4), 1185–1192.

Cumming, S. (2010). Word for linguistics: Typography. *University of California Santa Barbara faculty pages.* Retrieved on August 1, 2012 from http://www.linguistics.ucsb.edu/faculty/cumming/WordForLinguists/Typography.htm.

Cyphert, D. (2007). Presentation technology in the age of electronic eloquence: From visual aid to visual rhetoric. *Communication Education, 56*(2), 168–192.

Cyphert, D. (2004, March). The problem of PowerPoint: Visual aid or visual rhetoric? *Business Communication Quarterly, 67*(1), 80–84.

Duarte, N. (2011, January 22). Avoiding the road to PowerPoint hell. *Wall Street Journal–Eastern Edition.* p. C12. Retrieved on September 15, 2012 from Business Source Premier.

Eilks, I., Witteck, T., & Pietzner, V. (2009). A critical discussion of the efficacy of using visual learning aids from the internet to promote understanding. *EURASIA Journal of Mathematics, Science & Technology Education, 5*(2), 145–152.

Few, S. (2010, September). Data visualization for human perception. In: M. Soegaard, & R. F. Dam (Eds.), *Encyclopedia of human–computer interaction.* Aarhus, Denmark: The Interaction Design Foundation. Online at http://www.interaction-design.org/encyclopedia/data_visualization_for_human_perception.html.

Foss, S. K., & Kanengieter, M. R. (1992, July). Visual communication in the basic course. *Communication Education, 41*(3), 312–323.

Fried, J. (2004, August). A little Tufte recap. *Signals vs. noise.* Accessed from http://37signals.com/svn/archives/000831.php.

Friend, J., Adams, A., & Curry, G. (2011, December). Breaking news: Utilizing video simulations to improve educational leaders' public speaking skills. *Journal of Research on Leadership Education, 6*(5), 234–249.

Gallo, C. (2010). In defense of PowerPoint. *Business Week*, p. 9. Retrieved on September 15, 2012 from Business Source Premier.

Garcia-Retamero, R., & Galesic, M. (2010, April). Who profits from visual aids: Overcoming challenges in people's understanding of risks. *Social Science & Medicine, 70*(7), 1019–25.

Genard, G. (January 1, 2005). Picture it: The power of visual speaking. *Harvard Business Publishing Newsletters.*

Gieseke, J. (2010). Show them what you mean. *Public Management, 92*(2), 10–14. Retrieved on September 15, 2012 from Business Source Premier.

Glover, D., Miller, D., Averis, D., & Door, V. (2007). The evolution of an effective pedagogy for teachers using the interactive whiteboard in mathematics and modern languages: An empirical analysis from the secondary sector. *Learning, Media and Technology, 32*(1), 5–20.

Greco, M., Stucchi, M., Zavagno, D., & Marino, B. (2008). On the portability of computer-generated presentations: The effect of text-background color combinations on text legibility. *Human Factors: The Journal of the Human Factors and Ergonomics Society, 50*(5), 821–833.

Gurrie, C., & Fair, B. (2010). PowerPoint—from fabulous to boring: The misuse of PowerPoint in higher education classrooms. *Journal of the Communication, Speech & Theatre Association of North Dakota*, 2323–2330. Retrieved on September 15, 2012 from Communication & Mass Media Complete.

Heap, I. M., Burrill, L. C., Dewey, S. A., & MacDonald, G. E. (1994). Eradication of noxious visual aids: Slides and overheads that work. *Weed Technology, 8*(3), 649–657.

Heath, M. (2009). Use of visual aids in public speaking. *Whitman College Rhetoric and Public Address Department.* Retrieved on June 18, 2009 from http://www.whitman.edu/rhetoric/84zvas2.htm.

Humar, I., Gradizar, M., & Turk, T. (2008, November–December). The impact of color combinations on the legibility of a Web page text presented on CRT displays. *International Journal of Industrial Ergonomics, 38*(11–12), 885–899.

Kay, T. (2011). Building solidarity with subjects and audience in sociology and documentary photography. *Sociological Forum, 26*(2), 424–430.

Levasseur, D. G., & Sawyer, J. K. (2006). Pedagogy meets PowerPoint: A research review of the effects of computer-generated slides in the classroom. *The Review of Communication, 6*(1), 101–123.

Levie, W. H., & Lentz, R. (1982). Effects of text illustrations: A review of research. *Educational Communication and Technology, 30*(4), 195–233.

Li, Y., & Suen, C. Y. (2010). Typeface personality traits and their design characteristics. In *Proceedings of the 9th IAPR International Workshop on Document Analysis Systems (DAS '10)*. ACM, New York, NY, 231–238.

Lowenthal, P. (n.d.). Improving the design of PowerPoint presentations. *CU Online*. Retrieved February 17, 2010 from http://www.ucdenver.edu/academics/CUOnline/FacultyResources/additionalResources/Handbook/Documents/Chapter_12.pdf.

Mann, M., & Hill, T. (1984). Persuasive communications and the boomerang effect: Some limiting conditions to the effectiveness of positive influence attempts. *Advances in Consumer Research, 11*(1), 66–70. Retrieved from Business Source Premier database.

Martin, D. Z. (1992, May). Overhead transparencies designed to communicate. *Arts & Activities, 111*(4), 42–46.

Murcia, K., & Sheffield, R. (2010). Talking about science in interactive whiteboard classrooms. *Australasian Journal of Educational Technology, 26*(4), 417–431. Retrieved from Education Research Complete database.

Nonis, S., & Swift, C. O. (2001). An examination of the relationship between academic dishonesty and workplace dishonesty: A multicampus investigation. *Journal of Education for Business, 77*(2), 69–77.

Norman, D. (2004). In defense of PowerPoint. *Don Norman: Designing for People (Nielsen Norman Group)*. Retrieved February 15, 2010, from http://www.jnd.org/dn.mss/in_defense_of_p.html.

Ogg, E. (2010, June 7). Even Steve Jobs has demo hiccups. *CNET News*. Retrieved on August 1, 2012 from http://news.cnet.com/8301–31021_3-20007009-260.html.

OSHA Office of Training and Education. (1996). Training technology. *US Department of Labor*. Retrieved on July 26, 2012 from http://www.osha.gov/doc/outreachtraining/htmlfiles/traintec.html.

Perry, M., & O'Hara, K. (2003). Display-based activity in the workplace. *INTERACT '03, IFIP*, 591–598.

Phillips, A., & Donohue, P. (2010, September 20). New Yorkers outraged as bureaucrats order city to change lettering on every single street sign. *New York Daily News*. Retrieved on May 29, 2011 from http://www.nydailynews.com/ny_local/2010/09/30/2010-09-30_bureaucrats_order_city_to_change_every_street_sign_leading_ny_to_say__it_is_just.html.

Reynolds, G. (2008). Presentation tips: Top 10 slide tips. *Garr Reynolds*. Retrieved August 28, 2012 from http://www.garrreynolds.com/presentation /slides.html.

Rosenthal, M. (2012, February 20). Last word: Hear ye, hear ye. *Trainingmag*. Retrieved September 16, 2012 from http://trainingmag.com/article/last-word-hear-ye-hear-ye.

Rotman, E. (2009, July/August). Enhance your effectiveness with visual aids. *Legacy Magazine: National Association for Interpretation, 20*(4), 32.

Ruffini, M. F. (2009, December). Creating animations in PowerPoint to support student learning and engagement. *EDUCAUSE Quarterly Online*. Retrieved August 8, 2012 from http://www.educause.edu/ero/article/creating-animations-powerpoint-support-student-learning-and-engagement.

Sawyer, J. K. (2011). *PowerPoint reality: Slides in real time for real audiences with real easy steps*. Boston: Allyn & Bacon.

Schramm, W. (1954). How communication works. In W. Schramm (Ed.), *The process and effects of communication* (pp. 3–26). Urbana, IL: University of Illinois Press.

Schuck, S., & Kearney, M. (2007). Exploring pedagogy with interactive whiteboards: A case study of six schools. *Australian Educational Computing, 23*(1), 8–13.

Schuck, S., & Kearney, M. (2008). Classroom-based use of two educational technologies: A sociocultural perspective. *Contemporary Issues in Technology and Teacher Education, 8*(4), 394–406.

Schwartz, J. (2003, September). The level of discourse continues to slide. *The New York Times*. Retrieved February 22, 2010, from http://ied.unipr.it/~silve/tesi/the-level.pdf.

Shaikh, A. D., Chaparro, B. S., & Fox, D. (2006). Perception of fonts: Perceived personality traits and uses. *Usability News, 8*(1). Retrieved September 15, 2012 from http://www.surl.org/usabilitynews/81/PersonalityofFonts.asp.

Sheedy, J. E., Subbaram, M. V., Zimmerman, A. B., & Hayes, J. R. (2005). Text legibility and the letter superiority effect. *Human Factors, 47,* 797–815.

Sims, R. L. (1993). The relationship between academic dishonesty and unethical business practices. *Journal of Education for Business, 68*(4), 207–211.

Smith, S. M., & Woody, P. C. (2000 Summer). Interactive effect of multimedia instruction and learning styles. *Teaching of Psychology, 27*(3), 220–23.

Speaking Tips. (2004, January 26). Using flip charts. Speaking Tips. Retrieved on July 31, 2010 from http://www.speaking-tips. com/Articles/Using-Flip-Charts.aspx.

Tang, A., Lanir, J., Greenberg, S., & Fels, S. (2009). Supporting transitions in work: Informing large display application design by understanding whiteboard use. *Proceedings of the ACM 2009 international conference on supporting group work.* 149–158.

Thompson, C. (2003, December). PowerPoint makes you dumb. *The New York Times Magazine,* 688.

Tufte, E. (2003, September). PowerPoint is evil. *Wired News.* Retrieved February 18, 2010 from http://www.wired.com/wired/archive/11.09/ppt2. html.

Tufte, E. (2006). *The cognitive style of PowerPoint* (2nd ed.). New York: Graphics Press.

Unger, P., & Jenson, N. (2009). Powerpoint storyboarding in the courtroom. Presented at the American Bar Association Tech Show. March 25, 2010, 1–19.

Winterstein, A. G., & Kimberlin, C. L. (2010). Usefulness of consumer medication information dispensed in retail pharmacies. *Archives of Internal Medicine, 170,* 1314–1324. Retrieved on July 9, 2012 from http://archinte. jamanetwork.com/article.aspx?articleid=775631.

Wyatt, A. (n.d.) Developing visual aids. Pathways to tomorrow MMHS. Retrieved on July 31, 2010 from http://www.longview.k12.wa.us/mmhs/ wyatt/pathway/dvaid.html.

Xiao, Y., Lasome, C., Moss, J., Mackenzie, C. F., & Faraj, S. (2001). Cognitive properties of a whiteboard: A case study in a trauma centre. *ECSCW Kluwer Academics Publishers,* 259–278.

Zaichkowsky, J. (2010). Strategies for distinctive brands. *Journal of Brand Management, 17*(8), 548–560. Retrieved September 15, 2012 from Business Source Premier.

Chapter Six—Words, Voice, and Movement: Delivering Your Business Talk

Allen, M. T. (1989). A comparison of self-report, observer, and physiological assessments of public speaking anxiety reduction techniques using meta-analysis. *Communication Studies, 40*, 127–139.

Arnold, K. (2010). *Boring to bravo: Proven presentation techniques to engage, involve and inspire your audience to action.* Austin, TX: Greenleaf Book Press.

Ayres, J., & Hopf, T. (1999). Vividness and control: Factors in the effectiveness of performance visualization? *Communication Education, 48*(4), 287.

Briñol, P., & Petty, R. E. (2008). Embodied persuasion: Fundamental processes by which bodily responses can impact attitudes. In G. R. Semin & E. R. Smith (Eds.), *Embodiment grounding: Social, cognitive, affective, and neuroscientific approaches.* Cambridge, England: Cambridge University Press. (pp. 1–33).

Bodie, G. D. (2010). A racing heart, rattling knees and ruminative thoughts: Defining, explaining and treating public speaking anxiety. *Communication Education, 59*(1), 70–105.

Borrego, M. C., Gasparini, G., & Behlau, M. (2007, July). The effects of a specific speech and language training program on students of a radio announcing course. *Journal of Voice, 21*(4), 426–432.

Clark, T., & Greatbatch, D. (2011, February). Audience perceptions of charismatic and non-charismatic oratory: The case of management gurus. *The Leadership Quarterly, 22*(1), 22–32.

Don. (2009). Steve Ballmer monkey dance. *Know Your Meme.* Retrieved on June 25, 2012 from http://knowyourmeme.com/memes/steve-ballmer-monkey-dance.

Ellis, J. (2009). How to overcome public speaking anxiety. *How to Stop Anxiety & End Panic Attacks.* Retrieved July 1, 2012 from http://www.stop-anxiety-panic-attack.com/blog/how-to-overcome-public-speaking-anxiety.

Ezenyimulu, L. O. (2010). *Stealth of confidence: confidence is a retaining 'asset.'* Durham, CT: Eloquent Books.

Field, A. (2000, October and 2005, June). What is business casual. *Business Week, 3705.* Accessed on December 14, 2011 from http://www.businessweek.com/ 2000/00_44/b3705141.htm.

Garber, R. I. (2009, October). The 14 worst human fears in the 1977 Book of Lists: Where did this data really come from? *Joyful public speaking (from fear to joy).* Retrieved July 23, 2010 from http://joyfulpublicspeaking.blogspot.com/2009/10/14-worst-human-fears-according-to-1977.html.

Haefner, R. (2008, July 30). How to dress for success for work. *CNN.com*. Retrieved January 27, 2009, from http://www.cnn.com/2008/LIVING/worklife/07/30/cb.dress.for.success/index.html.

Hall, S. (1997). *Integrating pronunciation for fluency in presentation skills*. Paper presented at the Annual Meeting of the Teachers of English to Speakers of Other Languages (31st, Orlando, FL, March 11–15, 1997).

Hart, R. P. (1994). *Seducing America: How television charms the modern voter*. New York, NY: Oxford University Press.

Hayakawa, S. I. (1949). *Language in thought and action*. New York, NY: Harcourt, Brace.

Henderson, J., & Henderson R. (2007). *There's no such thing as public speaking: Make any presentation or speech as persuasive as one-on-one conversation*. New York, NY: Penguin Group.

Huchendorf, L. (2007). The effects of color on memory. *UW-L Journal of Undergraduate Research X*, pp. 1–3.

Jerry Seinfeld quotes. (2012, August 1). Retrieved on September 16, 2012 from http://thinkexist.com/quotes/jerry_seinfeld/.

Kaylor, B. T. (2012). A new law: The covenant speech of Barbara Jordan. *Southern Communication Journal, 77*, 10–23.

Keller, A. (2009). Odor memories: The first sniff counts. *Current Biology, 9*. Retrieved July 5, 2012 from http://vosshall.rockefeller.edu/reprints/KellerCB2009.pdf

Kiddie, T. (2009, September). Recent trends in business casual attire and their effects on student job seekers. *Business Communication Quarterly, 72*(3), 350–354.

Lynch, J. (2005, June 6). Tom & Katie: Truly, madly, deeply. *People Magazine*. Retrieved June 2011 from http://www.people.com/people/archive/article/0,,20147743,00.html

Maricchiolo, F., Gnisci, A., Bonaiuto, M., & Ficca, G. (2009). Effects of different types of hand gestures in persuasive speech on receivers' evaluations. *Language & Cognitive Processes, 24*(2), 239–266.

McNeill, D., Cassell, J., & McCullough, K. (1994). Communicative effects of speech-mismatched gestures. *Research on Language & Social Interaction, 27*(3), 223. Retrieved from Academic Search Complete database on September 15, 2012.

Merten, R. K. (1948). The self-fulfilling prophecy. *Antioch Review, 8*, 193–210.

Meyers, P. & Nix, S. (2011). *As we speak: How to make your point and have it stick.* New York, NY: Atria Books.

Miers, J. (October/November). Pause and effect. *HR Professional, 26*(6), 35–35.

Nash, D. B. (2010, June). Interdependence. *Pharmacy and Therapeutics, 35*(6), 306. Retrieved on September 16, 2012 from http://www.ncbi.nlm.nih.gov/pmc/articles/PMC2888549/.

Ogg, E. (2010, June 7). Even Steve Jobs has demo hiccups. *CNET News.* Retrieved on August 1, 2012 from http://news.cnet.com/8301-31021_3-20007009-260.html.

Ou, W., & Huang, X. (2008). A perfect match of style and subject: Remarks on the style of world leaders pay tribute to Reagan. *International Education Studies, 1*(2), 129–131.

Pearce, C. L., Manz, C. C., & Sims Jr., H. P. (2009). Is shared leadership the key to team success? *Organizational Dynamics, 38*(3), 234–238. Retrieved on September 16, 2012 from http://cte.rockhurst.edu/s/945/images/editor_documents /PEARCE%20MANZ%20SIMS%20%20%20Shared%20Ledership.pdf.

Pearce, W. B., & Conklin, F. (1971). Nonverbal vocalic communication and perceptions of a speaker. *Speech Monographs, 38*(3), 235–241. Retrieved September 15, 2012 from Communication & Mass Media Complete database.

Propp, K. M. (2008). Here's looking at you, kid: Enhancing eye contact in public speaking. *Paper presented at the National Communication Association*, 1–6.

Reddick, E. (2007, August). Casual dress—the new elephant in the room. *The Enterprise, 9*, 15.

Reimold, C., & Reimold, P. (2006, February). Back to basics: Quick and easy ways to develop a great presentation (part 4): Deliver your message clearly and enthusiastically. *Solutions! For People, Processes & Paper* [serial online]. *89*(2), 6. Retrieved on September 16, 2012 from Environment Complete.

Russ, T. L. (2012). The relationship between communication apprehension and learning preferences in an organizational setting. *Journal of Business Communication, 49*(4), 312–331.

Sato, W., & Yoshikawa, S. (2007). Enhanced experience of emotional arousal in response to dynamic facial expressions. *Journal of Nonverbal Behavior, 31*(2), 119–135.

Schramm, W. (1954). How communication works. In W. Schramm (Ed.), *The process and effects of communication* (pp. 3–26). Urbana, IL: University of Illinois Press.

Simon, S. (1998). *Now you see it, now you don't: The amazing world of optical illusions*. New York, NY: HarperCollins.

Smith, T., & Frymier, A. (2006). Get 'real': Does practicing speeches before an audience improve performance? *Communication Quarterly, 54*(1), 111–125.

UNC Speaking Center. (2009). Making friends with your public speaking anxiety monster. *The University of North Carolina Greensboro*. Workshop presented at the 2009 National Association of Communication Centers Mini-Conference. Retrieved June 24, 2012 from http://speakingcenter.uncg.edu/resources/anxiety/Anxiety_participants.pdf

Van Petten, V. (2007). *Ten minutes to the speech: Your last-minute guide and checklist for speaking in public*. Beverly Hills, CA: Tallfellow Press.

Wachsmuth, I. (2006). Gestures offer insight. *Scientific American Mind, 17*(5), 20–25. Retrieved from Academic Search Complete database on September 15, 2012.

White, M. (1964). The speaker's stand. *Today's Speech, 12*(2), 6. Retrieved September 15, 2012 from Communication & Mass Media Complete database.

Zarefsky, D. (1998). *Public speaking: Strategies for success*. Boston, MA: Allyn & Bacon.

Chapter Seven—Résumé and Cover Letter Communication

Adams, S. (2012). New expert tips for using LinkedIn, *Forbes*. 35. Retrieved June 13, 2012, from Business Source Premier.

Amare, N., & Manning, Y. (2009). Writing for the robot: How employer search tools have influenced résumé rhetoric and ethics. *Business Communication Quarterly, 72*, 35–60.

Brumberger, E. (2003). The rhetoric of typography: The persona of typeface and text. *Technical Communication, 50*(2), 206–223.

CareerBuilder. (2008). Nearly half of all employers have caught a lie on a resume, Careerbuilder.com survey shows. Retrieved on September 12, 2012 from http://www.careerbuilder.com/share/aboutus/pressreleasesdetail.aspx?id=pr448&sd=7%2F30%2F2008&ed=7%2F30%2F2099.

Casserly, M. (2011). The most over-used business buzzwords of 2011. *Forbes, 37.* Retrieved June 13, 2012 from Business Source Premier.

Casserly, M. (2012). Stop lying! And the nine other mistakes you're making on LinkedIn. *Forbes, 30.* Retrieved June 13, 2012 from Business Source Premier.

Condon, J. (2009, April). An online toolbox starts with a polished résumé. *New York Times.* Retrieved June 13, 2012, from http://www.nytimes.com/2009/04/02/technology/personaltech/02basics.html.

Crosby, O. (2009). Résumés, applications and cover letters. *Occupational Outlook Quarterly, 53*(2), 18–29. Retrieved June 9, 2010 from Business Source Premier.

Donlin, K. (2008). Three resume and cover letter myths exposed. *Star Tribune.* Retrieved June 22, 2010 from http://www.startribune.com/jobs/career/11436521.html.

Furtmueller, E., Wilderom, C., & Tate, M. (2011). Managing recruitment and selection in the digital age: e-HRM and résumés. *Human Systems Management, 30*(4), 243–259. Retrieved June 13, 2012, from Business Source Premier.

Half, Robert. (2008, September 17). Employment seekers increasingly turn to video over paper resumes. *Shaker.* Retrieved September 16, 2012 http://www.shaker.com/node/3357/print

Hauser, S. G. (2011). Tech turbo boosters on hyperdrive. *Workforce Management, 90*(8), 24–26. Retrieved June 13, 2012, from Business Source Premier.

Hoheb, M. (2002). Résumé writing. *Scholastic Choices, 18*(3), 19–23. Retrieved June 7, 2010 from Primary Search.

Hornsby, J., & Smith, B. (1995). Resume content: What should be included and excluded. *SAM Advanced Management Journal, 60,* 4–9.

Jacobs, D. L. (2012). The high price of career lies. *Forbes, 49.* Retrieved September 12, 2012 from Business Source Premier.

Kidwell Jr., R. E. (2004). 'Small' lies, big trouble: The unfortunate consequences of résumé padding, from Janet Cooke to George O'Leary. *Journal of Business Ethics, 51*(2), 175–184. Retrieved September 12, 2012 from Business Source Premier.

Koedel, C., & Tyhurst, E. (2012). Math skills and labor-market outcomes: Evidence from a résumé-based field experiment. *Economics of Education Review, 31*(1), 131–140. Retrieved June 13, 2012, from Business Source Premier.

Kluemper, D. H., Rosen, P. A., & Mossholder. (2012). Social networking websites, personality ratings, and the organizational context: More than meets the eye? *Journal of Applied Social Psychology, 42*(5). Retrieved June 13, 2012, from Business Source Premier.

Knowledge@Wharton. (2012a). Hold that password: The new reality of evaluating job applicants. *Knowledge@Wharton.* Retrieved June 13, 2012 from http://knowledge.wharton.upenn.edu/article.cfm?articleid=2978.

Knowledge@Wharton. (2012b). Why the job search is like throwing paper airplanes into the galaxy. Retrieved June 13, 2012, from http://knowledge.wharton.upenn.edu/article.cfm?articleid=2947.

Markey, B. T., & Campbell, R. L. (1996). A resume or curriculum vitae for success. *AORN Journal, 63*, 1, 192–202.

McGregor, J. (2010). Job sites: Are they worth it? *Fortune International (Europe), 161*(8), 27–28. Retrieved June 13, 2012, from Business Source Premier.

National Association of Colleges and Employers (NACE). (2011). Job outlook: The candidate skills/qualities employers want. *National Association of Colleges and Employers.* Retrieved August 13, 2012, from http://www.naceweb.org/s10262011/candidate_skills_employer_qualities/.

Needleman, S. E. (2009). Creating a résumé that sells. *Wall Street Journal—Eastern Edition, 254*(124), D1–D8. Retrieved June 7, 2010 from Business Source Premier.

Olsen, P. R. (2006). In a ghost-written résumé, your best incarnation. *The New York Times.* Retrieved September 15, 2012 from http://www.nytimes.com/2006/05/14/business/yourmoney/14resume.html?scp=2&sq=&st=nyt&_r=0.

Praetorius, R., & Lawson, L. (2004). The perfect resume: What you need to know to have one! *The New Social Worker, 11*, 18–20.

Potvin, K. (2009). Landing the interview: How to get to the top of the résumé pile. *Public Relations Tactics, 16*(5), 20–20. Retrieved June 9, 2010 from Business Source Premier.

Ross, C. M., & Young, S. J. (2005). Résumé preferences: Is it really 'business as usual?' *Journal of Career Development, 32*, 153–164. Retrieved June 7, 2010 from Sage Premier database.

Russo, F. (2011). The new online job hunt. *Time, 178*(13), B14–B16. Retrieved June 13, 2012, from Business Source Premier.

Ryan, L. (2009). Six tips for following up on your résumé. *Business Week Online,* 10. Retrieved June 9, 2010 from Business Source Premier.

Schriver, K. A. (1997). *Dynamics in document design: Creating texts for readers.* New York, NY: Wiley Computer Publishing.

Schullery, N. M., Ickes, L., & Schullery, S. E. (2009). Employer preferences for résumés and cover letters. *Business Communication Quarterly, 72*(2), 163–176. Retrieved January 20, 2010, from Business Source Premier.

Schultze, Q. J., Kim, B. J., & Bolles, R. N. (2012). *Resume 101: A student and recent grad guide to crafting resumes and cover letters that land jobs.* Boston, MA: Ten Speed Press/Random House.

Shaikh, A. D., Chaparro, B. S., & Fox, D. (2006). Perception of fonts: Perceived personality traits and uses. *Usability News, 8*(1). Retrieved September 15, 2012 from http://www.surl.org/usabilitynews/81/PersonalityofFonts.asp.

Smith, C. (2011). Selling yourself in today's job market: Put your professional face forward on the web. *ONS Connect, 26*(1), 22. Retrieved June 13, 2012, from Academic Source Complete.

Smith, J. (2012). New research shows where employers find their new hires. *Forbes, 9.* Retrieved June 13, 2012, from Business Source Premier.

Smith, P.G. (2002). Creating the perfect résumé. *Career World, 31*(3), 18–21. Retrieved June 7, 2010 from Education Research Complete.

Southam, K. (2006, May 13). Email addresses that kill off job chances. *The (Adelaide) Advertiser.* Retrieved on July 22, 2010 from Newspaper Source.

Thoms, P., McMasters, R., Roberts, M., & Dombkowski, D. (1999). Resume characteristics as predictors of an invitation to interview. *Journal of Business and Psychology, 13,* 339–356.

Twardowski Career Development Center. (n.d.). Résumé and cover letter writing. *West Chester University.* Retrieved January 27, 2010 from http://www.wcupa.edu/_SERVICES/STU.CAR/students/RESUME2.asp.

Volmar, P. (2010). 10 tips to obtain PR jobs through social media. *Public Relations Tactics, 17*(8), 7. Retrieved June 13, 2012, from Business Source Premier.

Washington, T., & Kanter, G. (2009). *Resume Empower: Shattering the Paper Ceiling.* Laurel, MD: Mount Vernon Press. Retrieved on September 6, 2012 from http://www.careerempowering.com/resume-empower/the-objective.html.

Weber, L., & Emma Silverman, R. (2012). Your résumé vs. oblivion. *Wall Street Journal—Eastern Edition.* B1–B6. Retrieved June 13, 2012, from Business Source Premier.

Weinstein, D. (2012, January–February). The psychology of behaviorally-focused résumés on applicant selection: Are your hiring managers really hiring the 'right' people for the 'right' jobs? *Business Horizons*, 55(1), 53–63.

Workbloom (2012). Professional resume layouts & designs. *Workbloom*. Retrieved on September 15, 2012 from http://workbloom.com/resume/resume-layouts.aspx.

Zupek, R. (2010). Top 10 tips for your 2010 résumé. Careerbuilder, Retrieved January 21, 2010 from http://msn.careerbuilder.com/Article/MSN-2143-Cover-Letters-Résumés-Top-10-Tips-for-Your-2010.

Chapter Eight—Interviews as Business Talk

Bhattacharyya, E., Patil, A., & Sargunan, R. A. (2010,November). Methodology in seeking stakeholder perceptions of effective technical oral presentations: An exploratory pilot study. *The Qualitative Report*, 15(6), 1549–1568. Retrieved on March 16, 2011 from http://www.nova.edu/ssss/QR/QR15-6/bhattacharyya.pdf.

Bibey, C. (2010). How to prepare for an online video. *MoneyCrashers*. Retrieved July 22, 2010 from http://www.moneycrashers.com/how-to-prepare-for-an-online-video-interview/.

Bowers, T. (2009, October). How to research a company before your interview. *TechRepublic*. Retrieved August 16, 2012 from http://www.techrepublic.com/blog/career/how-to-research-a-company-before-your-interview/1307.

Cardon, P.W., & Okoro, E. (2009). Professional characteristics communicated by formal versus casual workplace attire. *Business Communication Quarterly*, 72(3), 355–360.

Cejka, S., & Taylor, M. W. (2007). People persons—and the job interview. *The Physician Executive (May/June)*, 68–70.

Chan, C. (2010). Cabela's: Nearly 1,000 apply for 40 jobs at Glendale store. *The Arizona Republic*. Retrieved July 17, 2010 from http://www.azcentral.com/news/articles/2010/07/16/ 20100716glendale-cabelas-hiring-jobs.html.

Chia, Y. M. (2005). Job offers of multi-national accounting firms: The effects of emotional intelligence, extra-curricular activities, and academic performance. *Accounting Education*, 14(1), 75–93. Retrieved June 24, 2010 from Education Research Complete.

Conklin, J. (2007). Turning the tables: Six questions to ask your interviewer. *Quality Progress*, 40(11), 55.

Coombes, M. (2006). Interview blunders often culprit for missed opportunities. *Wall Street Journal Executive Career Site*. Retrieved July 17, 2010 from http://208.144.115.170/jobhunting/interviewing/20051115-coombes.html.

Cox, C. L., & Glick, W. H. (1986). Resume evaluations and cosmetics use: When more is not better. *Sex Roles, 14*, 1–2, 51–58.

Crawford, H. (2007). Job interviewing: Ten tips for success. *Contract Management, 47*(8), 4–6.

Development Dimensions International (2007, August 7). Interview impasse: Two out of three job seekers will evaluate a job based on the interviewers they encounter. *Development Dimensions International*. Retrieved September 16, 2012 from http://www.ddiworld.com/global-offices/canada/canada-press-room/interview-impasse--two-out-of-three-job–seekers-wi.

Field, A. (2000, October and 2005, June). What is business casual. *Business Week, 3705*. Accessed on December 14, 2011 from http://www.business-week.com/ 2000/00_44/b3705141.htm.

Friedman, A. (2011, May). Don't wear flip-flops to the interview. *Wall Street Journal—Eastern Edition*. A17. Retrieved from Business Source Premier database.

Giles, K. (2010). Nonverbal cues for interview success. *Employment Guide*. Retrieved July 22, 2010 from http://www.employmentguide.com/careeradvice/Nonverbal_Cues_for_Interview_Success.html.

Haefner, R. (2008, July 30). How to dress for success at work. *CNN Living*. Retrieved September 16, 2012 from http://www.cnn.com/2008/LIVING/worklife/07/30/cb.dress.for.success/index.html.

Hansen, K. (2006). Mastering the Case Interview. *Quintcareers*. Retrieved July 17, 2010 from http://www.quintcareers.com/case_interviews.html.

Hansen, K., & Hansen, R. (2006). Promising interview-prep technique: Composing written responses to interview questions. *Quintcareers*. Retrieved July 19, 2010 from http://www.quintcareers.com/interview-prep_technique.html.

Hansen, K. (2012). Behavioral job interviewing strategies for job-seekers. *Quintcareers*. Retrieved September 5, 2012 from http://www.quintcareers.com/behavioral_ interviewing.html.

Hayes, J. (1994). *Interpersonal skills: goal-directed behaviour at work*. London: Routledge.

Hilpern, K. (2003, October 12). Clean break with tradition. *The Guardian*. Retrieved on August 14, 2012 from http://www.guardian.co.uk/money/2003/oct/13/careers.jobsadvice.

Hiring managers share the most memorable mistakes in annual CareerBuilder survey. (2012). Retrieved June 28, 2012, from http://www.careerbuilder.com/share/aboutus/pressreleasesdetail.aspx?id=pr680&sd=2/22/2012&ed=12/31/2012.

Hoffman, E. A. (2008, September). The emotionally challenging, open-ended interview. *Business Communication Quarterly*, 387–390. Retrieved June 24, 2010 from Business Source Premier.

Hsu, T. (2012, February 19). Job interviewing, to the extreme. *Los Angeles Times*. Retrieved on March 19, 2012 from http://articles.latimes.com/2012/feb/19/business/la-fi-extreme-interviewing-20120219/1.

Joss, M. (2003). Tips and templates for creating an interview follow-up letter. *Techrepublic*. Retrieved July 18, 2010 from http://articles.techrepublic.com.com/5100-10878_11-1057839.html.

Kiddie, T. (2009). Focus on business practices: Recent trends in business casual attire and their effects on student job seekers. *Business Communication Quarterly*, 72, 350–354.

Kiviat, B. (2009). How Skype is changing the job interview. *Time*. Retrieved on July 21, 2010 from http://www.time.com/time/business/article/0,8599,1930838,00.html.

Krumhuber, E., Manstead, A. S. R., Cosker, D., Marshall, D., & Rosin, P. L. (2009). Effects of dynamic attributes of smiles in human and synthetic faces: A simulated job interview setting. *Journal of Non-verbal behavior, 33*(1), 1–15. Retrieved June 24, 2010 from Communication & Mass Media Complete.

Lazarus, A. (2004). Preparation is key to successful job interviews. *The Physician Executive (May/June)*, 48–50.

Lipovsky, C. (2006). Candidates' negotiation of their job expertise in job interviews. *Journal of Pragmatics*, 38, 1147–1174.

Mavunga, G., and Kumber, F. (2008, June). Interviews as forms of negotiation. *Journal of Language and Communication*, 66–77.

Messmer, M. (2004, August). Top 10 questions to ask during job interviews. *Strategic Finance*, 11–12. Retrieved June 24, 2010 from Business Source Premier.

Muir, C. (2005, February). Managing the initial job interview: Smile, schmooze, and get hired? *Academy of Management Executive*, 156–158. Retrieved June 24, 2010 from JSTOR Arts and Sciences VI Collection.

Muir, C. (2008). Job interviewing. *Business Communication Quarterly, 71*(3), 374–390. Retrieved June 24, 2010 from Business Source Premier.

Nash, R., Feldman, G., Hussey, T., Lévéque, J., & Pineau, P. (2006). Cosmetics: They influence more than Caucasian female facial attractiveness. *Journal of Applied Social Psychology, 36*(2), 493–504. Retrieved June 24, 2010 from SocINDEX.

Navarro, A. (2006). Employers want to know, "What can you do for me?" *The Physician Executive,* (September/October), 70–72.

Neuliep, J. W., Hintz, S., & McCroskey, J. C. (2005). The influence of ethnocentrism on perceptions of interviewee attractiveness, credibility, and socio-communicative style. *Annual convention of the International Communication, 53*(1), 41–56.

Neuson, B. A. (2007, February). Avoid discrimination claims when interviewing job candidates. *Nursing Management,* 16–18. Retrieved June 24, 2010 from Business Source Premier.

Oliphant, G. C., Hansen, K., & Oliphant, B. J. (2008, September). A review of a telephone-administered behavior-based interview technique. *Business Communication Quarterly, 71*(3), 383–386. Retrieved June 24, 2010 from Business Source Premier.

Paul, J., & Strbiak, C. A. (1997, April). The ethics of strategic ambiguity. *Journal of Business Communication, 34*(2), 149–159.

Pearce, S. (2010, March). A marathon, not a sprint. *Accountancy Magazine,* 48–49.

Pepitone, J. (2012, May 12). Yahoo confirms CEO is out after resume scandal. *CNN Money.* Retrieved September 16, 2012 from http://money.cnn.com/2012/05/13/technology.yahoo-ceo-out/index.htm.

Powers, L. (2000, October). Anatomy of an interview. *AORN Magazine, 72*(4), 671.

Psychometric-success.com. (2009). Aptitude tests—What you need to know. *Psychometric-success.com.* Retrieved July 22, 2010 from http://www.psychometric-success.com/aptitude-tests/aptitude-tests-introduction.htm.

Privacy Rights Clearinghouse. (2010). Social networking privacy: How to be safe, secure and social. *Privacy Right Clearinghouse.* Retrieved September 16, 2012 from http://www.privacyrights.org/social-networking-privacy.

Reddick, E. (2007, August). Casual dress—the new elephant in the room. *The Enterprise, 9,* 15.

Remillard, B. (2012). Two reasons interviewing fails so often. *Supervision, 73*(6), 3–5. Retrieved September 15, 2012 from Business Source Premier database.

Rennar, H. S. (2005, July/August). Interviewing: Positioning yourself to get the offer. *Financial Executive,* 60–61. Retrieved June 24, 2010 from Business Source Premier.

RGL Consultants. (2011). Interviewer bad behavior. *RGL Consultants*. Retrieved September 16, 2012 from http://www.rglconsultants.com/2011/09/01/ interviewer-bad-behavior/.

Rutgers. (2010). Conducting an interview. *Rutgers Human Resources department*. Retrieved on July 19, 2010 from http://uhr.rutgers.edu/stf/ ConductinganInterview.htm.

Schawbel, D. (2010, June). Manage your online reputation—before someone else does. *Wall Street Journal Blog/Hire Education*. Retrieved on July 17, 2010 from http://blogs.wsj.com/hire-education/2010/06/25/ manage-your-online-reputation-before-someone-else-does/.

Schramm, W. (1954). How communication works. In W. Schramm (Ed.), *The process and effects of communication* (pp. 3–26). Urbana, IL: University of Illinois Press.

Spolsky, J. (2006, October). The Phone Screen. *Joel on Software*. Retrieved on January 26, 2012 from http://www.joelonsoftware.com/articles/The PhoneScreen.html.

Straus, S. G., Miles, J. A., & Levesque, L. L. (2001). The effects of videoconference, telephone, and face-to-face media on interviewer and applicant judgments in employment interviews. *Journal of Management, 27,* 363–381. Retrieved June 24, 2010 from Business Source Premier.

Thornbory, G., & White, C. (2006). How to… be successful at job interviews. *Occupational Health, 58*(9), 22. Retrieved June 24, 2010 from Business Source Premier.

UC Davis. (n.d.). Guidelines for writing, sequencing, and asking interview questions. Tobacco Control Evaluation Center. *UC Davis*. Retrieved July 19, 2010 from ucce.ucdavis.edu/files/filelibrary/5715/22448.doc.

U.S. Equal Employment Opportunity Commission. (2010). Federal laws prohibiting job discrimination questions and answers. *U.S. Equal Employment Opportunity Commission*. Retrieved from http://www.eeoc.gov/facts/qanda. html.

Wiesnerf, W. H., & Cronshaw, D. F. (1988). A meta-analytic investigation of the impact of interview format and degree of structure on the validity of the employment interview. *Journal of Occupational Psychology, 61,* 275–290.

Williams, K. (2006, May). Can you ace 10 tough job interview questions? *Strategic Finance, 87,* 23. Retrieved June 24, 2010 from Business Source Premier.

Woloshin, M. (2008, July). Starting over: On layoffs and new job searches. *Public Relations Tactics, 15*. Retrieved June 24, 2010 from Business Source Premier.

Using consumer reports: What employers need to know. (2012, January). *Bureau of Consumer Protection*. Retrieved on August 21, 2012 from http://business.ftc.gov/documents bus08-using-consumer-reports-what-employers-need-know.

Chapter Nine—The Talk of Teams: Meeting and Leading at Work

Baker, H. (2010). *Successful minute taking: Meeting the challenge*. Universe of Learning, Ltd. [online book].

Beebe, S. A., & Masterson, J. T. (2003). *Communicating in small groups: Principles and practices*. (7th ed.). Boston, MA: Allyn & Bacon.

Benne, K. D., & Sheats, P. (1948). Functional roles of group members. *Journal of Social Issues, 4*, 41–49.

Bianco, L. (2007). Making it happen: Conflict is good. *Main Today*. Retrieved on August 10, 2012 from http://business.mainetoday.com/smallbusiness/strategic/008822.html.

Bormann, E. G., & Bormann, N.C. (1988). *Effective small group communication*. Minneapolis, MN: Burgess Publications.

Bormann, E. G. (1990). *Small group communication: Theory and practice* (3rd ed.) New York, NY: Harper & Row.

Borysowich, C. (2005, May 24). Why your meetings suck! [blog entry]. Retrieved 12/26/2010 from http://it.toolbox.com/blogs/enterprise-solutions/why-your-meetings-suck-4310.

Buschschluter, V. (2010, October). Celebrations as last trapped Chile miner is rescued. *BBC News*. Retrieved on September 8, 2012 from http://www.bbc.co.uk/news/world-latin-america-11518015.

Chong, E. (2007). Role balance and team development: A study of team role characteristics. *Journal of Behavioral and Applied Management, 8*, 202–217.

Dewey, J. (1933). *How we think: A restatement of the relation of reflective thinking to the educative process* (revised ed.). Boston, MA: D.C. Heath.

Dimitroff, R. D., Schmidt, L., & Bond, T. D. (2005). Organizational behavior and disaster: A study of conflict at NASA. *Project Management Journal, 36*(2), 28–38. Retrieved on September 15, 2012 from Business Source Premier.

Fisher, B. A. (1968). *Decision emergence: A process model of verbal task behavior for decision-making groups.* Unpublished Ph.D. dissertation, University of Minnesota.

Fisher, B. A. (1970). Decision emergence: Phases in group decision making. *Speech Monographs, 37,* 53–66.

Fisher, B. A. (n.d). Interact system model of decision emergence. *Group and public communication.* (pp. 253–263). Retrieved September 16, 2012 from http://highered.mcgraw-hill.com/sites/dl/free/0073385026/228359/intersys.pdf.

Goleman, D. (2006). *Working with emotional intelligence.* New York, NY: Bantam Books.

Gouran, D., & Hirokawa, R. Y. (1996). Functional theory and communication in decision-making and problem-solving groups. In Hirokawa, R. Y., & Poole, M. S. (Eds.), *Communication and group decision making,* 2nd ed. (pp. 55–80). Thousand Oaks, CA: Sage.

Guttman, H. M. (2009). Leading meetings 101. *Leadership Excellence, 26*(7), 18. Retrieved September 15, 2012 from Business Source Premier.

Hermann, A., & Rammal, H. G. (2010). The grounding of the 'flying bank.' *Management Decision, 48*(7), 1051.

Hersey, P., & Blanchard, K. H. (1969). *Management of organizational behavior—utilizing human resources.* Englewood Cliffs, NJ: Prentice-Hall.

Hersey, P., Blanchard, K. H., & Johnson, D. E. (2007). *Management of organizational behavior* (9th ed.). Englewood Cliffs, NJ: Prentice-Hall.

Janis, I. L. (1972). *Victims of groupthink: A psychological study of foreign-policy decisions and fiascoes.* Boston, MA: Houghton Mifflin.

Janis, I. L. (1982). *Groupthink: psychological studies of policy decisions and fiascoes* (2nd ed.). New York, NY: Houghton Mifflin.

Janis, I. L., & Mann, L. (1977). *Decision making: A psychological analysis of conflict, choice, and commitment.* New York, NY: Free Press.

Kauffeld, S., & Lehmann-Willenbrock, N. (2012). Meetings matter: Effects of team meetings on team and organizational success. *Small Group Research, 43*(2), 130–158. Retrieved September 15, 2012 from Business Source Premier.

Knowledge@Wharton. (2012). Lessons on leadership and teamwork—from 700 meters below the earth's surface. *Knowledge@Wharton.* Retrieved September 5, 2012, from http://knowledge.wharton.upenn.edu/article.cfm?articleid=2607.

Krattenmaker, T. (2007). Make every meeting matter. *Harvard Management Update. Harvard Business Publishing Newsletters.* Retrieved on September 15, 2012 from http://blogs.hbr.org/hmu/2008/02/make-every-meeting-matter.html.

Lloyd, J. (2012). Why you really need meetings. *Receivables report for America's health care financial managers, 27*(3), 8–9. Retrieved September 15, 2012 from Business Source Premier.

Mandell, B., & Pherwani, S. (2003). Relationship between emotional intelligence and TL style: A gender comparison. *Journal of Business & Psychology, 17*(3), 387–404.

Marriot. (n.d.). Step-by-step planning guide. Marriott. Retrieved September 6, 2012 from http://www.marriott.com/meeting-event-hotels/event-planning-guide.mi.

Millard, D. (2007). Make the most of meetings by planning and following up. *Indianapolis Business Journal, 28,* 44, 19–19.

Morreale, S., & Pearson, J. (2008). Why communication education is important: The centrality of the discipline in the 21st century. *Communication Education, 57*(2), 224–240.

Moorhead, G., Ference, R., & Neck, C. P. (1991). Group decision fiascoes continue: Space shuttle Challenger and a revised groupthink framework. *Human Relations 44*(6), 539–550.

National Association of Colleges and Employers (NACE). (2011). Job outlook: The candidate skills/qualities employers want. *National Association of Colleges and Employers.* Retrieved August 13, 2012, from http://www.naceweb.org/s10262011/candidate_skills_employer_qualities/.

Osborn, A. (1953). *Applied imagination.* New York, NY: Charles Scribner's Sons.

Parayitam, S., & Dooley, R. S. (2009, August). The interplay between cognitive and affective conflict and cognition and affect-based trust in influencing decision outcomes. *Journal of Business Research, 62*(8), 789–796.

Pearce, C. L., Manz, C. C., & Sims Jr., H. P. (2009). Is shared leadership the key to team success? *Organizational Dynamics, 38*(3), 234–238. Retrieved on September 16, 2012 from http://cte.rockhurst.edu/s/945/images/editor_documents/PEARCE%20MANZ%20SIMS%20%20%20Shared%20Ledership.pdf.

Pozen, R. C. (2011, May). Extreme productivity: A veteran executive outlines the principles for getting a lot done. *Harvard Business Review,* pp. 127–131.

Rowan, J. M. (2003). Seating arrangements should support goal of meeting. *San Antonio Business Journal*. Retrieved June 12, 2010 from http://www.bizjournals.com/sanantonio/stories/2003/11/10/focus3.html.

Stogdill, R. M. (1948). Personal factors associated with leadership: A survey of the literature. *Journal of Psychology, 25*, 35–71.

Swain, M. (1998). Focus on form through conscious reflection. In C. Doughty & J. Williams (Eds.), *Focus on form in classroom second language acquisition* (64–83). Cambridge: Cambridge University Press.

Thomas, K. W., & Kilmann, R.H. (1974). Thomas-Kilmann conflict mode instrument, *Consulting Psychologists Press*.

Thomas, K. W., & Thomas, G. F. (2004). *Introduction to conflict and teams*. Mountain View, CA: CPP Inc.

Tuckman, B. (1965). Developmental sequence in small groups. *Psychological Bulletin, 63*, 384–399.

Tuckman, B. W., & Jensen, M.C. (1977). Stages of small group development revisited. *Group and Organizational Studies, 2*, 419–427.

Willets, A. (2011). Escape the time trap—Make meetings work for you. *Public Relations Tactics, 18*(9), 6. Retrieved on September 15, 2012 from Business Source Premier.

INDEX

C

M

P